# SPYCOPS
## Secrets and Disclosure in the Undercover Policing Inquiry

Raphael Schlembach

First published in Great Britain in 2024 by

Policy Press, an imprint of
Bristol University Press
University of Bristol
1–9 Old Park Hill
Bristol
BS2 8BB
UK
t: +44 (0)117 374 6645
e: bup-info@bristol.ac.uk

Details of international sales and distribution partners are available at policy.bristoluniversitypress.co.uk

© Bristol University Press 2024

British Library Cataloguing in Publication Data
A catalogue record for this book is available from the British Library

ISBN 978-1-4473-6536-5 hardcover
ISBN 978-1-4473-6537-2 paperback
ISBN 978-1-4473-6538-9 ePub
ISBN 978-1-4473-6539-6 ePdf

The right of Raphael Schlembach to be identified as author of this work has been asserted by him in accordance with the Copyright, Designs and Patents Act 1988.

All rights reserved: no part of this publication may be reproduced, stored in a retrieval system, or transmitted in any form or by any means, electronic, mechanical, photocopying, recording, or otherwise without the prior permission of Bristol University Press.

Every reasonable effort has been made to obtain permission to reproduce copyrighted material. If, however, anyone knows of an oversight, please contact the publisher.

The statements and opinions contained within this publication are solely those of the author and not of the University of Bristol or Bristol University Press. The University of Bristol and Bristol University Press disclaim responsibility for any injury topersons or property resulting from any material published in this publication.

Bristol University Press and Policy Press work to counter discrimination on grounds of gender, race, disability, age and sexuality.

Cover design: Nicky Borowiec
Front cover image: Adobe/Andrii Yalanskyi

# Contents

| | | |
|---|---|---|
| List of abbreviations | | iv |
| About the author | | v |
| Acknowledgements | | vi |
| Preface | | vii |
| | | |
| 1 | An (un)acknowledged truth | 1 |
| 2 | The undercover policing scandal | 22 |
| 3 | Deviant knowledge and activist research | 46 |
| 4 | The public inquiry as a site of struggle | 67 |
| 5 | Dirty data and devices of dis/closure | 95 |
| 6 | Human rights and data protection | 122 |
| 7 | In and against the Undercover Policing Inquiry | 147 |
| 8 | Public inquiries at a crossroads | 164 |
| | | |
| Appendix A: Terms of Reference | | 171 |
| Appendix B: Timeline | | 173 |
| Notes | | 180 |
| References | | 183 |
| Index | | 204 |

# List of abbreviations

| | |
|---|---|
| ACPO | Association of Chief Police Officers |
| CPS | Crown Prosecution Service |
| ECHR | European Convention on Human Rights |
| GDPR | General Data Protection Regulation |
| ICO | Information Commissioner's Office |
| IOPC | Independent Office for Police Conduct |
| IPCC | Independent Police Complaints Commission |
| IPT | Investigatory Powers Tribunal |
| MPS | Metropolitan Police Service |
| NCND | Neither Confirm Nor Deny |
| NDEDIU | National Domestic Extremism and Disorder Intelligence Unit |
| NPCC | National Police Chiefs' Council |
| NPOIU | National Public Order Intelligence Unit |
| PCA | Police Complaints Authority |
| RIPA | Regulation of Investigatory Powers Act 2000 |
| ROA | Rehabilitation of Offenders Act 1974 |
| SDS | Special Demonstration Squad |
| UCPI | Undercover Policing Inquiry |
| URG | Undercover Research Group |
| VSC | Vietnam Solidarity Campaign |
| WLF | Women's Liberation Front |
| YRE | Youth against Racism in Europe |

# About the author

Raphael Schlembach teaches criminology and sociology at the University of Brighton, UK. He has a long-standing interest in the politics of social movements and their criminalisation. He has been involved as an activist with various social and climate justice groups. It was here that he encountered 'Mark Stone' and 'Marco Jacobs', who, as he later found out, were undercover police officers. Their exposures renewed his interest in the policing of protest and led to the present book. He is the author of *Against Old Europe: Critical Theory and Alter-Globalization Movements* (Routledge, 2014) and has contributed to academic journals such as *Criminology & Criminal Justice*, *Social Movement Studies*, *Critical Social Policy*, *Citizenship Studies* and *Environmental Politics*.

# Acknowledgements

The analysis of the Undercover Policing Inquiry that I have attempted here is informed to a great extent by the meticulous research carried out by people outside the academy. Without the undercover profiles compiled by the Undercover Research Group, the daily digests from oral hearings by the Campaign Opposing Police Surveillance, the stories of deception and resistance compiled by Police Spies Out of Lives, the live Tweets and podcasts to name just a few, this book would not exist. These groups and individuals have worked tirelessly to make the Inquiry as transparent and accessible as possible and so my appreciation goes out to Tom, Merrick and many others. I am specifically grateful to Eveline Lubbers, Chris Brian and Dónal O'Driscoll who have read drafts of this book and fact-checked them. Several of the women whose stories of relationships with undercover officers are represented in this book also kindly checked through draft sections for accuracy. Any errors that remain are entirely mine.

I want to extend special thanks to Nicola Clewer, who read drafts of all chapters along the way and whose invaluable comments added clarity and perspective. Other friends and colleagues, too, have offered continuous support and intellectual companionship; in particular Deanna Dadusc, Roxana Pessoa Cavalcanti, Lambros Fatsis and Emily Luise Hart. Further gratitude is due to everyone at Policy Press and to the two peer reviewers who gave constructive feedback on the manuscript.

In the end, this book sees the light of day against the backdrop of a difficult working environment in the English higher education sector and an exceptionally hostile atmosphere at my own place of work. Much of it was written during periods of leave from my university employer to counteract the diminishing resources and rising workloads that stand in the way of sustained intellectual work. The final manuscript was put together at a time when the university had put my post at risk of redundancy alongside those of almost 400 other academic colleagues. The shameful and unjustified sacking of highly talented close friends and colleagues overshadows the completion of this book. My UCU branch has been a much-needed source of community and solidarity throughout.

Some of the materials collected here have been published in different forms before. Across Chapters 1–2 and again in Chapter 4, I have drawn on a paper that was published as 'The Pitchford inquiry into undercover policing', in *Papers from the British Society of Criminology Conference 2016*. Chapter 3 is an updated and extended version of a chapter published as 'Resisting the surveillance state: Deviant knowledge and undercover policing', in E. L. Hart, J. Greener and R. Moth (2020) *Resisting the Punitive State* (Pluto Press). Many thanks to the British Society of Criminology and Pluto for granting me the permissions to reproduce these here.

# Preface

I have not been able to find out when exactly the word 'spycops' was first used to describe the British undercover police officers who infiltrated protest groups, but it gained some popularity as a hashtag on Twitter from 2011 onwards. Since then, a community of activists, lawyers, journalists and researchers has injected the term with its specific meaning relating to undercover cops who assumed false identities to gain trust within the targeted groups.

Various elements of the spycops scandal have been investigated by over a dozen official inquiries. They have all been superseded by the Undercover Policing Inquiry, which was set up to get to the truth about undercover policing across England and Wales from 1968 to the present and to learn lessons for the future. At the time of writing, it is not yet at all clear what impact the Undercover Policing Inquiry will have and what its final recommendations will be. When the Inquiry publishes its final report, currently expected to be in 2026, it will have sat for more than ten years and cost more than £100 million.

One milestone was reached on 29 June 2023 when Sir John Mitting, the Chair of the Undercover Policing Inquiry, published an interim report about undercover policing in the period from 1968 to 1982. In those years, the Metropolitan Police had established and operated the Special Demonstration Squad (SDS), a specialist spycops unit attached to its Special Branch and with links to the Security Service. SDS officers infiltrated and disrupted scores of campaigning organisations on the left of the political spectrum.

Mitting investigated whether the deployment of undercover officers to infiltrate protest and political groups was a legitimate exercise of police functions. His answer is plain: 'I have come to the firm conclusion that, for a unit of a police force, it [was] not; and that had the use of these means been publicly known at the time, the SDS would have been brought to a rapid end' (UCPI [Undercover Policing Inquiry], 2023a, p 96). As was widely reported at the time, Mitting finds that, for the most part, spycops policing was not a justified tactic to inform public order responses to protests or to monitor 'subversive' groups and individuals. In short, the (political) ends did not justify the (policing) means. It was a headline-grabbing diagnosis and vindicated the campaigners who had been spied on.

Beyond this, Mitting's report is actually a very timid document that avoids making judgment calls and papers over the cracks in the Inquiry's own proceedings.

When the Undercover Policing Inquiry – first announced in 2014 and then formally established in 2015 – was issued with its Terms of Reference, the Home Office expected a final report within three years. The Chair's interim conclusions are published a full eight years after the Inquiry began its work. The report itself obscures this huge delay. There is no commentary on the complexities of investigating secret state activities. Moreover, there is no word on the struggles within the Inquiry over what evidence could be voiced and heard. The glacial pace with which the Inquiry has progressed needs to be interrogated as part of the spycops scandal itself.

The evidence that underpins the interim report only pertains to a single undercover unit, the SDS (known at first as the Special Operations Squad), and only to a restricted time period, from the unit's founding in 1968 to the arbitrarily chosen year 1982. The report's structuring narrative is that the Inquiry's investigation is concerned with a matter that lies *in the past*. Mitting refers to the Undercover Policing Inquiry as a 'historical inquiry' and the undercover units that are being investigated as 'historical policing units'. This is the result of a choice made to divide the Inquiry's work into 'modules' and 'tranches' and to organise the investigation in a chronological order. What helps the Inquiry to manage its work also serves to produce the fiction that political spying was a novel tactic born from the specific necessity to monitor changes in socialist and communist politics in the late 1960s.

Mitting himself does not overemphasise the role of his interim conclusions. In his own metaphor, they are only 'the first fruit' (UCPI, 2023a, p v). This qualification allows him to sidestep some of the crucial matters which have brought spycops policing to public attention. 'Some issues are better addressed when all of the evidence about them is in', he writes (UCPI, 2023a, p vi). These include, by his own admission, the claim that an institutionalised culture of sexism underpinned the deployment of male undercover officers who deceived women into intimate relationships, the practice of building cover legends based on the identities of deceased children and the intelligence gathering on racial and family justice campaigns. There is no word at all on the undercover unit's possible role in the blacklisting of workers – a practice of economic policing that was long denied by the state and by industry.

The historicising lens allows Mitting to avoid commenting on some of the key political questions that have engulfed the Metropolitan Police in recent years, too. Do the deceitful sexual relationships that male undercover officers engaged in with members of the public further demonstrate that Britain's largest police force was institutionally misogynist? On this question, Mitting simply points to his final report, not expected until at least 2026. What about institutional racism? The words 'race' and 'racism' are entirely absent from the interim report, other than when they form part of the names of the anti-racist and anti-fascist groups that were infiltrated or reported on by the SDS.

Mitting finds, further, that there should be no concern that the Metropolitan Police was politically biased. During the period under investigation from 1968 to 1982, the SDS did not infiltrate the far Right (despite considerable threats to public order from their demonstrations and increasing racist violence). This, however, 'did not result from political bias', Mitting assures us. How can he be so certain? He simply reiterates points made by police witnesses that the Metropolitan Police had sufficient intelligence on the activities of fascist groups and that their infiltration would be too risky. The counterclaim, that police decision-makers harboured stereotypes of left-wing protesters and cultural sympathies with the politics of the Right, receives no further comment.

While Mitting says little of substance about the tactics and targets of the SDS, he is critical of its purpose. Most of the groups that were infiltrated planned for demonstrations and rallies in open planning meetings. If some additional intelligence about protests and direct actions could be gathered by deceptive means, its contribution to preventing public disorder 'should not be overstated' (UCPI, 2023a, p 90). He questions the logic of police managers deploying undercover officers into groups that 'posed no threat to public order or to the state' (UCPI, 2023a, p 34). Mitting reasons that by the standards of the time (he refers here to the era of the Cold War and of the 'Troubles'), the infiltration of subversive organisations 'could have readily been justified' if they posed internal dangers to the state. By his own application of these standards, only three of the targeted groups posed such a threat – the Provisional Sinn Féin (its Hammersmith branch was infiltrated by an undercover officer who went on to be elected as its Branch Chair and finance officer for the London district) and two further groups that he does not name. This is a rare example of spycops activity that Mitting believes to have been of 'undoubted value' (UCPI, 2023a, p 27).

Conversely, on the matter of whether the spying on political expression and activity constitutes itself a subversion of democratic principles, the Inquiry's report remains silent. In fact, the Chair comments with misplaced confidence that he has 'refrained from expressing any view' on issues such as 'the proposition that the SDS was one of the instruments set up by a conservative state to suppress the aspirations of those who wished to produce radical change by political means' (UCPI, 2023a, p vi). His reasoning reveals something about the views held by a senior retired judge of the function of public inquiries. Rather than allowing the evidence he collects about the political police's anti-democratic mandate to inform his conclusions, the issue of those units' wider political role is relegated to a matter of personal 'opinion', and should the Chair add his own opinion, this would, in his words, 'serve no useful purpose' (UCPI, 2023a, p vi). Those radical activists who were spied on would be forgiven for coming to the view that Mitting himself forms part of the conservative state that suppresses their aspirations.

As was perhaps expected from an establishment judge, Mitting takes the opportunity to remind the reader of his respect for the role of the undercover police officer. The 'great majority' of them, the Chair observes, 'performed their duties conscientiously and in the belief that what they were doing was lawful and in the interests of the public' (UCPI, 2023a, p 96). In this way, his report can invoke the image of the few 'bad apple' officers who have tarnished the reputation of their otherwise courageous and honest colleagues. It is an interpretation happily seized upon by the leadership of the Metropolitan Police who, in a brief acknowledgement of the Inquiry report, frame the issue as a familiar story of police personnel working hard to keep Londoners safe, only to be let down by the 'unacceptable and immoral behaviour by *some* undercover officers' (Metropolitan Police, 2023, emphasis added). The Metropolitan Police reassures us that 'radical reform' has taken place and that the policing in the 1970s 'bears no relation to how it is conducted today'.

The interim report completes the Inquiry's investigation into 'Tranche 1'. There are four more tranches to come; hearings covering the Tranche 2 period from 1983 to 1992 are to take place in 2024. This Inquiry has a long way to go.

# 1

# An (un)acknowledged truth

## The politics of public inquiries

What does a public inquiry do? Seen from one perspective, the answer is reasonably straightforward. As a formal process, the public inquiry offers some kind of redress for injustice and injury. It assembles evidence of past events, learns from institutional or procedural failures and makes recommendations for the future. Even though it sits outside the ordinary criminal justice process, it offers an appearance of justice. Perhaps, there's even a semblance of reconciliation or restoration of trust.

Invariably, there is a messier side to public inquiries. They are condemned as state-led processes that impose official narratives onto contested histories. Their simplified framings produce and reproduce hierarchies of blame and guilt. They can be perceived as a toothless irrelevance, as a white-wash and smokescreen, as a waste of money, as justice delayed, as Kafkaesque nightmares and legal labyrinths. They may conclude too hastily, with little regard for detail and complexity. They can test their protagonists' patience, getting caught up in minutiae and unresolvable arguments. In many cases, their final reports and recommendations leave all sides – if there are sides to take – exhausted and dissatisfied. And in the UK, the conclusions of public inquiries are not legally enforceable and may fail to translate into policy change.

So what's the point? This is essentially the question that has driven my interest in the public inquiry into undercover policing in England and Wales – the Undercover Policing Inquiry – which was set up in 2015 as a judge-led, statutory inquiry under the Inquiries Act 2005. If we consider the public distrust in elite-led processes and the scepticism directed at public authorities, why did so many people invest their time, effort and money in this Inquiry? Why, despite the endless talk of cover-ups and police favouritism, despite the personal costs and political doubts, did so many people welcome the establishment of the Inquiry and persist with it for so long? If such questions are troublesome, the paradox is even greater if we consider the political background of many of the Inquiry's core participants: what did activists with an inherent, and learned, disregard for the corruption at the heart of the British state and its legal institutions expect to gain in this process? As the reader will come to see, the answers I give in this book are as unsatisfactory as the Inquiry itself.

In a small but crucial way, the events surrounding the British undercover policing scandal – or the spycops scandal, as I will refer to it at times – have impacted on my own personal and political sense of reality. I was in and around the non-hierarchical networks of committed activists and friends when a police officer, Mark Kennedy, was publicly exposed as a 'spy' and I saw the diverse ways in which people reacted. There was a widespread sense, nonetheless, that a door had opened into a murky, previously invisible world of police activity, which everyone had known existed, though rarely dared to speak of. With the first concrete proof of police 'covert human intelligence sources' embedded in progressive social movements, what had belonged to the realm of tin foil hats and conspiracy theories was elevated to the arena of serious political discussion and strategy. I argue in this book that the public inquiry – contested, biased, whitewashing it may be – included with it the promise that the role of state repression and police surveillance of protest movements could move from a fringe activist concern to the public sphere. In short, the public inquiry, taking the character that it does in British public administration, accords suspicions of police interference in political activity an official status, where the repressive state is forced to cede ground and affirm the existence of an *acknowledged truth*.

What do I mean by that phrase – an acknowledged truth? I have borrowed the term from the prominent human rights lawyer Imran Khan. In the public mind, Khan remains best known for his role in the Stephen Lawrence murder case, in which he represented the Lawrence family during the Macpherson Inquiry and their private prosecution. But when a government-commissioned report found in 2014 that there were grounds to suspect that activists involved with the Lawrence family campaign had been monitored by undercover police officers, Khan experienced both shock and vindication. He told *The Guardian* newspaper that reading an official report all but confirming his suspicions of the state abusing its powers gave a new impetus to his work. 'It was shocking to read it', Khan is quoted in his interview. 'A shock in the sense of a victim seeing someone acknowledge what has happened to them; in the sense of, finally, someone gets it. Finally, someone in authority has matched it all up, drawn it all out and given a conclusion I always knew to be the case' (Khan, cited in Muir, 2014). This sense that knowing the truth is not enough, but that it finds another, more viscerally real, dimension in public and official acknowledgement is central to the argument in this book.

Acknowledgement, or recognition, also goes to the heart of the matter in public inquiries, in which victims of state abuse or state negligence invest their hopes of gaining justice. Justice, other than in an adversarial court process that pitches prosecutors against defendants, is here seen as the official recognition of what really happened, an acknowledged truth. To be sure, in international legal scholarship, investigatory truth and reconciliation commissions following civil conflicts or human rights abuses are frequently viewed as establishing an account of truth *as* justice. On the flip side, there is nothing straightforward about the concept of truth. The search for truth, as we will see, can easily come into conflict with other social values, including those of individual privacy or national security. The publication of truthful accounts of fact may even be regarded as *un*just, for example when such disclosures are devoid of context or unresponsive to unequal relations of power between conflicting parties. The troubled dialectic of disclosure and non-disclosure is also the basis for the recuperation of secrecy for democratic ends proposed by some scholars of contemporary culture. Clare Birchall (2021) has termed this 'radical secrecy', a term that denotes an understanding of 'secrets' without the usual negative connotations and envisaging a political strategy that goes beyond the common calls for more transparency. And as we will see, even though calls for the disclosure of state secrets were at the heart of the spycops scandal and its public inquiry, the relationship of transparency to secrecy was by no means one of binary opposition.

Responding to such complexities in the relation between 'truth' and 'justice', some have therefore offered a moral defence of truth commissions, especially in cases where commonly understood conceptions of 'justice' are sacrificed for the purpose of a reconciliatory ideal (see Rotberg and Thompson, 2000). They tie the success of truth commissions to a conception of deliberative democracy. If justice is usually conceived of as criminal justice – not necessarily, but frequently, enacted through punishment for the offender and redress for the victim – commissions of inquiry subordinate this aim to the pursuit of a historical truth and a cathartic reckoning with the past. In some instances, perpetrators of atrocities and abuse are offered amnesty in return for their testimony. This dispensation with criminal justice can only be defended, according to political philosophers Amy Gutman and Dennis Thompson (2004), if it is done in the context of democratisation. The success, and moral justification, of such inquisitorial institutions and practices is therefore bound up with their ability to command a process of social cooperation in which both agreements and disagreements can be respected by most.

Yet, where the deliberative democratic ideal rests on the existence of reciprocal relationships between mutually understanding adults, others stress the ubiquity of power relations that subordinate some truth(s) to others. I do not want to relativise the existence of truth by pluralising the word unnecessarily. But the Foucauldian notion of 'regimes of truth', a phrase that Foucault used in his *Discipline and Punish* (1991) to refer to the entanglement of a set of scientific and epistemic discourses with political power, allows us to think of a subaltern truth as opposed to official discourse. This way of thinking along Foucauldian lines has had a large impact on British political sociology and on those trying to theorise state accountability, criminal justice and social marginalisation. It has had a particular impact on those who study prisons and other total institutions. Phil Scraton, now best known for his investigatory work into the state's response to the Hillsborough Stadium disaster in 1989, which claimed the lives of 97 Liverpool football supporters, and his membership of the Hillsborough Independent Panel, articulated the conflict between 'hidden voices' and official narratives in this way:

> The advanced democratic state, supposedly underpinned by the checks and balances of interrelated, formalised processes of legal, political and professional accountability, claims transparency for its public institutions. Yet behind the high walls of special hospitals, the bolted doors of psychiatric units and prison wings, those imprisoned continue to be subdued by a lethal mix of tranquillising and anti-psychotic drugs, supervisory neglect, staff brutality and defensive managements. Like the abandoned mental institutions, high security special hospitals form a closed world. (Scraton, 2002, p 108)

The voices of the detained could rarely be heard outside these closed worlds.

Both conceptualisations – truth as reconciliation and truth as the exercise of power – lend themselves to the analysis of public inquiries. But neither quite fit with my experiences of the conflict surrounding the Undercover Policing Inquiry. On the one hand, reconciliation with the police's political-repressive undercover units was never on the cards for those subjected to long-term surveillance, although some may have agreed to sacrifice the prospect of criminal sanctions in return for answers and explanations. But truth and justice did not operate as binary categories here: at best they were two sides of the same coin. On the other hand, the desire to influence the 'official discourse' of the state remained a key reason why intergenerational activists from a vast range of groups and groupuscules, spanning some 40 years of campaigning against injustice, came to the public inquiry. They were not content with having their voices finally heard; they asked for meaningful participation in the process. If this gets us somewhat closer to the notion of an acknowledgement that I have been working with to understand the Undercover Policing Inquiry, 'truth' as a philosophical category remains elusive. But, as we will see, it was a crucial conceptual tool employed by those with high expectations for the Undercover Policing Inquiry.

Dave Smith is a former construction worker and trade unionist from East London who was blacklisted after he raised concerns about building site safety issues with his employers. In 2009, he discovered that he was listed in confidential files kept in the small offices of the Consulting Association, an organisation that catalogued information about workers' employment details, political beliefs and union activities passed onto it by over forty large construction companies. A raid on the offices by investigators from the Information Commissioner's Office laid bare the extent of the secret database, which, as Smith found, 'acted as a covert vetting service funded by the industry' (Smith and Chamberlain, 2015a). The blacklisting had a profound impact on his life and that of thousands of other workers, as they were routinely and repeatedly denied work. Some of the information in the Consulting Association files was public knowledge, but specific details appeared to have originated from undercover police officers in Special Branch units. To aid in the investigation of these claims, Dave Smith has been given 'core participant status' in the Undercover Policing Inquiry.

In a pointed challenge to the way that the Undercover Policing Inquiry had erred on the side of non-disclosure and secrecy, Smith used his opening statement to impress upon it the anti-democratic character of police organisations in their apparent role in blacklisting workers from construction sites. Smith, who has also co-authored the excellent *Blacklisted: The Secret War between Big Business and Union Activists* (2015b), accused the Inquiry of acting akin to the Magisterium in Philip Pullman's fantasy novels *His Dark Materials*, which maintains strict control of its fictional society through a totalitarian organisation of knowledge:

> And, actually, coming into this public inquiry seems like stepping into an alternate universe, you know? And just to be clear, it's the alternate universe that's a bit sinister, where the Magisterium cling onto power by holding on to an outmoded view of the world, denying people to be able to see the truth, and deciding what people are allowed to know and what they're not allowed to know. (UCPI[1], 2020a, p 26)

Such sentiments kept recurring in a variety of ways during the opening statements made by or on behalf of non-police, non-state core participants. Imran Khan continues to represent Doreen Lawrence in the Undercover Policing Inquiry, alongside a number of trade union members of the Blacklist Support Group. Khan, in his opening statement on behalf of Baroness Lawrence, spelled out how learning the truth remained the main hope – a hope quashed – for Stephen's mother:

> She [Doreen Lawrence] is losing confidence, if she has not already lost it, in this Inquiry's ability to get to the truth. The truth as to why she, her family and supporters were spied upon by the police. This Inquiry is not delivering on what she was promised, and is not achieving what she expected. (UCPI, 2020b, p 2)

That this idea of truth appears interchangeable with 'knowledge' – what happened and why – should not diminish the fact that answers to such questions need to take the form of *public* acknowledgement. As Khan went on:

> It is ... a source of great shame and concern that what she was promised has not been delivered. What she expected has not been achieved. What Baroness Lawrence believes is actually happening is a 'secret inquiry', in which officer after officer is hiding behind a pseudonym and screen. Not only does she not know who most of them are but neither does the public ... This is certainly not what she expected. Baroness Lawrence has been through a proper inquiry. She knows what it is supposed to be like. (UCPI, 2020b, p 20)

The idea that the Stephen Lawrence Inquiry was conducted *properly*, while the Undercover Policing Inquiry was not, is one that shapes Baroness Lawrence's submissions to the latter. While, in this book, I explore the Undercover Policing Inquiry on its own terms, references and comparisons to other past and ongoing public inquiries were frequently made by the people I spoke to for my research. I shall return to this theme at the end of the book. Meanwhile, let me briefly explain what the Undercover Policing Inquiry is and what sparked my interest in it.

## Inquiring into police secrets

At the time of writing the introduction to this book, the Undercover Policing Inquiry is ongoing. For the past few years, and still today, it has offered an extraordinary chance for academic scrutiny – both of the role that undercover policing has played in the suppression of progressive social change and of the flawed, state-controlled accountability process that has followed. Surprisingly, given this opportunity, both matters have been somewhat neglected in recent academic analysis of police accountability.[2]

Launched by the Home Office in 2015 and with evidence hearings that finally began in November 2020, the Undercover Policing Inquiry investigates the infiltration of hundreds of political campaign groups since 1968, with evidence given, among others, by police officers and by activists who were spied on. Two undercover units are of particular interest to the Inquiry: the Special Demonstration Squad (SDS) and the National Public Order Intelligence Unit (NPOIU). These units deployed over a hundred undercover police officers into a huge range of large and small social movement organisations and campaigns. The tactics used to develop and maintain cover identities by officers in these units are at the centre of concern: undercover policing through infiltration has involved the use of intimate and sexual relationships, often over a period of years, the use of dead children's identities as aliases without the knowledge of the deceased's parents, and the withholding of information from courts and juries. In some instances, police officers fathered children with the activists they had targeted, raising important questions concerning the ethics of undercover policing.

The Inquiry's final report, delayed again and again, will be an important milestone in the regulation of police surveillance in England and Wales, though many fear that the document will do little more than historicise police abuses of power and leave current practices by undercover police untouched. They may well be right: at the end of 2020, in the middle of a lockdown to stem the spread of COVID-19 in England and just weeks before the Brexit transition period came to an end, the Johnson-led Conservative government decided to push a new intelligence services bill through parliament that effectively further diminished the safeguards against criminal activity committed by officers deployed undercover as 'covert human intelligence sources'. The resulting Covert Human Intelligence Sources (Criminal Conduct) Act 2021 offers immunity to those authorised to commit crimes in their deployments to gather covert intelligence.

But the Inquiry process itself is also a test of the ability to use an inquisitorial mechanism to disclose state secrets (related to undercover policing) and to satisfy both the police's interest in maintaining secrecy and the competing demand (from victims, media organisations, researchers and campaign groups) for transparency and accountability. It is my aim in this book to report on the first eight years of the Undercover Policing Inquiry, to understand how it is contested by different interested parties and to make a contribution to the study of inquiries more broadly.

## Background to the research

This book was not conceived as a study of a public inquiry. My initial interest had been in some particular stories woven into the emerging fabric of the undercover policing scandal, which I explore in some detail in Chapter 2, with personal, political and academic motivations. One of the threads that connected my political engagement and my academic home discipline of criminology – a 'home' which I inhabit rather reluctantly – had been the policing of protest. When the story broke, in 2011, of a police infiltrator in the British anarchist and direct action milieu, I quickly became aware that I had been on the periphery of the activist groups targeted for infiltration. I had met Mark Kennedy, the police 'spy' in question, on several occasions over the preceding years, on social occasions and at political events.

Kennedy had worked for the NPOIU, infiltrating environmental, anarchist and other direct action groups. He spent seven years deep undercover, much of that time living with a group of environmentalists in Nottingham. I had never warmed much to Mark Kennedy in the time I knew him, but I was not suspicious. Looking back, our paths would have crossed numerous times; we were in the same campaign meetings, went to the same protests and he came to the parties in the communal housing cooperative where I lived at the time. His 40th birthday party was the last time I saw him. The discovery of his passport by 'Lisa', the woman he had deceived into a long-term relationship, led to his outing a year later.

Later on, by the time that the exposures of undercover officers had snowballed into a national scandal with international ramifications, I remembered a fleeting encounter with another infiltrator, which had left a sour taste. This happened in 2007 when I took part in a protest to prevent the building of a gas pipeline right through the middle of the Brecon Beacons National Park in Wales. The protest was not authorised, but it was not illegal either. For some protesters who stood on a private access road it was at best a case of civil trespass. I had travelled to Wales with friends and attended a protest meeting. With nowhere to stay, we met 'Marco', a local activist who let us sleep over in his flat and drove us to the protest the next day. But as soon as I arrived at the demonstration, still on public land, I and several others were arrested under suspicion of conspiracy to cause aggravated trespass. The exact location of the protest was not advertised, so it was a surprise to find a large number of police officers waiting there. I was held for 24 hours in custody at the local police station and during that time officers searched my house and confiscated pretty much all my PhD work, including my laptop, voice recorder and literature. They kept it for the following eight months and it was only returned after I threatened to recover the value of the items through the small claims court. This would be a fairly ordinary story – as social movement researchers sometimes describe it, arrest and prosecution are part of the 'normal events in the life cycle of many protest movements' (Barkan, 2006, p 183) – apart from the fact, and this makes the story more complex, that the local activist who helped me to attend the demonstration, who offered me to stay the night before in his flat, who drove me to the protest and who apparently got arrested next to me was 'Marco Jacobs', an undercover cop.

I remember my housemate telling me about the search back at home. Officers from Greater Manchester Police had demanded entry and announced their intention to take computer equipment and documents. When my housemate protested, an officer told him calmly: "If this was Northern Ireland, we'd just shoot you." While exaggerated of course, and probably more intended as a way to intimidate than as a credible threat or even a comparative analysis of police styles, the officer in question was, inadvertently, right to contextualise policing on the British mainland. The reference to policing in Northern Ireland is ubiquitous in policing discourse that I traced throughout the public inquiry. Repeatedly, national security and state secrets are invoked as justifications for undercover operations in social justice circles. The colonial mindset of mainstream policing is clear to see here in the enemy narrative that paints protesters as subversives and extremists (Bell, 2013). The experiences of policing in Northern Ireland are points of reference both to raise the level of threat and to differentiate mainland policing from its paramilitary cousin. I hope to have largely avoided such qualifying comparisons in my own description of the spycops scandal; this is a story of injustice, violence and abuse on its own terms.

It should be said at the outset, however, that the stories that inform this book are not my own. I am indebted to the work of many activists who first uncovered the presence of undercover officers in campaign groups and then exposed them to a wider public. As I will describe in Chapter 2, the Inquiry was set up to investigate a scandal of huge political significance and which is intimately tied to 50 years of British social and political history. It is a response to two distinct, yet allied, structural injustices implicating police practice and policy – that of institutional racism and that of a sexist police culture. My own personal encounters with spycops are peripheral at best to these injustices. But they also speak precisely to a problem addressed in this book: that the Inquiry has sought to restrict itself to such outwardly expressions of injustice while at the same time negating or belittling the mundane function of police surveillance and political repression or its impact on democratically expressed dissent. In what follows, I work with an expansive understanding of the effects of undercover policing, not just on the trust in the police institution among the wider public but incorporating the repressive effects on progressive activism and dissent.

While my interest is centred on the extent of police infiltration of progressive social movements and on its impact on groups, causes and individuals, the specific focus of this book is on the public inquiry as a vehicle for acknowledging the truth. The Undercover Policing Inquiry was announced by the then Home Secretary Theresa May in 2014 and established in 2015. The expectation at the time was that, in line with other inquiries, it would carry out a background investigation, hold a series of public evidence hearings and then report back to the Home Office with its findings and recommendations. Most accounts at that point expected the final report by 2018. As I am writing this introductory chapter, now almost eight years after the Inquiry was set up, the Undercover Policing Inquiry has held just three rounds of evidence hearings that have only considered police operations up to the early 1980s, and the next phase is not expected for another year. It has divided its work into 'tranches', which enables the Inquiry to approach its work in broadly chronological order. Tranches 1, 2, 3 and 4 cover the periods 1968–82, 1983–92, 1993–2007 and the more recent NPOIU deployments respectively. So far, the Inquiry has only published an interim report on the first tranche, in June 2023. It is yet to hear public evidence on any police operations within the past 40 years. More than this glacial pace in considering evidence, which only in part can be ascribed to the impact of the COVID-19 pandemic, the Inquiry has been caught up in a legal battle over its remit, its organisation and its processes during a lengthy 'preliminary phase' of its work. Most significantly here, it has been delayed again and again by police applications for anonymity or restrictions to disclosure and public deliberation.

In this way, my initial research project, to study undercover policing, shifted to the public inquiry. Looking back, when the Inquiry was announced by the Home Office, I shared the view of many activists that this represented an uncertain, yet significant, victory. In the words of Imran Khan, the state's recognition that the widespread infiltration of political activist groups was real took it from the realm of paranoia to an acknowledged truth. As the proceedings slowly began, my primary interest in this public inquiry was essentially the same as that of the other activists I knew – finding out what happened, why it happened and how it could have been different. But over the years that followed, the conversations I had with people shifted. Their initial hopes that some light would be shed on the scandal of undercover policing gave way to boredom and frustration with the slow pace of the official process. In contrast, my fascination moved increasingly away from the content of the Inquiry – the specific policing units tasked with infiltrating and monitoring political campaigns since 1968 – and to the protracted, bureaucratic and legalistic contradictions that held back the official investigation. In short, I diverged from many of the activists in that my interest in the Inquiry processes increased, while theirs waned.

## The Terms of Reference

As a statutory, judge-led inquiry, the Undercover Policing Inquiry was set up in accordance with the Inquiries Act 2005 and the Inquiry Rules 2006. The Terms of Reference are rather broad, although there are some notable omissions from its remit. As both Chairmen of the Inquiry – Sir John Mitting and before him Sir Christopher Pitchford – have been keen to stress, its priority is the understanding of what happened: the truth. It is tasked to 'inquire into and report on undercover policing operations conducted by English and Welsh police forces in England and Wales since 1968', a period of 48 years. The stipulation of the year 1968 refers to the establishment of one undercover police unit in Special Branch, the SDS. The NPOIU, an offshoot of and successor to the SDS, will also be scrutinised. While the Inquiry does not restrict itself to undercover operations conducted in order to gather intelligence on political campaigns, the nature of these two units already suggests an emphasis on what critics call 'political policing'. This is interesting insofar as public inquiries into policing matters are frequently restricted by very narrow Terms of Reference that rarely look beyond the improvements that can be made to police management. From the outset, these broader political perspectives had to compete with smaller administrative ones. For example, the restriction of the Inquiry to police operations in England and Wales only is a major bone of contention. The NPOIU, for example, was centrally involved in gathering intelligence for the purposes of informing public order policing in Scotland, as well as internationally in countries such as Germany, Iceland, Italy, France and Spain. A number of stakeholders have made repeated calls to the Home Secretary to broaden the remit to include at least Scotland and Northern Ireland. The Scottish government, for example, has formally requested inclusion in the Terms of Reference. The issue has also been raised by senior politicians in Ireland and Germany.

The Terms of Reference (reproduced in Appendix A) asks the Inquiry to pay particular attention to six aspects of undercover policing. In brief, these can be summed up as: (1) the aims and achievements of undercover policing; (2) its rationale, and its effects on the public; (3) its justification; (4) knowledge of undercover policing methods in government; (5) oversight and governance; and (6) selection process, training and management, and support available to undercover officers. It is worth noting also what the Inquiry does *not* cover, despite valid arguments that omitting these matters only allows for a partial picture to emerge. Such issues include any undercover police work conducted outside of England and Wales (despite frequent trips abroad by a number of known former undercover officers); corporate intelligence gathering on political activism (despite clear links between private security operations and the public police); and anything that involves the security services (despite clear evidence that the SDS routinely passed information to MI5).[3]

One of the concerns of the Inquiry is the potential of miscarriages of justice, resulting, for example, from cases where intelligence gathered through undercover operations has not been made available to the defence in criminal trials. This concern is in part informed by an earlier review into a specific account of miscarriages of justice where the work of one officer – Mark Kennedy – had led to the pre-emptive arrest and eventual prosecution of a group of environmental activists (Rose, 2011). The fact that Kennedy had infiltrated the protest group was not disclosed to the activists' defence team, although it was known to the prosecution. In the event, the Court of Appeal quashed the sentences of several activists, deeming their convictions unsafe. While the Inquiry is not itself responsible for investigating miscarriages of justice, in the event of identifying any potential unsafe convictions it is obliged to report these to a justice panel.[4]

## Preliminary matters

For an incredibly lengthy period of five years, after which core participants were finally able to make their opening statements, a large part of the work of the Inquiry had consisted of determining preliminary legal issues and setting out guidance principles. In cases where submissions to the Inquiry needed further exploration, often because they were contested, the Inquiry held preliminary oral hearings in the Royal Courts of Justice. There have been a series of these hearings and they have spanned a wide range of matters, including the determination of applications for core participant status, the allocation of legal representation and public funding, the legal approach to be taken in relation to application for restriction orders, the terms of an undertaking sought from the Attorney General, the state's duty to disclose to the parents of a deceased child that the child's identity was used for police purposes, considerations of SDS officers' anonymity applications and the consideration of spent convictions under the Rehabilitation of Offenders Act 1974. I cover many of these issues and the controversies that accompanied them in this book, drawing on my observations and document analysis. I also draw on discussions and interviews with core participants.

## The core participants

At the end of 2022, the Inquiry had 247 designated core participants. A core participant is a formally designated person or organisation under the Inquiry Rules 2006 with a significant interest in a public inquiry's subject matter. Core participants have participatory rights in inquiry proceedings and may access funded legal representation. They can be provided with disclosure of evidence that is not in the public domain, have the opportunity to make opening and closing statements or suggest lines of questioning of witnesses.

In some of the existing academic literature on public inquiries, especially within political science research on public administration, attention is paid to the Chair's significant role in setting the agenda and determining outcomes. In the UK system of inquiries, Chairs are often – though not always – appointed from a narrow pool of male, white, retirement-age judges. To some extent, this role for the judiciary underlines the supposedly impartial and politically independent nature of what is, in theory, an inquisitorial process. On the other hand, senior judges retain an image of being close to the conservative establishment, or, in the words of criminologist and Hillsborough Independent Panel member Phil Scraton, they are 'achievers within the status quo' (Scraton, 2013a, p 48). An Institute for Government analysis points to the ludicrous reflection of this status quo in the appointment of inquiry Chairs, when it notes that between 1990 and 2017 there were fewer inquiries chaired by women than by individuals with their given names being either Anthony or William (Institute for Government, 2018).

In this book, however, the emphasis is elsewhere, namely on the core participants themselves. There are two initial observations I could make in this regard. First, core participant status matters. Controversially, the Inquiry rejected several applications from prospective core participants who believed that they had been spied on, including some from high-profile campaigners such as Ricky Tomlinson, Peter Tatchell and Jenny Jones. The rejections have usually been on the grounds that there was no evidence that the police monitoring of the applicant had been made through the manipulation of relationships by authorised covert human intelligence sources. Yet, as the applicants and their supporters have pointed out, to prove beyond doubt that such targeted surveillance occurred would necessitate a prior disclosure of police authorisation documents and therefore the inclusion as interested parties in the Inquiry. We will come back to this overarching paradox that beset the Inquiry early on – of being a *public* inquiry into *secret* activity.[5] Second, there are in effect two separate categories of core participants in the Undercover Policing Inquiry. They are referred to as 'state core participants', a group that includes police officers and organisations, and 'non-police, non-state core participants', sometimes and inconsistently abbreviated in official documentation to NSCPs, NPNSCPs or NSNCPs.

There are three categories of state core participants with letter cyphers in the Inquiry:

A. Police institutions
B. Government
C. Police officers

Non-police, non-state core participants are also subdivided into categories for the purposes of the Inquiry's work and they are in effect 'the victims' of spycops policing:

D. Political organisations and politicians
E. Trades unions and trades union members
F. Relatives of deceased children
G. The family of Stephen Lawrence, Duwayne Brooks OBE and Michael Mansfield
H. Individuals in relationships with undercover officers
I. Miscarriage of justice
J. Justice campaigns
K. Political activists
L. Social and environmental activists
M. Families of police officers

At times, these categories hide considerable social or generational differences between those grouped together. While most would have been involved in political activity around broadly progressive social and environmental causes, this activity stretched across almost half a century and involved people from contrasting demographic backgrounds and with irreconcilable political beliefs. More fundamentally, the relationship between state and most non-state core participants is marked by opposing positions which have placed conflicting demands on the Inquiry. A ruling by the Chair Sir Christopher Pitchford in 2016 recognised the contrasting interests of police and state witnesses and of everybody else.

> There is a difference in status or position of witnesses within the Inquiry between (a) police officers and state employees and (b) those non-police, non-state witnesses who have been affected by undercover police operations. The main purpose of the Inquiry is to investigate undercover policing and not the conduct of those who were affected by it. To the extent that the conduct of non-police, non-state witnesses is examined it is a collateral effect of the main focus of the Inquiry. (UCPI, 2016, p 9)

In the sense that police witnesses were accused of wrongdoing, this was also a recognition that what was set up as an inquisitorial process was inhabited by participants engaged in adversarial conduct.

## Methods

To paraphrase the one-time president of the British Society of Criminology, Maureen Cain, sociological ignorance of secret policing stems from a methodological conundrum: it is neglected theoretically because of the obvious obstacles in studying it empirically (Cain, cited in McLaughlin, 2007, p 61). This is beginning to change, not least in newer fields of research, such as critical security studies and even in relation to state secrets (see, for example, Walters, 2021). Among a flurry of methodological approaches and tools – from freedom of information requests to whistleblower testimony – it has also been recognised that 'the public inquiry form is a promising setting for secrecy research' (Walters, 2021, p 24). The Undercover Policing Inquiry is a case in point.

The empirical research for this book was carried out between 2015 and 2023. There was considerable ebb and flow during the research process. At times, my engagement with the study was intense and focused, while at other times it lay dormant for longer periods. As will become clear in the pages that follow, my approach observed a rigorous methodology, and yet was partisan in nature. The aim was to subject the Inquiry to academic scrutiny and contribute to the activist campaign for more transparency. The empirical research began in earnest when the Inquiry held its first preliminary meeting. At the end of 2016 and in the first half of 2017, I interviewed some two dozen activists who had discovered that they had been targeted by covert human intelligence sources because of their political activities, views or associations. The majority of the interview participants had contacted the public inquiry and been designated as core participants. The interviews focused on one key theme: the relative legitimacy of the Inquiry in the eyes of those who were the targets of intrusive surveillance by undercover police. I wanted to know what hopes and fears those 'non-police' core participants had for the Inquiry.

The second aspect of the research took me to the Royal Courts of Justice for observations of a number of preliminary oral hearings that were open to the public. While I made initial contact with the Inquiry's press secretary to reveal my presence as a researcher to the Inquiry team, I soon found it more practicable to observe the hearings from the public gallery, frequently sitting among the non-police, non-state participants who were there to witness the legal arguments that would define the Inquiry's mode of operation. When hearings were conducted remotely to comply with COVID-19 restrictions I tried to follow the proceedings online as best as possible. Public hearings have been crucial to facilitate the academic scrutiny of the Inquiry's work. At other times, restrictions to public access have been insurmountable obstacles. For much of the process, I have shared the non-police, non-state participants' frustration with a lack of transparency. But being around others, for example during hearings, at protests outside the hearing rooms or in meetings and conversations, helped me to understand how the Inquiry's work was perceived.

Finally, a substantial element of what I present in this book is based on the analysis of publicly available documents that can be accessed on the Undercover Policing Inquiry website. They include a huge range of resources. Among the most useful have been the transcripts of hearings produced by the Inquiry team. There are also a number of publications by the Inquiry Chair and counsel to the Inquiry, such as statements, directions or 'minded-to' notes. In addition, there are a huge number of legal submissions on matters of importance in the preliminary phase from those acting on behalf of various core participants. Finally, I have relied on the applications for restriction orders by or on behalf of former police officers and their associated risk assessments and supporting documentation, despite the fact that many of them were heavily redacted.

My reading of these publicly accessible documents tries to make a small contribution, not just to the academic study of policing and of public inquiries, but also to the efforts of those who have been subjected to undercover policing strategies, in order to bring some light into this darkness. My account is necessarily partial and reflects my own position and interests and my familiarity within the discussions among activists with social and environmental justice backgrounds. While I have sought to be systematic in my analysis, there are several and perhaps important omissions. These are not oversights, however. It is simply the case that there are other people much better placed than me to complete the partial account I have provided here. Nonetheless, some activists may read these following pages and find their stories missing, perhaps even misrepresented. They would be right to criticise.

As this book is focused on matters of secrecy, disclosure and privacy in the procedures of the public inquiry, and much less so on the evidence provided to it, I have not been able to do full justice to the experiences of the women who found out that they had been deceived into intimate relationships with undercover policemen. Yet, their experiences must remain central to any discussion of the spycops scandal. Several of the women subjected to sexual infiltration have taken leading roles in the campaign for transparency and so their stories are present in this book. But they themselves are better placed than me to expand on these and they have done so publicly many times. I would encourage any reader new to the spycops scandal to pause here and to first seek out some of their personal accounts. Good places to start are the website of the support group Police Spies Out of Lives, the co-authored book *Deep Deception* (Alison et al, 2022) and Donna McLean's *Small Town Girl* (2022).

The second omission in this book is that of the continuing problem of institutional racism in the British police and the experiences of anti-racist family justice campaigns. Chapter 2 will briefly explain how Theresa May was driven to announce a full public inquiry into undercover policing by the finding of the Stephen Lawrence Independent Review in 2014 that there had been a SDS deployment into the Lawrence's family campaign for justice. It is a great shame that the accounts of people, families and organisations that have campaigned for racial equality, accountability and truth around police violence against black people in Britain have again been sidelined in the public inquiry. They are not easily silenced, however. Alongside the Lawrence family, the family friend Duwayne Brooks and their lawyer Michael Mansfield, justice campaigns in the Undercover Policing Inquiry are grouped under category 'J' as non-police, non-state core participants. These include the families of Blair Peach, of Cherry Groce, of Joy Gardener, of Roger Sylvester and of Jean Charles de Menezes, all of whom died as a direct result of police action.

They also include the family of Ricky Reel and the Justice for Ricky Reel campaign. Ricky was 20 years old, a student at Brunel University London, when he went missing on 14 October 1997. A week later his body was recovered from the river in Kingston upon Thames. On the day of his disappearance, Ricky and a group of friends were racially abused and attacked. The friends were all Asian men studying at Brunel; Ricky was a British Sikh from West Drayton in London. Despite protestations from the family, the police investigation recorded an accidental death and refused to contemplate any suspicious circumstances. Ricky's parents, Sukhdev and

Balwant Reel, feared that their son had been murdered by racists. The police did not take them seriously. The matter was referred to what was then the Police Complaints Authority (PCA). Its inquiry found failures and flaws in the initial police response and neglect in the subsequent investigation. The PCA report was released to the Reel family only under the condition that it would remain confidential. It took their local MP, John McDonnell, who had supported the family from the start, to use his parliamentary privilege to bring the findings into the public domain. As McDonnell (2022, p 5) recalls, '[t]he use of the redaction of reports provided to the family and me by the police rendered them farcical at times as only individual words were revealed and we were not allowed to take away our individual copies in case we put them together to make sense of sentences'. A later inquest questioned the initial 'accidental death' report and returned an 'open verdict'.

Ricky's family held on to the memory of their son and to their belief that he was murdered in a racist attack. They now also felt that the police response to them and to their enquiries was marked by racism. Sukhdev Reel, Ricky's mother, worked closely with the anti-racist charity Southall Monitoring Group, established by Suresh Grover following other racist killings in London. Now known as The Monitoring Group, the charity has organised legal defence campaigns and supported grieving families seeking justice since 1979.

Many of these families found out that there had been undercover police involvement in or around their campaigning for justice and accountability only when officers from Operation Herne, the police-internal criminal investigation into spycops policing, told them of such accusations. This is what happened to Sukhdev Reel when in 2014 a letter from the Metropolitan Police asked her to meet with officers from the Operation Herne team. She was told that there were accusations of police spying on the Justice for Ricky Reel campaign and she was later given (with the condition not to share them with anyone, even within her family) 13 heavily redacted intelligence files produced by the SDS. In a report by Operation Herne (2014a), accusations that category 'J' core participants were the targets of SDS undercover officers are to be treated as specifically 'sensitive'. The campaigns had typically arisen out of family concerns that police conduct or negligence had led to the death of a family member while in police custody or after contact with the police, or resulted from unanswered questions about the criminal investigations into murders – as was the case with Stephen Lawrence and Ricky Reel.

The police have maintained that the families' campaigns themselves had *not* been placed under surveillance; rather they had been victims of 'collateral intrusion'. The true targets of police infiltration – if indeed there had been any – had been the revolutionary activities of the support groups associated with the family campaigns. Needless to say, the justice campaigns that for years had found the police less than willing to allow scrutiny of their actions and all too eager to evade accountability remained unconvinced by the story of 'collateral intrusion'. In her book *Silence Is Not an Option*, Sukhdev Reel writes of the meeting with the Operation Herne investigators: 'it plays on my mind and it leaves me angry' (Reel, 2022, p 169). 'They said the surveillance of our Campaign was simply "collateral intrusion". This was the exact term used as if the damage done to us was simply "collateral".' Sukhdev and her family began looking for evidence which could show that SDS officers were centrally involved in the campaigns themselves. But, like other activists, they encountered the problem that the names and photographs of any contemporaneous spycops were kept secret.

Stafford Scott is also a core participant in the public inquiry and co-founder of the Broadwater Farm Defence Campaign in 1985. He is now the director of Tottenham Rights, part of The Monitoring Group, and a core participant in the Inquiry. Scott's characterisation of his experiences with the Undercover Policing Inquiry is illustrative of the Inquiry's blindness to racism:

> As a black activist who has been campaigning against racism and discrimination for decades I find myself being forced together with other activists with whom I share very little in common and who incidentally have very little in common with me. I am compelled to go to legal meetings where the vast majority of lawyers are white, have no understanding of institutional racism and are therefore unable to empathise with and understand my experience. Yet, somehow these legal experts are supposed to represent my interests? (Scott, nd)

Not to be dismissed as collateral, these stories are in fact crucial to understanding the impact of undercover operations on democratic political activity. Readers are encouraged to seek them out to complement my limited description of the undercover policing scandal here. There are few better voices to listen to than Sukhdev Reel's (2022).

Despite these gaps, my analysis of the controversies in and around the Undercover Policing Inquiry reveal a remarkable coming together of people from different walks of life with different political priorities and diverse personal experiences of injustice in a powerful movement for truth and accountability. They have come together to be heard and to push the British state to fully investigate the repression they experienced.

## Structure of the book

The presentation of my analysis in this book follows a thematic rather than strictly chronological structure. There are overlaps between the two, however, and a timeline of key occurrences in and around the Undercover Policing Inquiry in Appendix B should aid the reader in gaining an overview of the sequence of events. Before the book looks more closely at the most significant disagreements that arose in the preliminary phase of the Inquiry, I have found it necessary to provide some background in Chapters 2 and 3.

Chapter 2 introduces the spycops scandal and follows some key narratives as they unfolded. Towards the end of 2010, a group of activists confronted their friend 'Mark Stone' with the suspicion that he was in fact an undercover police officer, whose real name was Mark Kennedy. The Kennedy story quickly spiralled into the wider public debate, helped in large part by investigations carried out by *The Guardian* journalists Rob Evans and Paul Lewis. Their book, *Undercover: The True Story of Britain's Secret Police* (2013), is still one of the best accounts of how the spycops scandal unfolded. In close cooperation with a group of activists with their background in environmental direct action and animal rights, the investigative reporters revealed how clandestine police units had been set up from the 1960s onwards to conduct surveillance operations targeting British 'subversives' and later 'domestic extremists'. What began with the infiltration of the Vietnam Solidarity Campaign in 1968 spiralled into a nebulous network of police infiltrators who went undercover in political groups as diverse as the Socialist Workers Party, the Campaign for Nuclear Disarmament and the Camp for Climate Action. Over the next few months in 2011, the allegations against police spies multiplied and led to collapsed prosecutions and the quashing of convictions of environmental protesters. In 2015, eventually, the Home Secretary established the public inquiry, responding to concerns that the Metropolitan Police had subjected the Stephen Lawrence family campaign to covert surveillance. Quite to the contrary of the often-assumed character of British policing as *policing by consent,* the chapter picks up on the idea that this was *policing by deception.*

Chapter 3 offers some further methodological reflections, but mostly at a theoretical level. How can academic researchers break into the hidden worlds of secret police activity if opportunities for public scrutiny are largely foreclosed? My answer to this question can best be thought of as an answer to a methodological challenge that I have been confronted with repeatedly when talking to criminology colleagues about my research. They put to me, often as a fundamental objection, that without *police knowledge* I could not make sense of the role of spycops and the confidentiality needed to protect them. To recall just one example: at a conference, a retired-officer-turned-academic said that he had authorised a number of undercover deployments in his police career and that if I only knew the circumstances I "would be glad about it". This theme, that only those with policing experience can fully appreciate why secret activity is justified, is not novel. That working relationships between academic researchers and police organisations are mutually beneficial has become a dominant catchphrase. Yet when it comes to political policing, this is highly doubtful. To make my point, I contrast the insistence on police knowledge with Reece Walters' notion of *deviant knowledge* (Walters, 2003). Investigating the politics of criminological knowledge production, Walters' work allows us to refocus attention on the need for critical distance to corporate and state interests, research integrity and intellectual autonomy. Simply put, my argument is that Special Branch does not make for a good research partner.

Chapter 4 focuses on the police's initial insistence that they could 'neither confirm nor deny' their use of covert human intelligence sources to monitor political campaign groups. This line of quasi-denial was repeated over and over, but the chapter shows how it was also a policy *invention*. Police institutions went to great lengths to demonstrate that their stance of not commenting on any such allegations was born from principle but tied themselves in knots and contradictory arguments. Moreover, their attempts to block or derail any investigation into political undercover policing were ruptured at key moments by new exposures and allegations. Finally, in 2015, following an out-of-court settlement with seven women who had launched legal action against the police over the deceitful relationships they had entered into with undercover policemen, the Metropolitan Police issued a formal apology, accepting that 'these relationships were a violation of the women's human rights, an abuse of police power and caused significant trauma' (cited in Evans, 2015a). It was now clear that some form of acknowledgement had been conceded in the campaign against police surveillance of political activity. In the Undercover Policing Inquiry, however, the Metropolitan Police lawyers continued a strategy of intransigence and denial. The chapter therefore looks at the contested arena of the Inquiry's preliminary phase as a *site of struggle*.

In Chapter 5, I analyse much of the material that is held by the Inquiry as 'dirty and hidden data'. The term derives from the work of the surveillance studies scholar Gary Marx (1984) but is applied here more broadly to encompass the wealth of data that is available to the public inquiry but remains out of the public view. Police intelligence files undergo strict processes of redaction and are subjected to risk assessments before they are made available to core participants. This chapter also analyses the struggles over public disclosure and evidence gathering approaches adopted by the Inquiry. It emerged as a particular problem that the Inquiry was prepared to keep many of the cover names used by undercover police officers confidential, thereby cutting off an avenue for participation by activists who now would not be told that their campaign groups had been infiltrated. What appeared as a process to maintain police secrets, however, was more complex than that. The chapter engages with recent work by the political sociologist William Walters (2021) to think through the complexities involved in inquiring publicly into state secrets. Far from state secrets being totalising, they figure in a public 'covert imaginary' and are made intelligible through what Walters calls 'devices of dis/closure'.

Chapter 6 considers the legal strategy by the police and lawyers acting on behalf of former undercover officers, which is frequently based on human rights. The relationship between criminal justice and privacy is a complex one. But as the spycops scandal broke, much of the early discussion was understandably framed in terms that linked covert policing to violations of privacy rights. Yet, as the preliminary stages of the public inquiry went underway, it was, perversely, the police who sought to protect the human rights of its officers. They sent big batches of applications to the Inquiry Chair, asking him to issue restriction orders which would keep the identities of former undercover officers secret and allow for the heavy redaction of any police files that would have to be made public. With remorse for past wrongdoings apparently gone, the cruel irony that police had discovered the importance of privacy rights under Article 8 of the European Convention on Human Rights was not lost on those who were still awaiting answers about the extent of police infiltration into their lives.

Chapter 7 highlights some of the tactics used by the victims of abusive undercover policing and their supporters to bring the Inquiry's shortcomings to public attention and to participate effectively in its work. Most campaigners for transparency and accountability in policing found that the public inquiry offered them little in the way of disclosure. Their frustrations with the huge expenses, the delay and the apparent stonewalling was clearly on show in their protests outside the hearing venues and in their attempts to intervene into the Inquiry process itself. This fight back against excessive secrecy was specifically driven by the women who were deceived into long-lasting, intimate relationships with male undercover officers. They valued the potential of the public inquiry, but they were also determined to push beyond its limits.

In the final chapter of the book, I situate the conflicts and contestations in the Undercover Policing Inquiry in a broader debate about the role of inquests and inquiries. The Inquiry appears as a whitewash; few readers of this book will come to a different conclusion. But to name it as such, and only as such, is to erase the struggles of those who have fought for greater openness and accountability. The levels of public access and ability to participate in the proceedings were continually contested, while attempts to limit them were resisted and police strategies of obfuscation were called out. These struggles in and around the public inquiry were therefore crucial. They gave voice to the pain and feelings of betrayal by those subjected to intrusive police surveillance. They shifted activist priorities. They exposed police leadership closing ranks. And they systematically demonstrated the limitations of the public inquiry as a method for police accountability.

# 2

# The undercover policing scandal

### Unravelling threads of deception

The unmasking of Mark Kennedy, which became public in a post made on the then popular activist publishing platform *Indymedia UK*, slowly rippled through the milieu of British direct action and anarchist groups. But there was no 'big bang', no sudden change of direction. Kennedy had played his part largely in horizontally organised activist communities and so the news spread rhizomatically, with different groups and networks making sense of it on their own terms. I do not think that anyone in those days had yet understood the magnitude of the discovery. Nor could they have done, because there had not yet been any official police acknowledgement that one of their own had been unmasked. *The Guardian* journalists Rob Evans and Paul Lewis worked right in the middle of the exposures, often in tandem with the affected activists themselves. As they describe it in their book *Undercover: The True Story of Britain's Secret Police*:

> [T]he process of realisation was a gradual one. There was no sudden deluge of revelations, no decision from on high to come clean about the dark truth of covert policing. None of those who were spied upon were granted permission to visit a police warehouse, open their file and discover which friends and lovers had betrayed them. All of that is perhaps still to come. (Evans and Lewis, 2013, p 3)

If the journalists doubted that disclosure and full public debate about covert policing would follow, they were right to do so. Despite the public inquiry, no one from up high has come to the decision to 'come clean'. To find any answers at all, to gain any permission to open the files, has been a constant struggle and contestation between arguments for openness and arguments for secrecy.

And yet there are stories to be told. Evans and Lewis write that 'one of the most tightly guarded secrets the British police had ever kept from the people unravelled slowly, like an old jumper finally worn thin' (Evans and Lewis, 2013, p x). This chapter follows the thread as it unravels and examines the road to the public inquiry. How did the exposure of the undercover operative Mark Kennedy raise the alarm to sufficiently trouble the Home Secretary to order a full, statutory public inquiry? Who were Kennedy's colleagues in the police, what did they aim to achieve and what were their methods? And how did a group of environmental and anarchist protesters secure public acknowledgement of a surveillance operation of such proportions?

This chapter serves as an introduction to the spycops deployments. As an area of sociological and criminological research, knowledge of political undercover policing remains limited. The 'closed world' of covert surveillance all too often remains closed off also to academic scrutiny. This difficulty notwithstanding, for some time in the early 2010s, the unmasking of field officers such as 'Lynn Watson', Jim Boyling, Bob Lambert and 'Marco Jacobs' received a tremendous amount of coverage in the British and international media. Their exposures also led to a number of investigations into the issue of police spying on left-wing political activists and campaigners, notably the inquiry led by the prominent barrister Mark Ellison and the Metropolitan Police's own investigation known as Operation Herne.

As this book is about the public inquiry that followed, rather than the scandal itself, the introduction to what actually happened is necessarily limited. But the chapter highlights three 'ingredients' to the scandal that, together, have moved undercover policing into the national spotlight. First, the practices and strategies of the undercover policing units cannot be divorced from institutional racism. Second, the revelations that undercover police targeted women for infiltration, deceiving many into intimate relationships that lasted years, extended the narratives of abuse to a latent, yet institutionalised, sexism at the heart of policing. Third, the infiltration of primarily progressive causes and their retroactive construction as 'subversive' or 'extremist' brought the charge of political bias. It appeared that a particular model of British undercover policing had been employed to protect conservative, elite and business interests from grassroots dissent. To conclude, the chapter examines the way that the scandal has progressed in many ways because of the tenacity of those most affected by police infiltration, a broad and diverse church of activists who have in effect become campaigners for accountability in and beyond the public inquiry. While their backgrounds are diverse, they are all brought together by a desire to find an acknowledged truth.

## The making of a scandal

The exposure of Mark Kennedy as a covert human intelligence source, placed right in the heart of the horizontal direct action networks of the British Left, quickly unfolded as a crisis for police legitimacy. It is probably fair to say that conservative politicians and security advisors had little sympathy for the infiltrated protest groups. How, then, did it come about that a state-sponsored, full inquiry was deemed necessary?

In a short overview of the UK system of inquiries, the Institute for Government notes that '[t]he only justification required for a public inquiry is the existence of "public concern" about a particular event or set of events' (Institute for Government, 2018). It is difficult to be precise about the term 'public concern'; what is the public concerned about? Why are inquiries appointed to look into some matters of concern, but not others? Research into these questions has pointed at various issues of salience, such as the visibility of failings and the presence of relatable victims (Sulitzeanu-Kenan, 2010; Thomas and Cooper, 2020). In other words, while some matters of public concern remain latent, others are elevated to the status of 'institutional scandals'.

The sociologists Chris Greer and Eugene McLaughlin (2016) note the proliferation of scandals engulfing Britain's public institutions – from local authorities to the BBC. Building on symbolic interactionist perspectives, they explain scandal proliferation as a process shaped by the dynamic interactions between a set of state and non-state actors. Here they grant a significant space to the power of the mainstream media to define and amplify public scandals. Greer and McLaughlin assert that transformations in the British media landscape make 'scandal hunting' a lucrative endeavour for the national press and internet news sites alike. Initially, the scandal might be largely concealed from public knowledge but latently present as an open secret within the institution. These open secrets may become activated where rumour or chatter on social media and online forums is picked up and verified by mainstream news agencies (Greer and McLaughlin, 2011). Thus validated, scandals provoke reaction, primarily by public institutions seeking to manage their institutional reputation. In cases where the scandal fits with the news agency's business model, a phase of 'trial by media' sets in, whereby individuals are blamed and institutional processes are scrutinised – leading to scandal amplification. The accountability phase of the scandal's lifecycle is characterised by 'the *separation* of the individual and institutional accountability' (Greer and McLaughlin, 2016, p 122, emphasis in the original). The authorities will seek to manage the institutional crisis by seeking to establish the 'official truth' and rectify the institutional failures. Applied to the infiltrations of political targets by the police's undercover units, this model can be usefully employed – yet, as we will see, with an important reservation:

1. *Latency.* In this phase social movement activists first suspected and then discovered the identity of undercover officers who had infiltrated environmental campaigns and other protest networks. They began to paint a picture of the police operations: 'spycops' – the umbrella term given by activists to the officers sent to infiltrate political groups – spent months, even years, living the lives of committed campaigners, taking leading roles in member-led organisations and influencing the activities of their campaigns.

2. *Activation.* A post on the activist website Indymedia UK alerted other activists to the police identity of Mark Kennedy. Working with the journalists Paul Lewis and Rob Evans from *The Guardian* newspaper, the scandal was brought to public attention in the national press.
3. *Reaction.* Kennedy and his former police employers reacted in various ways to contain and neutralise the scandal, as well as to shift the blame. Kennedy, for example, made frequent media appearances while the police launched an internal investigation into the allegations. Senior officers, at first, signalled that Kennedy was a lone, rogue officer. In fact, Kennedy's deployment into climate activism was preceded by dozens of others, with the main targets for infiltration being those with left-wing and progressive political affiliations.
4. *Amplification.* The uncovering of further police infiltrators served to amplify the scandal. A whistleblower, Peter Francis, alleged that he had been sent to monitor and smear the justice campaign run by Stephen Lawrence's family and his mother. These revelations and allegations proved toxic for the police. Francis, a former Special Demonstration Squad (SDS) undercover officer, was interviewed about his allegations in the national press and appeared in a Channel 4 *Dispatches* programme titled 'The Police's Dirty Secret'.
5. *Accountability.* A number of accountability mechanisms were employed, from official investigations to the quashing of sentences for falsely convicted activists. Eventually, the Home Secretary, Theresa May, recognised that the scandal had warranted enough public concern to establish a statutory inquiry.

While the model works, there is also a significant shortcoming in its applications to this case. In describing it as a 'scandal machine', Greer and McLaughlin themselves insinuate that there is something mechanical in the workings of their procedural model, although they warn against any sort of determinism. Reading it in this way, it appears as if the establishment of the Undercover Policing Inquiry was a natural and inevitable phase in the 'process' of the scandal proliferation model. In fact, a public inquiry into secret state activity was far from assured. Rather, the scandal proliferation that led to the public inquiry was driven by activists seeking to establish the truth very much against the official accountability processes.

Greer and McLaughlin propose that the modern regulatory state has lost its traditional deference to the sanctity of its own public institutions. Members of the British government and establishment are less adamant to protect public bodies from criticism and instead employ the mechanisms of audit, accountability and performance management to maintain the dynamic yet continuous legitimacy of state institutions. The sociologists mean to criticise the work of political scientists, who, in a functionalist manner, assume that state-sanctioned moral outrage about the failings of its own system components is an acceptable mechanism for the correction of individual faults. In the regulatory state, on the other hand, the public inquiry brings to the fore systemic and institutional failure. Clearly, such theorisation on institutional scandals is a noteworthy attempt to regenerate sociological state analysis by infusing it with the conceptual frameworks of media sociology and regulation. Thus, it goes beyond an analysis of the abstract role of the state to create, justify and enforce legal rules designed to maintain economic, racialised and gendered divisions in the accounts of many critical criminologists. It seeks instead to progress a more empirically grounded and interactionist understanding of the changing character of the state in different regimes of accumulation.

But what does this mean for political strategy and agency? Even though the model advocated by Greer and McLaughlin reintroduces an activation phase in the cycle of moral panic and scandal formation, it foregrounds the state's and mainstream media's response and inserts the conflicting interests of state control and its detractors only as an afterthought. The model describes the context of scandals as a business model of the press and a state increasingly prepared to allow the hollowing out of its own institutions. The agency of other actors only serves to activate and accelerate an already existing structural failure. By contrast, in the various stages of the undercover policing scandal, campaigners and activists played a pivotal role. The process of the Undercover Policing Inquiry, too, is very much driven by those who want to see justice done. Those who are engaging in the process, the so-called non-police, non-state core participants, are a vital public from where the Inquiry receives legitimacy and acknowledgement. Without the active and critical participation of those whose lives were infiltrated, the Undercover Policing Inquiry would have resembled an establishment cover-up much more than the eventual site of contestation that it became.

## The greatest possible scrutiny?

The findings and recommendations of public inquiries or royal commissions frequently leave their imprint on public policy and discourse. But few have had as enduring an impact as the final report of the Stephen Lawrence Inquiry. Over 389 pages, its Chair Sir William Macpherson of Cluny examined the matters arising from the murder of the black London teenager Stephen Lawrence and made his recommendations for the investigation and prosecution of racially motivated crimes. The Macpherson report, which was sent to the Home Secretary Jack Straw in February 1999, has become synonymous with the recognition of institutional racism in London's Metropolitan Police and police forces more widely. In its well-known formulation, institutional racism is referred to as:

[T]he collective failure of an organisation to provide an appropriate and professional service to people because of their colour, culture or ethnic origin. It can be seen or detected in processes, attitudes and behaviour which amount to discrimination through unwitting prejudice, ignorance, thoughtlessness, and racist stereotyping which disadvantage minority ethnic people. (Macpherson, 1999, paragraph 6.34)

The concept of institutional racism highlights how racist attitudes do not simply play out as individual attributes but are woven into the fabrics of institutions. This was not exactly a new 'discovery'. Macpherson recognised that the term had long been used by racial justice activists and academics, as well as many campaigners on the Left. In fact, several of them contributed to his findings. Albeit it in a different context, in their 1967 book *Black Power*, the Trinidad-born civil rights organiser Stokely Carmichael (later Kwame Ture) and the political scientist Charles Hamilton had already argued that institutional racism:

[O]riginates in the operation of established and respected forces in the society. It relies on the active and pervasive operation of anti-black attitudes and practices. A sense of superior group position prevails: whites are 'better' than blacks and therefore blacks should be subordinated to whites. This is a racist attitude and it permeates society on both the individual and institutional level, covertly or overtly. (Ture and Hamilton, 1992, pp 20–1)

But what the Stephen Lawrence Inquiry did was to give official acknowledgement to the fact of discriminatory policing experienced by black and ethnic minority communities in London. It shifted the discourse from one of the denial of racism to one of an acknowledged truth. To stress the importance of the Stephen Lawrence Inquiry report is not to canonise it as the final word – Macpherson was careful to stress this point himself. Similarly, in this book, the findings and processes of public inquiries are treated as inherently contested. While the report of the Stephen Lawrence Inquiry found widespread recognition, it continues to be at the sharp end of political challenges from those seeking to deny the presence of racism at the heart of policing.

To name just one high-profile example, the then Metropolitan Police's Commissioner Cressida Dick used an appearance before the Home Affairs Committee in July 2019 to reject the label of institutional racism. Being questioned on her force's progress in implementing the recommendations of the Macpherson report, Dick told the Committee that the Metropolitan Police was no longer institutionally racist and stressed that the label itself was 'toxic' and 'unhelpful'. Insisting that policing in the capital had been 'utterly transformed' in the past 20 years, the Commissioner added:

> The label now does more harm than good, it is something that is immediately interpreted by anybody who hears it as not institutional but racist – full of racists, full stop, which we are not … For me it is not a useful term at all. It is a label that puts people off from engaging with the police. It stops people wanting to give us intelligence, evidence, come and join us, work with us. (Dick, 2019)

To dismiss the charge of institutional racism as an 'unhelpful label' was wishful thinking. Little did the police chief know that the following two years would prove to be rocked by further scandals, putting public trust in the Metropolitan Police further into question, not least the use of force and containment tactics against Black Lives Matter demonstrations in 2020 (Elliott-Cooper, 2020). The Commissioner had repeatedly argued that it was for others to judge whether institutional racism still characterised the attitudes and processes in the force; and so they did. In February 2022, having lost the faith of London mayor Sadiq Khan in her leadership, Dick stood down from her role amid claims that the capital's police force had remained institutionally racist and sexist.

Against this backdrop of institutional failure, the legacy of Stephen Lawrence remains firmly wedded to fights for equality in British public life. The enduring significance of the Macpherson Inquiry and its report also made itself felt soon after the exposure of Mark Kennedy as a police officer working in the National Public Order Intelligence Unit (NPOIU). As we will see, questions about the botched Metropolitan Police investigation into Stephen Lawrence's killing bubbled back up to the surface, some 20 years after the murder.

## The Home Secretary's announcement

On 12 March 2015, Theresa May established the public inquiry into undercover policing in England and Wales. The inquiry was to be statutory, held under the 2005 Inquiries Act and chaired by an independent senior judge, Sir Christopher Pitchford. Already a year earlier, May had addressed parliament to set out the need for a judge-led inquiry. It followed the conclusion of an investigation into the Stephen Lawrence case that had landed on the Home Secretary's desk. In 2012, she had asked for a review to examine allegations of corruption linked to the initial police investigation of the murder. She commissioned Mark Ellison, a leading barrister with expertise in serious fraud cases, to carry out the review. Ellison was the ideal candidate. Based on new forensic evidence, he had led the prosecution of

Gary Dobson and David Norris some 19 years after the killing and secured their conviction for Lawrence's murder in early 2012.

Ellison's probe into corruption, which became known as the Stephen Lawrence Independent Review, certainly left its mark on the Home Secretary. She told parliament:

> 'I don't say this lightly, but I think that the greatest possible scrutiny is now needed into what has taken place. And so, given the gravity of what [has] now been uncovered, I have decided that a public inquiry, led by a judge, is necessary to investigate undercover policing and the operation of the SDS. Only a public inquiry will be able to get to the full truth behind the matters of huge concern contained in Mark Ellison's report.' (May, 2014)

We cannot quite know what swayed May in her decision. Was it the desire to preserve the integrity of the Macpherson report? Was her legacy as Home Secretary so tied up with the incorporation of the Lawrence campaign for justice into the mainstream of British politics? What we do know is that the unravelling undercover policing scandal added an incendiary ingredient to the allegations of corruption.

## Officer A: the whistleblower

The idea that the Metropolitan Police had at the very least attempted to undermine the Macpherson Inquiry into Lawrence's murder investigation was given fuel by an unlikely source. In March 2010, *The Observer* newspaper ran a story of a whistleblower, a former police officer referred to only as Officer A, who said that he had been deployed undercover by the SDS between 1993 and 1997. The newspaper's exposé sensationalised his role as that of a 'hardcore Trotskyist agitator with a passion for heavy drinking, a deep-seated hatred of the police and a predilection for extreme violence' (Thompson, 2010). In reality, he joined Youth against Racism in Europe (YRE), a Trotskyist organisation launched by Militant Labour, the forerunner to the Socialist Party. Some months later, *The Guardian*'s Paul Lewis and Rob Evans revealed Officer A's cover identity as 'Peter Black' and in 2013 he identified himself as Peter Francis in the Channel 4 *Dispatches* documentary 'The Police's Dirty Secret'.

Francis's allegations made in the media sent shockwaves through the police establishment. It was not the first time that someone from within its own ranks began to spill its secrets, but the former SDS officer did so without authorisation and at a time of heightened interest in the police's secret political units. Francis reported on the tactic of 'sexual infiltration', the use of police cover identities to deceive women into casual sex and long-term relationships. He revealed how cover personas were 'stolen' from the identities of deceased children, using public birth and death records. And, in the *Dispatches* documentary, he described his own task as seeking to 'smear' the campaign for justice that rallied around the Lawrence family. On this matter, Francis's allegations were the most explosive and they implicated two other SDS officers who were in the field with him and had infiltrated groups that supported the Lawrences and their campaign for justice. The SDS leadership came in for heavy criticism:

> They wanted any intelligence that could have smeared the campaigns … so had I through my circles come up with something along the lines of they, the family were political activists, if someone in the family were involved in demonstrations, drug dealers, anything … There were rumours and conjecture that the family itself may have not been a loving caring home. That was passed on about the family that could have, may have been used if they were really desperate to try and smear the family. (Francis, cited in Operation Herne, 2014b, p 7)

The possible presence of specialist undercover officers within the family campaign, including at the time of the Macpherson Inquiry, was perhaps reason enough for Theresa May to commission Ellison KC to investigate. In any case, she expanded his terms of reference to include the Francis allegations. They now included the question: 'Was there inappropriate undercover activity directed at the Lawrence family?' Mark Ellison's report, published as the Stephen Lawrence Independent Review, corroborated many, though not all, of Francis's accounts. Undercover officers were indeed present in the groups that supported the family campaign, yet this is explained as information gathering about the possibility of public disorder, rather than attempts to smear the family. However, Ellison acknowledged that the absence of surviving documents proving Francis's claims could not be seen as evidence that they were false. In fact, he eventually admitted that he was 'unable to reject' the allegations that the whistleblower had made 'simply because other SDS officers deny them' (Ellison, 2014, p 30).

Peter Francis's role in the anti-racism movement features heavily in the book *Undercover* by Rob Evans and Paul Lewis (2013) and the former SDS officer has made some high-profile media appearances. The journalists suggest that it was perhaps the excitement of being in the thick of confrontational demonstrations against the British National Party's presence in suburban East London that appealed most to Francis, who had adopted the cover name 'Peter Black'. The undercover identity was not picked at random. Like other officers, Francis visited St Catherine's House in Central London, which at the time held Britain's family records, including the births and deaths indexes. Using the death certificates of boys who were deceased at a young age and who would be of similar age to the undercover officers afforded the deployments an additional layer of protection from being discovered.

The early 1990s was an intense period of racist attacks in East London. The British National Party, led then by the neo-Nazi and former National Front chairperson John Tyndall, had set up shop in Bexley in 1989 and sought to radicalise English nationalism in the area. Stephen Lawrence was murdered on the streets of nearby Eltham. There had been other racially motivated killings in the area, including that of 15-year-old Rolan Adams whose family are core participants in the Inquiry. While police investigations at the time tried to 'de-racialise' the attacks, YRE was at the centre of a campaign that put the blame for racist violence on organised fascist mobilisations. Strategically, the group was also a response to the more moderate and Labour-entryist Anti-Racist Alliance and the re-launched Anti-Nazi League initiated by the Socialist Workers Party. YRE saw itself as part of a mass socialist movement, combative and militant via socialist agitation, rather than targeted violence. Its position was summarised neatly in the slogan 'Jobs and homes, not racism' and a key part of its activism in London centred on building mass opposition to the BNP headquarters in Bexley. The infiltration of a revolutionary group whose activists took part in confrontational street demonstrations against the far Right would have been seen by senior officers to deliver useful public order intelligence. But Francis's deployment went far beyond passing on information about possible disorder. As other SDS officers before him, he took active part in political activity and accepted leadership positions. Rising through the group's ranks, he ended up as an elected branch secretary for Militant Labour in Hackney. This not only allowed him access to key information about the forerunner to the Socialist Party but also participation in its democratic processes.

By the late 1990s, the SDS's purpose appeared to be focused on longer-term decision-making within the police and government. A Metropolitan Police review itself found that the previously tactical justification for undercover deployments into activist groups – namely the prevention of public disorder – had given way to a strategic one. The 2009 report is cited in the Ellison review:

> Over time the main objective of the SDS operation changed. It became focussed on obtaining strategic intelligence on the direction of subversive, extremist and other target groups for the purpose of informing decision making within the Police Service and Government. The objective was to know where a target organisation would be in five years and who would be leading or directing them. In this regard the SDS were successful and managed on many occasions to engineer their field officers into key positions within target groups. Tactical intelligence became a bi-product of the operation and secondary to

their long-term aim. (Metropolitan Police Service, cited in Ellison, 2014, p 22)

In reality, the public order purpose of the spycops operations provided a convenient fig leaf, hiding the wider, political role of the SDS. Many of the groups and individuals targeted by undercover officers provided little risk to public order, or none at all. Evidence heard during the Inquiry's Tranche 1 investigation showed that, instead, much of the impetus for the police spying came from the relationship between Special Branch and the Secret Service.

Ellison's report also highlighted what he called the 'wholly inappropriate' presence of an undercover officer at the time of the Macpherson Inquiry. The officer, referred to by the cypher N81, is described as 'an MPS [Metropolitan Police Service] spy in the Lawrence family camp during the course of judicial proceedings in which the family was the primary party in opposition to the MPS' (Ellison, 2014, pp 23–4). Years later, the Undercover Policing Inquiry released N81's cover name, 'David Hagan', and named his deployments as targeting the Movement for Justice, the Socialist Workers Party, Class War and the Movement against the Monarchy.

Apart from these findings, one other thing stands out from Ellison's review. The Metropolitan Police, it seemed, had not approached even the Macpherson Inquiry into its own failings with the required candour and transparency. In August 1998, the SDS arranged for N81 to meet Richard Walton, then a detective inspector seconded to the team tasked with writing the police submissions to the Macpherson Inquiry. This, at least, was Walton's initial admission to the Ellison review investigators, though when informed that criticism of the meeting would be contained in the final report, he quickly challenged the assumption that he was part of the MPS inquiry team at the time of meeting with N81, a change of mind described by Ellison as 'unconvincing' (Ellison, 2014, p 25). The report found that the meeting, held in the garden of another SDS officer (HN10 – Bob Lambert), was 'completely improper' and had it been made public at the time 'it would have been seen as the MPS trying to achieve some secret advantage in the Inquiry from SDS undercover deployment' (Ellison, 2014, p 26).

By the time Ellison reported, Walton had been promoted into one of the most senior roles in the Metropolitan Police, as head of Counter Terrorism Command or SO15, the successor unit to its Special Branch. Walton's role during the Macpherson Inquiry thus came under major scrutiny and it appears that he was temporarily moved to a non-operational role while his conduct was referred for investigation by the Independent Police Complaints Commission (IPCC). Scotland Yard could not wait for the outcome. While still under investigation by the IPCC, Walton resumed his role leading Counter Terrorism Command until his early retirement in January 2016. This was convenient timing. Leaving the force in 2016 meant that Walton could avoid any disciplinary hearings following the IPCC investigation. Baroness Lawrence, Stephen's mother, suspected more foul play: 'I find it upsetting to think that Commander Walton might be able to retire without being held to account ... He shouldn't be allowed to retire just when the IPCC says there's a case to answer' (cited in Wright, 2016). Richard Walton, meanwhile, continued in his post-police career as a public commentator on counter-terrorism strategies and consultant for think tanks. Despite the circumstances under which he left the Metropolitan Police, Walton also continued to show an interest in political activism. In 2019, for example, he co-authored a report for the influential conservative think tank Policy Exchange on the tactics of the environmental direct action network Extinction Rebellion, in which he argued that its non-violent outlook masked an extremist and anti-democratic ideology (Wilson and Walton, 2019).

The difficulty of gaining reliable information from the Metropolitan Police showed that Ellison was on to something and Theresa May had to make a decision. She gave public backing to an investigation by the National Crime Agency into the corruption allegations in the original Lawrence murder investigation, a criminal investigation overseen by Chief Constable Mick Creedon and the related, yet non-statutory, Daniel Morgan Independent Panel. The latter would conclude years later, in June 2021, that the Metropolitan Police's denial of its own failings constituted institutional corruption and made the recommendation that law enforcement agencies should be subject to a statutory duty of candour. Most importantly, however, the calls for a public inquiry into undercover policing had grown louder. May agreed.

The Home Secretary showed herself clearly dissatisfied with the "extraordinary level of secrecy observed as to any disclosure that might risk exposing an undercover officer" (May, 2014). The continuing obfuscation around the role and purpose of the SDS had left all other avenues exhausted. May told the House of Commons:

> 'In policing as in other areas, the problems of the past have a danger of infecting the present, and can lay traps for the future. Policing stands damaged today. Trust and confidence in the Metropolitan Police, and policing more generally, is vital. A public inquiry, and the other work I have set out, are part of the process of repairing the damage.' (May, 2014)

Peter Francis, to date still the only whistleblower from within the SDS or NPOIU ranks, told Channel 4 News of his 'relief' that a public inquiry had been announced and of his belief that he could tell his story in a public forum (Channel 4 News, 2014). If Francis's disclosures over the years have been behind much of what we know about these undercover deployments, it is extraordinary that the public inquiry has still not requested his witness testimony at the time I am writing this in 2023. At the end of 2020, when the public evidence phase finally started, the whistleblower's legal representatives gave voice to his frustrations:

> Some five years in, he [Francis] still awaits the formal request for a witness statement under Rule 9 of the Inquiry Rules as well as his 'witness pack'. He wants to speak formally through the Inquiry process, but it does not wish to hear from him any time soon. This is a source of real upset and concern to him. After all, it was his disclosures, his account to the Ellison Review, that triggered this Inquiry. (UCPI, 2020c, paragraph 41)

Francis's lawyers are right here to highlight the information he gave as 'Officer A' and his subsequent self-disclosure as Peter Francis as key steps en route to the public inquiry. The Home Secretary, in announcing the public inquiry, placed the emphasis on the Ellison report herself. However, other issues had come to capture public attention in the months preceding the publication of the report. The wrongful convictions of possibly thousands of activists through undisclosed undercover operations, the adoption of deceased children's identities as cover and the police's role in passing on information on trade union activists to construction companies all led to calls for a judge-led inquiry, independent from police and government, but with the necessary powers to demand access to intelligence files. Parliament, too, began to take note of the potentially anti-democratic nature of the undercover operations, not least because it was claimed that up to ten Labour members of parliament had been spied on by the units. Peter Francis said that he had seen intelligence reports on politicians including Jeremy Corbyn, Dianne Abbott, Harriet Harman, Jack Straw and Peter Hain among others. An urgent question in the House of Commons, tabled by the latter, led to calls by affected MPs to see their police files. The Speaker of the House, John Bercow, assured members that their concerns would be impressed on the Undercover Policing Inquiry and promised that 'this matter will not go away' (House of Commons, 2015, column 1952).

The spycops scandal had made itself felt at the top of the British policing hierarchy and reverberated around the walls of Westminster. But it was the stories of the women who discovered that their trusted, intimate partners and political soulmates were in fact undercover policemen deployed to gather information on them and their friends that generated the most outrage and disbelief (see Alison et al, 2022). It is beyond doubt that their relentless resolve to find answers turned the infiltration of political activism by the SDS and NPOIU into the undercover policing scandal. In this book, I cannot do full justice to the harm and trauma experienced by the women who found out that their partners and lovers had hidden behind elaborate and police-sanctioned cover stories, constructed to maintain sexual infiltration as a tactic in the monitoring of progressive activism. But I cannot avoid their experiences either. The exposures that many of these women faced, the experiences that they have re-told, their pursuit of the truth about formative chapters in their lives, are at the centre of the spycops scandal.

## The personal is political

Just months after the public inquiry began its work, the Metropolitan Police issued a public apology to seven women who had pursued a civil case in the courts. The case had originally been brought by eight women altogether, who had found out that they had been deceived into intimate and sexual relationships with undercover policemen. Their legal action ensured that the undercover policing scandal continued to receive public attention. But now the focus was on the apparent culture of misogyny within the secret police units.

The SDS was formed in 1968, at a time when student radicalism, anti-imperialist agitation and new feminist thinking began to coalesce in North America and Western Europe. These new social movements were influenced at times by the democratic cracks appearing in the Stalinist grip on Soviet countries and by the principle that apparently personal problems can only be addressed through collective action. Women's liberation groups worked within this political intersection, combining revolutionary demands for equality with the Marxist-Leninism of workers' movements. One such group was the Women's Liberation Front (WLF), which was infiltrated by a female officer known in the Inquiry by the cypher HN348. The undercover officer joined the Metropolitan Police's Special Branch in 1971 and used the alias 'Sandra' in her deployment into the WLF's north London branch. HN348 was one of the first officers to be called to give evidence to the Undercover Policing Inquiry. Now in her seventies, her real identity remained protected by the Inquiry, with Sir John Mitting deferring to her concern 'that the publication of her real name would lead to unwelcome media attention and, perhaps, to damage to her reputation amongst her wider social circle' (UCPI, 2018a, p 7). Other campaigns led by women were infiltrated too, for example the Greenham Common Peace Camp by 'Kathryn Lesley Bonser' between 1983 and 1987 and the Aldermaston women's peace camp by 'Lynn Watson' (Syal and Wainwright, 2011). These former officers are yet to give evidence to the Inquiry.

The battle for women's liberation was one area of political activity monitored by undercover police. But the infiltration of the women's movement was also an anomaly of sorts – most SDS and NPOIU field officers were male. It is a crucial fact if we want to understand the claim that the undercover policing units reflected the institutional sexism at the heart of the Metropolitan Police and other police forces.

In the early 2010s, several exposures of undercover officers in the environmental direct action scene led to the discovery that the infiltration of activist networks rested heavily on a horrendous undercover tactic: the manipulation of personal interactions into long-term sexual relationships. The US-based social movement researcher Michael Loadenthal has tried to make sense of such police tactics as cases of 'sexual infiltration'. The insertion of police 'into the private sphere of activists' sexual relationships', he argues, 'serves to not only disrupt the target communities but also to reverberate throughout social networks and create inactivity' (Loadenthal, 2014, p 24). What does it mean when the personal and the political become so conflated that they both become targets for police interference? Loadenthal's claim is that the presence of undercover officers not only in the public-political sphere – for example as plain clothes observers – but as long-term infiltrators embedded in activists' personal lives, aims at producing movement inertia. He suggests that the deployment of such 'deep swimmers' in mostly non-violent campaigns reflects counter-terrorism strategies that are 'traditionally reserved for the investigation of violence-prone groups' (Loadenthal, 2014, p 25).

Drawing on Michel Foucault's theoretical re-examination of the architectural panopticon as a metaphor for social control, Loadenthal is able to conceptualise the impact of such undercover strategies on social movements. He suggests that:

> [T]he activist is thrust into the outer ring of the panopticon, and with informants and undercover officers in the central tower, the state is able to see all and record completely whilst remaining unseen … If one's partner/spouse is a secretive agent, the site of the home can function similarly to the site of the prison; both acting as venues of observation and data collection. (Loadenthal, 2014, p 33)

The outwardly repressive function of the police state in this way is enhanced by a surveillance operation that aims to produce political inactivity. However, if the objective of undercover deployments was to produce the kind of insecurity and suspicion that would paralyse movement activism, how could this be achieved through the near-total secrecy surrounding the police's political units? In any case, the exposure of spycops in the midst of campaigns also had a contrasting effect: it generated new arenas for political activism.

The criminologist Nathan Stephens-Griffin has been one of those who have pursued such an understanding of the effects of undercover policing on progressive activism in the UK. Rather than totalising power over social movements, Stephens-Griffin proposes that the surveillance operations had a 'derailing' effect. Sure enough, he argues, Loadenthal was right to conceptualise the way that infiltration atomises individual activists and can turn them away from politics. At the same time, however, research with those targeted by spycops policing shows continuities of activism and demonstrates their 'resilience' when confronted with the surveillance operations against them. Stephens-Griffin writes that '[s]ome activists transitioned away from environmentalism into anti-state surveillance activism, thus opening up opportunities for anti-state surveillance activism for others ... Activists may have been derailed but not always in ways that saw them desist from activism' (2021, p 473). Nowhere is this more prominent than in the continued political activism of those who shared parts of their lives with the fictional personas created and deployed by the British police. Their mobilisations against the state's surveillance powers and their abuses are central to understanding the spycops scandal.

As details of the undercover units emerged, it became clear that the relationships between officers and members of the target groups were commonplace at least from the mid-1970s onwards. It is widely accepted, including in statements made by the Inquiry team, that 'deceitful sexual relationships were one of the principal issues of public concern which led to this public inquiry being established' (UCPI, 2021a, p 53). Of the estimated 139 officers who infiltrated political campaigns (117 in the SDS, 22 in the NPOIU; UCPI, 2019a), it is now believed that at least 20 deceived women into sexual relationships, several of them long-lasting. Often, the male undercover officers had intimate relationships with several women during their deployments. As some of these women asserted through their legal representatives in the Inquiry, there were by the end of 2020 'more than 30 women who know that they were deceived into such relationships by undercover police officers spying on campaign groups' (UCPI, 2020d, p 1). I was told by campaigners at the start of 2023 that they now believe it to be more than 50 women affected in this way.

It also appears to have been common practice that officers selected for SDS and NPOIU deployments were married, perhaps in the hope that a stable family life would ease their transition back into 'ordinary' police work at the end of their undercover tours and limit the chance of their 'defection' to their target communities. Their wives and children were apparently kept in the dark about the nature of the undercover work and this adds to the sense that they, too, were treated as objects in an effort to build credible and long-lasting cover identities. As the lawyer acting for those former wives grouped together under core participant category 'M' in the public inquiry put it:

> None of them had any idea that in the name of policing their husbands were having sexual relationships with other women. All were left

shocked and devastated by the media coverage as it unfolded, and the media intrusion that accompanied it, which affected not only them but also their children and wider families. (UCPI, 2020e, p 3)

Some officers moved in with the women they had deceived, manipulating their trust by insinuating that they were in love, wanted to marry and have children. At least three officers – Bob Lambert, Jim Boyling and 'Jim Pickford' – fathered children with women they met during undercover deployments. There might have been more. One activist, who went public using her first name Jacqui, was in a relationship with Lambert and gave birth to their son in 1985. A photograph shows Lambert, who used the identity of the animal rights campaigner 'Bob Robinson', holding his new-born child on the maternity ward. He abandoned the family he had created in his undercover role two years after it was taken. Upon discovering Lambert's true identity many years later, Jacqui spoke about the relationship in the starkest terms. It was 'like being raped by the state', she told *The Guardian*. 'I was not consenting to sleeping with Bob Lambert, I didn't know who Bob Lambert was. I had a spy living with me, sleeping with me, making a family with me, and I didn't do anything to deserve that' (Lewis et al, 2013).

Were these relationships sanctioned tactics to build credible legends for officers tasked with monitoring political campaigns? Were they wilfully overlooked or even encouraged by handlers and police managers? The search for answers to these questions puts the legality of the undercover operations carried out by the SDS and the NPOIU into sharp focus.

Legal action began in December 2011, with a case lodged by the human rights law firm Birnberg Peirce against the MPS and the Association of Chief Police Officers (ACPO) (Police Spies Out of Lives, 2011). The claimants asserted that they had been deceived into having long-term intimate relationships with five undercover officers belonging to the SDS and the NPOIU, with the relationships lasting between seven months and nine years. This, the women argued, had breached their rights under the European Convention on Human Rights, particularly Article 3 (freedom from torture and inhuman or degrading treatment) and Article 8 (respect for private and family life, including the right to form relationships without unjustified interference by the state). In addition, their case against the police included common law claims, including assault, deceit, negligence and misfeasance in public office. In a press release issued as they commenced their legal action, the women said:

> We believe our case highlights institutionalised sexism within the police. It is incredible that if the police want to search someone's house they are required to get the permission of a judge, yet if they want to

send in an agent who may live and sleep with activists in their homes, this can happen without any apparent oversight! (Police Spies Out of Lives, 2011)

Undercover officers initiated and continued intimate relationships for extended periods of time, sometimes for years. They reported daily to their team of handlers and supervisors and the targets of undercover deployments therefore claimed that the practice of manipulating women in this way was commonly known and sanctioned across the policing units. These were not rogue officers who had developed genuine feelings for members of the public that they had encountered in the field. They were, instead, trained police sources who used a well-developed tactic to build and maintain cover identities.

Both the common law cases and the human rights case were fought by the police. They argued, successfully, that human rights claims should be heard in closed session in the secretive Investigatory Powers Tribunal, rather than in open court. But after four years, as part of an extensive settlement agreement resulting from the women's common law claims, the MPS issued an unprecedented apology. On 20 November 2015, Assistant Commissioner Martin Hewitt apologised to the women who had brought their case over such relationships with undercover officers in a pre-recorded message. He stated that:

> [I]t has become apparent that some officers, acting undercover whilst seeking to infiltrate protest groups, entered into long-term intimate sexual relationships with women which were abusive, deceitful, manipulative and wrong. I acknowledge that these relationships were a violation of the women's human rights, an abuse of police power and caused significant trauma. I unreservedly apologise on behalf of the Metropolitan Police Service ... relationships like these should never have happened. (Hewitt, cited in Evans, 2015a)

For the eight women – Helen, Kate, Lisa, Rosa, Belinda, Naomi, Ruth and Alison – the police acknowledgement of the abuse was a huge victory, even though the potential for having to pay exorbitant legal costs meant that seven of them had to settle out of court. What they were still denied, however, were answers about the spycops deployments and any insight into their police-held files.

## The Tradecraft Manual

It is clear that one of the Inquiry's main lines of investigation is the extent to which 'sexual infiltration' was permitted or encouraged. And although we still know relatively little about the chain of command which oversaw such practices, some snippets of information have begun to emerge – many of them unearthed by the tenacity of the affected women themselves.

A good place to start would be a guidance document addressed to undercover officers in the SDS, compiled by Andy Coles, who was an undercover officer between 1991 and 1995, using the cover name 'Andy Davey'. In the document, titled 'Special Demonstration Squad Tradecraft Manual', Coles gives advice on the infiltration of campaign groups. It makes for shocking reading. In a discourse analysis of the Tradecraft Manual, Chris Brian (2019) has highlighted how the document is littered with 'othering' discourses that serve to justify the tactics used to infiltrate animal rights and environmental protesters. If the repeated use of the term 'the wearies' to describe political campaigners isolates them from the general population, the police document does little to hide the author's outright contempt for certain groups of activists. Anarchists are referred to as 'nihilistic crusty low-life' and officers are warned of the conditions in which they would have to work: 'The crusty lifestyle in particular is really unpleasant. You will be expected to eat food you wouldn't put in your bin, drink tea from cups which appear to have grown their own beards and sit on furniture that is alive' (cited in Brian, 2019, p 57). In a section he headed 'sexual liaisons', Coles further writes that 'one should try to avoid the opposite sex for as long as possible' or risk 'serious consequences'. But he also, quite openly, addresses instances where there may be 'no other option'. Then, Coles advises his SDS officers, 'you should try to have fleeting, disastrous relationships with individuals who are not important to your sources of information' (UCPI, 2018b, p 28). The Manual was made public by the Undercover Policing Inquiry, alongside other relevant documentation, but was still heavily redacted.

Coles's own activities in the field, reporting on an animal rights group, gives us some illustration of the nature of such 'fleeting' and 'disastrous' relationships. Coles was 32 when he reportedly entered a relationship with a woman the Inquiry named as 'Jessica'. Jessica was 19 at the time and describes how Andy Coles was her first serious boyfriend. She has told her story publicly and believes that her relative inexperience left her vulnerable to be 'groomed' by an undercover officer. Jessica described the manipulation of her emotional life in the starkest terms: 'I was groomed by someone much older, and far more experienced, and I was manipulated into having a sexual relationship with him. I didn't even know his real name', she told the Channel 4 News home affairs correspondent Simon Israel (Channel 4 News, 2017).

When she met Coles, Jessica had just moved out of her parent's home to be in London. There she got more involved in animal rights and other campaigning. For her, personally, this was a big step. As she described it:

I had never been in a proper relationship before. Events in my life had taught me it's best to keep people at arm's length. So I didn't know how to react when he made advances towards me. I was embarrassed, awkward, and what truly makes me feel sick now, is that I didn't want to hurt his feelings. I look back now and realise I was naive, idealistic, unsophisticated and a very young 19. (Police Spies Out of Lives, nd, Jessica's story)

Coles has publicly denied that the relationship took place, telling his local newspaper that the allegations made by Jessica 'are completely untrue' (Coles, cited in *Peterborough Telegraph*, 2018). Exposed by activists in 2017 and confirmed as a former undercover officer in the SDS by the Undercover Policing Inquiry in 2018, he has still not been called to give evidence in public at the time of writing. Years are passing by before the former officer can be questioned about the alleged relationship under oath.

For Jessica, the short-lived relationship with the man she knew as 'Andy Davey' was indeed disastrous. More than five years after finding out about his true identity, she is now waiting to give evidence to the Undercover Policing Inquiry. Coles, on the other hand, was elected as a Conservative councillor on Peterborough Council and became Deputy Police and Crime Commissioner in Cambridgeshire. He stepped down from the latter role following his exposure.

## Institutional sexism

There are other places we could look to learn about the impact on the women who were so deceived, often in similar circumstances to Jessica's. Donna McLean, at first using the pseudonym 'Andrea', was a politically active trade unionist when she was approached by a police infiltrator who had adopted the persona of 'Carlo Neri'. She has told of the life she lived together in a relationship with 'Neri' and the traumatic impact of his calculated disappearance in her hard-hitting book *Small Town Girl* (McLean, 2022). Donna met the SDS undercover officer in September 2002 at an anti-war demonstration in London. Their political bond rapidly turned personal: 'Carlo and I were inseparable', she explains. 'Within six weeks he'd moved in with me. We lived together for two years and in that time, we got engaged and talked about having children' (Police Spies Out of Lives, nd, Donna's story).

There has been some controversy in the Inquiry over the restriction order granted that protects the officer's true identity. Referred to in the Inquiry by the cypher N104, the anonymity application made by 'Neri' was published with redactions, yet Sir John Mitting ruled that the former officer's real identity should be kept secret, citing among other factors the possibility that disclosure would infringe on the private lives of the spycop's two teenage children. However, a combined investigation by some of the activists targeted by 'Neri', alongside the Undercover Research Group (URG), was able to confirm his real name. It was finally put into the public domain by an investigative journalist in 2019, yet Chair Mitting has insisted that he cannot be named within any of the Inquiry's proceedings or documents.

On her part, while waiting for the Inquiry to invite public evidence, after five years of using the name 'Andrea' in public, Donna McLean made the decision to drop her pseudonym. 'I did not want a false identity', she writes. 'This double life was forced on me by Carlo's deception' (McLean, 2022, p 216). Her book tells of her incredible experience of being deceived and manipulated by an undercover officer for the purposes of intelligence on protest activity. From her account, we learn about the extraordinary length to which 'Neri' went in developing his identity and maintaining his legend.

He had planned the day carefully. It was his idea to throw a party on New Year's Eve 2002 in Donna's flat, just three months after they met. They had invited friends, 'Neri' had put up the fairy lights and prepared cocktails for the occasion. When he kneeled in front of her and proposed, with the party in full swing, Donna had no doubt in her mind that this was a serious relationship that was meant to last a lifetime. In her book (McLean, 2022, p 89), Donna describes the scene afterwards: ' "Let's ring your mum!" 'Neri' said. "I want to tell her the good news".' The wedding never happened. Two years into the relationship, 'Neri' began showing signs of burnout and mental distress. It was part of an exit strategy used by several undercover officers. To Donna, he put this down to his upbringing in a difficult family setting and a recent realisation that there had been sexual abuse in his family. Donna was worried when he disappeared for longer periods of time and disclosed suicidal thoughts to her. It was no surprise therefore, if no less distressing, when he finally vanished for good.

How do you come to terms with your own sense of self after such a betrayal? Donna tried. 'When this happens', she explained, 'when your life narrative becomes a fiction, time itself becomes fragmented. There's a ripple effect. It impacts your family, your relationships, your career, your health' (Police Spies Out of Lives, nd, Donna's story).

When Donna found out, she was able to rely on the support of other women who had similarly been deceived. They included Helen Steel, a social justice activist and formerly a defendant against a McDonald's libel lawsuit in the infamous 'McLibel' case. Representing herself during parts of the Undercover Policing Inquiry, Steel has been granted the opportunity to address the Inquiry team in person, rather than through a lawyer, on several occasions. She is one of the women who have waived their anonymity in the hope that speaking out in their real names would increase public understanding of the spycops scandal. Steel was, alongside Dave Morris, a member of London Greenpeace. Not to be confused with the better-known pressure group, London Greenpeace was a small collective committed to environmentalism and anarchism.

Steel had a relationship with a man she knew as 'John Barker', who she met at London Greenpeace meetings. They were close friends, initially, during a time that Steel recalls 'Barker' sharing stories of personal loss and trauma – fabrications as they turned out to be. Steel recalls the impact of these stories on her:

> Those stories, seeking my empathy and involvement in his life, were a deliberate process of emotional manipulation. He was seeking to draw me closer to him, so that he could spy on me and my friends, to undermine the political movements we were involved in and ultimately to prevent change. This is not just what's happened to me, this is what has happened to the other women as well. (Police Spies Out of Lives, nd, Helen's story)

Following a routine that was also used by other undercover officers, 'Barker' left Steel's life gradually, displaying behaviour that suggested burnout and mental breakdown. He eventually vanished without a trace, other than a letter posted from South Africa.

Years went by before Steel found proof that the 'John Barker' she knew did not exist.

> One day ... as I passed what was then St Catherine's House, the registry of births, deaths and marriages, I just got this sudden instinct to go in and start looking through the death records. And I then found out he had been using the name of a child who'd died when he was eight years old.
>
> That left me with this great void. I'd been living with someone for two years and I now didn't even know what his name was. I was deeply in love with this person and I knew nothing about him. It really throws all your other relationships into doubt. (Police Spies Out of Lives, nd, Helen's story)

I will not get drawn into the question of whether, operationally, sexual deception might be a necessary part of the police's methods in order to successfully embed an undercover officer in a criminal target group. But let me raise a point aptly made by Helen Steel, using her pseudonym 'Clare', in response to hostile questioning from members of the parliamentary Home Affairs Committee in 2013.

> There was an interesting interview with Peter Bleksley, who was an undercover policeman, on Radio 5 a couple of months ago. He said that he had slept with a target in his investigations. He mentioned on the radio that she was a very attractive woman, and the radio presenter said, 'Would you have slept with this person if it had been a man?' and he said, 'No, I'm not gay.' I think that answers the question. This is not about a need to do it. It is about a desire to do it. They have the power and they think they can get away with it. (Home Affairs Committee, 2013a, p 24)

The Police Spies Out of Lives group represents the women who were thus targeted and abused. Their use of the term 'institutional sexism' is informed exactly by such realisations – that the abuse of women involved in progressive causes by undercover policemen was underpinned by stereotyping of left-wing groups as promiscuous, by the officers' own sexual interests and by the abuse of power in their undercover roles.

In their opening statement, women in the Inquiry's core participant category 'H' summed up their understanding of the term as 'reflecting the deeply sexist attitudes pervading the police in general and the undercover units in particular' (UCPI, 2020d, p 3). It is not difficult to see why. They blame the officers and decision-makers in the SDS and the NPOIU for treating women 'as mere objects, as props to shore up the fake identities of the officers'. The fact that some, though very few, female police officers went undercover as well does not change this: 'Only women could fall pregnant and give birth to the child of an officer. Only women could lose their child bearing years to the manipulations of the state' (UCPI, 2020d, p 3).

## Policing by deception

When the undercover policing scandal broke, and with activists mobilising for answers and accountability, politicians and police leaders could not avoid the fact that secretive policing units had existed virtually unchecked and had caused unjustifiable trauma and suffering to many who had become their targets. Crucially, the Stephen Lawrence case refused to go away. Institutional racism thus became central to the concerns that a public inquiry was asked to address. On top of that, the allegations that kept mounting – that police officers, possibly sanctioned by their superiors, had exploited their postings to strike up long-term intimate relationships with people often at the fringes of their investigations – captured some public interest. As we will see, the women who so painfully found out about the abuses they suffered refused to accept what had happened silently. They are, and must be, at the centre of the scandal engulfing undercover policing in Britain.

There is no doubt that the infiltration of social movement organisations by the British police – rationalised as the monitoring of subversives and extremists – has a longer history and continues beyond 2011. But a historical overview of the work of these two units, as we know it today, still serves the purpose of understanding the public inquiry's key priorities. As stated, the common justification of these two organisations within the British police, both historically and sometimes ex post facto, was to gather intelligence on political subversion for the purposes of informing public order policing and preventing political violence. But it appears that both units found themselves at a more specific crossroads between the secret services and mainstream policing. In this liminal space, managers, handlers and field operatives developed practices and policies that had little if anything to do with 'policing by consent'.

In this way, policing by deception contrasts to the mythical yet frequently parroted line that British policing rests on consent. In the area of 'political' policing at least, the picture that has emerged so far gives ground for a re-assessment of the character and legitimacy accorded to the 'British model of protest policing' (Schlembach, 2018). While in the past, the surveillance and infiltration of protest has often been neglected theoretically because of the obvious limitations placed on its empirical analysis, the public exposure of Kennedy and several of his former colleagues now warrants a thorough re-assessment of what we know about protester–police interactions, surveillance and repression in Britain over the past 50 years.

3

# Deviant knowledge and activist research

## Covert policing and academic knowledge

In the summer of 2016, police in Hamburg, Germany, went to remarkable lengths in an effort to clean up two large fly-posters (Trautwein, 2017).[1] At five o'clock in the morning, some 30 officers wearing fire-resistant clothing and protective helmets loaded extendable ladders and pots of black paint from their vans. Securing the area around a large, run-down building covered from top to bottom in colourful graffiti they began painting over the fly-posters. Minutes later, with their mission complete, they left. The offending items had been posted onto the façade of the left-wing cultural and political centre Rote Flora in the lively Schanzen district of the city. Written on them, the large lettering of the word 'FOUND' resembled that of a police officer recruitment campaign. Above it, the perpetrator had glued four portrait images showing the faces of undercover police officers, together with their names. The four had been outed as police infiltrators in the activist groups that met and socialised in the building.

Painting over the posters in the dawn operation might have been counterproductive for Hamburg's police, but it demonstrates the value it had placed on the anonymity of its undercover officers. It is true that the invisibility of police secrets is rarely maintained in such dramatic nighttime deployments. More typically, it consists of legal, administrative and intellectual strategies of neutralisation that implicate public authorities in denial and whitewash. But the Hamburg example illustrates the extent to which secrecy is central to the tradecraft of police infiltrators. Throughout this book I show that, while the public scrutiny of policing has undoubtedly led to new ways of accountability and democratic oversight, it has also been met with new ways of institutional reputation management. And, as I shall argue in this chapter, criminological knowledge encounters real problems of its own if it aims to study invisible policing practices. A more fruitful engagement is with various forms of social movement knowledge and activist research.

Chapter 2 described how the exposures of infiltrators in Britain's progressive social movements led to the undercover policing scandal. Much of what we know about the scandal has been uncovered by activists-turned-researchers, a whistleblower and investigative journalists. They were vindicated, at first, when the Metropolitan Police issued a wide-ranging apology and the announcement of the public inquiry provided further official acknowledgement of what had happened. There is another reason why the exposures of undercover police officers placed into political campaigns proved to be scandalous. The very existence of a political secret police – distinct from the secret services, yet in close collaboration – is considered anathema to the often-touted myth of a British way of doing police work, 'policing by consent'. The idea that the British policing tradition relies on the public's consent has become quasi-folkloric, notwithstanding its oppressive colonial roots. It is enshrined, for some, in Robert Peel's principles of policing issued in 1829. The 'general instructions' that police officers in the newly formed Police of the Metropolis received included some clues as to the origin of the term. They suggested a role for paid police in preventing outbreaks of disorder, as an alternative to the repressive function carried out by military force. It followed events such as the Peterloo Massacre in 1819, during which a privately funded, amateur cavalry brutally dispersed a radical gathering that demanded greater political representation and at least a dozen people were killed. Peel, who had masterminded the oppressive policing tactics designed to keep colonial subjects in check in Ireland, understood that policing on the mainland needed to offer a different justification for itself. Although it is the case that '[t]he policing of the English white working class was modelled after the policing of colonial (surplus) populations in Ireland, the Caribbean and the Indian subcontinent' (Fatsis and Lamb, 2022, p 25), the rationale for a professional police force on the mainland differed from that of counter-insurgency and supporting colonial administrations. Advancing the virtues of impartiality and independence from private capital, Peel's principles included the instruction to recognise that the police's powers are reliant on the public's approval of their existence and the manner of their exercise (Home Office, 2012). The origins of such an instruction may 'largely be an invention of twentieth century text book authors' (Lentz and Chaires, 2007, p 69), but it has been adopted in the government's definition of policing by consent. This, somewhat unsurprisingly, refers back to Charles Reith, the 'conservative "cop sided" police historian' (Bowling et al, 2016, p 137), who described Britain's philosophy of policing as 'unique in history and throughout the world because it derived not from fear but almost exclusively from public co-operation with the police' (Reith, cited in Home Office, 2012).

The undercover policing scandal upsets, at least to some extent, this still widely accepted narrative, where it is commonplace to assert the difference of the British style of policing and that of continental, American or post-colonial policing systems. 'Policing by deception', the term that I use in this chapter to describe the infiltration and manipulation of social movements, is then a variation on the notion of 'policing by consent', the foundation myth that continues to be the guiding principle of policing in (mainland)

Britain. Policing by consent proposes that the relationship between police and the public is one of cooperation and that, in turn, police are accountable to the communities they serve. Yet, accountability and transparency have always been partial at best, and perhaps necessarily so. Intelligence work, specifically when carried out by covert means, is by definition a form of statecraft based on secrecy and deception. This, the chapter argues, poses real challenges for independent academic research.

## Deviant knowledge

What strategies are available to expand the sociological or criminological understanding of such policing practices? Picking up on some discussions of 'activist' or 'alternative' criminology (Belknapp, 2015; Carlen and Ayres França, 2017; Canning et al, 2023), the chapter revisits Reece Walters's outline of a 'sociology of criminological knowledge', which casts a critical eye on the production of pragmatic knowledge. Walters's book *Deviant Knowledge* (2003) sets out to examine the politics of criminological research and how the production of knowledge in universities increasingly yields to the pressures of regulation and market governance. The effect has been a silencing of critical perspectives and an overly accommodating relationship between researchers and the institutions that set research priorities. I have a specific interest in the way that research, which exposes uncomfortable truths, can be seen as 'deviant knowledge' in this way. The political policing of social movements is underpinned by secrecy surrounding policies and practices that often evade accountability as cases rarely make it to court. In what follows I outline how deviant knowledge can play a role in rendering transparent some of those state secrets and what this means for the research relationships between (former) police officers and (academic) researchers.

The crucial issue here is the very understandable desire to produce knowledge that is useful, relevant, practical and instrumental. For some, such a desire results directly from institutional pressures on university-based researchers, a theme that is central to Walters's work on 'deviant knowledge'. He describes criminology, specifically, as a field of inquiry dominated by market demands and policy-relevance, unable to elevate critical and 'deviant knowledge' to the same level of importance as the utilitarian pragmatism of public authorities and civil servants. Famously, Michel Foucault also included criminological texts in his critique of disciplining knowledge:

> Have you ever read any criminological texts? They are staggering. And I say this out of astonishment, not aggressiveness, because I fail to comprehend how the discourse of criminology has been able to go on at this level. One has the impression that it is of such utility, is needed so urgently and rendered so vital for the working of the system,

that it does not even seek a theoretical justification for itself, or even simply a coherent framework. It is entirely utilitarian. (Foucault, cited in Carrabine et al, 2014, p 112)

Walters argues for 'knowledges of resistance' as a mode of critique that challenges power and maintains intellectual distance from governmental and market-led knowledge industries. As a starting point, for Walters this means that 'academics should refuse to participate in contract research where the methods, questions, content and conclusions of the research are framed, determined and even altered by government' (Walters, 2003, pp 166–7).

While such a position broadly informs my argument, I recognise that these matters are a bit more complicated than that. Academic knowledge does not become deviant or non-instrumental as soon as it becomes independent from state or market influence. In the light of the undercover policing scandal, what would such 'knowledges of resistance' that Walters speaks of look like? Is it not, in fact, the surveillance state that is engaging in resistance, including resisting against research by outsiders? In this context, deviant knowledge can mean recognising the limitations in accessing official accounts of undercover policing, and of treating with scepticism, if not outright suspicion, the narratives offered by those embedded within covert policing practices themselves.

## Political policing targeting the Left

Discussions of undercover policing frequently suffer from considerable conceptual confusion. What do we mean by 'undercover'; and what do we mean by 'policing'? Both terms come with narrow and expansive meanings attached to them. Even scholarly exchanges are at times unable to resolve the ambiguities of the terms of debate, because they are essentially talking about different things. In the UK, the police's use of undercover deployments has taken many forms, from classic 'sting' operations to the recruitment of informers. The former may involve the time-limited set up of fake environments – such as leaving valuables on display in areas plagued by burglary offences – while the latter can simply mean that incentives are offered to petty offenders to pass information about more serious crimes to the police.

There is no doubt that covert surveillance of citizens by public police organisations is now widespread and normalised. In part, this is due to the acceleration of technological communication. With the ubiquity of smartphones, to name just one example, state institutions including the police find it easier to intercept and monitor communication between private citizens. To take account of these new developments, the policing scholar Bethan Loftus argues that the use of covert surveillance has become 'normalised' (Loftus, 2019). She argues that contemporary policing practices are underpinned by 'the legal and cultural acceptance of covert tactics, as well as an external environment which advocates surveillance for the governance of security threats' (Loftus, 2019, pp 2070–1). Loftus's characterisation is based on one of the first ethnographic explorations into undercover policing in Britain, carried out together with Benjamin Goold and others (Loftus and Goold, 2012; Loftus et al, 2015). We can learn a lot from their observations, although their conclusions are necessarily limited by two methodological restrictions. First, their work deals with crime fighting in the narrow sense. So, it excludes, for example, counter-terrorism or political policing. Second, access to police participants in the research is facilitated and permitted by their employer. As the researchers readily admit (Mac Giollabhui et al, 2016, p 633), 'as with all police research, the terms of our access to [the police force we studied] determined the parameters of our research'.

The undercover policing scandal refers to much more precise, targeted and long-term deployments of existing police officers being seconded to specialist undercover units with the remit to monitor political activity. Some of this may have been justified with the explicit aim to prepare public order policing strategies in advance of major demonstrations. But frequently, the information collected by a single officer sent into the field was much more mundane than that. The Special Demonstration Squad (SDS) and the National Public Order Intelligence Unit (NPOIU) recruited police officers to act as 'spies', or what are now called 'covert human intelligence sources', within the meaning of section 26(8) of the Regulation of Investigatory Powers Act 2000. While covert human intelligence sources may also be a term used to describe civilians acting as police informants, in this instance it refers to police officers sent into political campaign groups, with fake identities and elaborate back-up stories, to lead double lives as activists.

The Undercover Policing Inquiry's Terms of Reference describe one of its purposes as an investigation into the motivation and scope of undercover policing operations, starting in 1968. What accounts for the development of these secretive units? What were their objectives? One narrative is that the existence of the SDS and NPOIU is to be explained as 'preventing political violence' and that, despite widespread wrongdoing, the units were successful in doing so. As an example, Stefano Bonino and Lambros Kaoullas, the authors of an 'evaluation of forty years of undercover policing of political groups involved in protest' (Bonino and Kaoullas, 2015) argue that the objectives of police infiltration were tied up with the British state's legitimate desire to neutralise threats to its security. Intelligence gathered and disseminated by officers embedded within political campaigns was intended to prevent criminal activity or aid planning for the potential of future disorder on demonstrations. An appraisal of the undercover policing of protest must be one that 'does not shy away from criticisms but, equally, recognizes successes' (Bonino and Kaoullas, 2015, p 826).

The authors go further, however. While there may be some merit in the critical view that would see in those undercover activities an unlawful infringement of civil liberties on an enormous scale, they propose that 'there exists a less conspiratorial and more politically aware side of the story':

> If the police fail to seize a drug shipment, the cost associated with media and public condemnation, and related growing social insecurities, will be minimal. However, if a single bomb goes off, not only will political violence and terrorism have scored a goal, but public confidence in the State and law enforcement agencies, and their capacity to protect the security of its citizens, will be undermined. (Bonino and Kaoullas, 2015, p 827)

Bonino and Kaoullas claim that theirs is the 'value-free, evidence-based account' (Bonino and Kaoullas, 2015, p 828) of the SDS and NPOIU. They conclude that the risks of doing nothing were simply too great to be acceptable to the state's security apparatus.

There is, however, nothing conspiratorial in the view that the SDS and its successor organisations within Special Branch permitted the unlawful and anti-democratic mass surveillance of mostly progressive social movements. While its raison d'être was at first the preparation of uniformed police responses to a single demonstration in 1968, it quickly outgrew this mandate, unchecked and with impunity, indiscriminately collecting information on activists aligned with a huge variety of causes. Their methods, too, became ever more extreme, intruding into the private lives of thousands of Britons. Although public order and the threat of subversion remained the justification in the unit's annual reports, its deployments diversified and became ever more intrusive. Far from informing the preparation of uniformed police for potential disorder at protests, Special Branch now compiled reports for the Home Office and the Security Service for the politically motivated fight against 'subversion'.

The more one delves into the files obtained and published by the Undercover Policing Inquiry, the more one gets the sense that not only was the justification for the SDS built upon a mirage, there was increasingly little that had to do with law enforcement or even 'keeping the peace'. In fact, as one submission by non-police, non-state core participants put it: 'there is a remarkable lack of reports on public order issues' (UCPI, 2022a, p 5).[2] The net was cast so widely that any reporting on potential law-breaking was incidental to the mundane intelligence gathering that became the routine practice. SDS officers recorded personal details of thousands of people involved in campaigns against racism, workplace activism, feminist groups and many more, and monitored the physical appearances, health, sexual preferences, personal finances, relationships and family arrangements and opinions held on a range of political and social matters. They attended weddings, birthdays and other significant family gatherings, they took active part in their targets' social lives, they befriended their friends and families and they babysat their kids. In collecting a huge amount of information about people involved, even if tangentially, in political activity, the SDS had an anti-democratic mandate. In the sense that this was done to collect intelligence about and against civil society organisations, rather than to investigate potential offences, this was political policing.

It was also economic policing. In producing files to be disseminated to MI5 and other 'clients', the SDS enabled vetting and blacklisting. Trade unionists lost their jobs or found themselves unable to gain new employment in their sectors. The opening statement made by James Scobie KC on behalf of Lindsey German, Richard Chessum and 'Mary' to the Tranche 1 of evidence hearings, covering the period from 1968 to 1982, interprets the bundle of evidence given by SDS managers that had been provided to them by the Inquiry. This disclosure, the submission states:

> [G]ives a great deal of insight into the liaison between MI5 and Special Branch on the issue of vetting. An example is a fractious exchange of documents between the two where MI5 set down a marker, that the passing of information to employers about their employees is the role of MI5, rather than that of Special Branch. The document is clearly meant (and taken) as a rebuke. (UCPI, 2022a, p 34)

The precise relationship between the Home Office, MI5 and the SDS is one to be determined by the Inquiry, hampered by missing or illegible files and the passing of time. It may well be that the submission on behalf of Tariq Ali, Piers Corbyn (Jeremy Corbyn's now-conspiracist brother) and Ernie Tate had it right. In it, the Security Service, rather than Special Branch, was regarded as the driving force behind the scramble for personal information: 'MI5 were the organ grinders, and SDS were the monkeys. Only the monkeys did not know to whose tune they were really dancing' (UCPI, 2022b, p 9). This is one of the reasons why the Inquiry remains important. The files, reports and witness statements it has received from police sources, however reluctantly, are invaluable in assessing the politicised nature of undercover policing. The evidence for these activists pointed at the fact that undercover policing of political groups was not the brainchild of rogue units but took direction from the top of the policing hierarchy.

## The Special Demonstration Squad

Tariq Ali and Ernest Tate were the first activists to give evidence to the Undercover Policing Inquiry, in November 2020, in the midst of the COVID-19 pandemic. Ali, regarded as one of the leading socialist intellectuals of the

New Left in Britain, had aroused the interest of the secret police some years before the first spycops unit was founded. Special Branch opened a file on him when he was president of the Oxford Union in the mid-1960s. Ali and Tate were leading members of the Vietnam Solidarity Campaign (VSC), a campaign group priding itself on transparent and non-violent methods of organising the opposition to the imperialist war in Vietnam. In 1968, they were both involved in organising a demonstration against the war, which escalated into a violent confrontation between protesters and police in Grosvenor Square, outside the US Embassy in London. Protesters pushed back police lines and mounted police responded with charges and mass arrests. Many of those in the crowd sustained injuries from the horse charges. The trouble in Mayfair was the impetus for a new, secretive unit reporting to Special Branch, eventually called the 'Special Demonstration Squad' (SDS).

From early documentation and reports, we know that the SDS – at first using the name 'Special Operations Squad' – was set up with the explicit and focused aim to monitor the mobilisation for a later protest in the same year and to prepare the public order policing strategy – ostensibly in order to avoid similar clashes. It was, of course, in the interest of the police to overestimate its own impact on the conduct of demonstrations. In reality, multiple factors may have led to the absence of large-scale disorder at the later demonstration, including the aims of the protest organisers and more disciplined stewarding provisions. The activist group Campaign Opposing Police Surveillance summed up this sentiment after hearing Tariq Ali's testimony during the Inquiry, when it described the SDS origin story – namely that the unrest at the Grosvenor Square demonstration was the result of a failure of intelligence – as an 'oft-repeated fable'. 'This lie', the group said, 'was the original sin that led to the founding of the SDS' (Campaign Opposing Police Surveillance, 2020a).

To 'get to the truth', the Undercover Policing Inquiry has opted for a chronological approach. Divided into 'modules', 'tranches' and 'phases', it invited opening statements from core participants across six days in early November 2020, after five years of preliminary work. Then, on 11 November 2020, as the UK government was making plans for the COVID-19 vaccination rollout, the Inquiry held its first evidence hearing, accessible to the public only via a stream to YouTube.

If we are to believe the 'scandal model' discussed in Chapter 2, then the public concern around undercover policing arose because of the abusive tactics of deception employed by field agents and apparently sanctioned by high-ranking officers. How a public inquiry fulfils its remit is a decision for the Chair, independent of political or ministerial direction. And yet it was remarkable to see that the lead counsel to the Inquiry, David Barr, had been instructed to devote the full first day of public evidence, after all these years of waiting, to questioning 77-year-old socialist intellectual Tariq Ali. Barr had done his homework and repeatedly referred to passages in Ali's book *Street Fighting Years: An Autobiography of the Sixties* (2018), originally published in 1987. Perhaps predictably, Ali was asked questions about his concept of militancy – was this just another word for political violence? – and his wider political outlook. As a socialist revolutionary, was his aim the overthrow of the British state?

Barr: Would it be fair to say that your ultimate aspirations were revolutionary?
Ali: Not in Britain, no.
Barr: Your view at the time was that you were not expecting this demonstration itself to precipitate a revolution; is that fair?
Ali: I mean, you would have to be slightly deranged to think that a VSC demonstration would trigger off a revolution in Britain.
Barr: So does that mean that, given the air of change that was in the wind, or the possibility of change, that you saw the March demonstration as not likely to cause a revolution here but as a step towards a piece of the jigsaw that would be put together eventually as part of a worldwide revolution with the ultimate aim of worldwide socialism?
Ali: [*Laughing*] No, not really. (UCPI, 2020f, pp 31–4)

At first, the purpose of the SDS was to gather intelligence on left-wing political causes and activists, especially those deemed 'subversive', and to prepare the police for potential disorder at demonstrations. Later on, the Squad also deployed officers into environmental and animal rights networks. Only very few spycops were deployed to infiltrate extreme right-wing groups.

## The National Public Order Intelligence Unit

The NPOIU evolved from the Animal Rights National Index in 1999 and was overseen by the Association of Chief Police Officers (ACPO). The ACPO acted as an independent company without statutory power, yet had a leading role in influencing government policy, especially in the area of police policy and until recently was not subject to freedom of information laws – useful of course to a company in charge of one of the UK's police intelligence units. The NPOIU's intelligence and undercover deployments largely left the language of 'subversion' behind and focused instead on what it called 'domestic extremism'. Other than animal rights activism, it appears that environmental and climate change protesters were considered as primary targets for infiltration. Undercover officers deployed by the NPOIU were seconded from police forces across the country and may have had prior experience of undercover work in areas such as organised crime or drugs. The NPOIU was Mark Kennedy's unit. He and his colleagues across the country were tasked with infiltrating and gathering intelligence from animal rights, environmental and political activists and they followed similar objectives as those given to their predecessors in the SDS.

Eventually, the NPOIU merged with other ACPO policing units, primarily the National Extremism Tactical Coordination Unit and the National Domestic Extremism Team, to form the National Domestic Extremism and Disorder Intelligence Unit (NDEDIU). In the wake of the Mark Kennedy scandal, the NDEDIU was brought under control of the Metropolitan Police.

The existence of the SDS, the NPOIU and other policing units with similar objectives should make us question to what extent the 'British model' of protest policing really is an extension of policing by consent. Is policing by deception a divergence from the principle or an integral part? In a written witness statement to the Inquiry, one senior officer in Special Branch in the 1970s and 1980s made the case that protest policing in mainland Britain developed *because* of the use of undercover policing methods. Summarising the rationale for the infiltration of protest groups, he wrote:

> After the large scale 'Vietnam' demonstration in the spring of 1968 where the police nearly lost control of public order, there was a choice of either escalating the number of police at such events and resorting to the use of things like rubber bullets, water cannons or tear gas or utilising intelligence to better police such events. (UCPI, 2022c, p 2)

According to this view, the rights of protesters are safeguarded precisely thanks to the infiltration tactics used by undercover police. Those who saw their task as tackling 'subversion' and of providing the state with intelligence against socialist and other revolutionary activists resorted to secret methods in order to keep alive the 'Peelian' narrative that the police in Britain were different from their colonial and continental neighbours. If true, consent-based policing is built on policing by deception.

## Public order policing and political protest

Anti-capitalist opposition and police violence have provided a common backdrop to major international summits from Seattle's WTO conference to

Hamburg's G20 meeting. This has renewed academic interest in the issue of protest policing in Western democracies. Much of this research is based on empirical observations of police and protester interactions in public order situations. There are indications in the literature that the ideals and values of liberal democracies find (flawed and contested) recognition in the styles of protest policing. As Donatella Della Porta and Herbert Reiter wrote in the late 1990s: 'A general trend emerges regarding protest policing styles, which … can be defined as "soft," tolerant, selective, legal, preventive, consensual, flexible, and professional' (Della Porta and Reiter, 1998, p 6).

This general trend is affirmed by much of the research on protest policing in Britain, although it rarely takes into account deceptive and undercover tactics. Take, for example, the work by P.A.J. Waddington, *Liberty and Order* (1994), which details his in-depth observation of the Metropolitan Police's Public Order Unit, or riot squad, in the early 1990s. The book-length study is often seen as a leading example of research into protest policing by a former police officer. The book's publication in 1994 followed the miners' strike in 1984 and the introduction of the Public Order Act 1986. The Act was seen by critics as an assault on civil liberties and the right to protest, granting the police powers to restrict and ban political assemblies which they deemed to be at risk of violent disorder. Waddington's book sought to assuage such fears. He argued that rather than representing a drift towards an authoritarian state, the new legislation had little impact on police strategy when dealing with protests in the capital. In any case, the practice of public order policing was more influenced by operational and pragmatic concerns, such as wanting to avoid 'on the job' and 'in the job' trouble. Waddington's work is not easily categorised as 'the police's view' – in fact, much of his exposition shows how police discretion and knowledge extend police power far beyond its legal constraints. But his account of protest policing by the Metropolitan Police, even though it extends into the control rooms and back-room negotiations, remains locked into a world of surface relations between protesters (and organisers) and officers (and police commanders).

The possible presence of undercover actors rarely features in such academic observations of protest policing, either empirically or conceptually. Where it is discussed, it often leads to a departure from the idea of policing as a political project and reduces it to crime fighting. As P.A.J. Waddington writes elsewhere about infiltration, it is the policeman's burden to tussle with the moral ambiguity of his profession and to 'perform dreadful deeds for the higher good'; and, 'moral ambiguity does not extend only to the use of force for police officers also lie, deceive and cheat for the greater good' (Waddington, 1994, p 113). When Waddington describes aspects of policing that are deceptive or manipulative, he considers them to be 'dirty work', a view that is also reflected in Gary Marx's account of undercover policing as a 'necessary evil' (1988). While Marx's starting point is the infiltration of the protest group he was involved with as a student, Waddington remains unperturbed by the threats to democracy in the wake of the spycops scandal. In fact, it is the 'dirty work' analysis that prevails even here in a blog post written in 2016 after new guidance on undercover policing was issued by the College of Policing. Waddington writes:

> Activist groups present a particularly seductive milieu for promoting identification. They are composed of 'true believers', eager to convince others of the truth that has been revealed to them. Often they feel beleaguered, a sense of threat that binds them closely together. Of course, they fear infiltration, and so any newcomer will need to establish the strength of their commitment, but an undercover agent will need to work especially hard at doing so. In order to accomplish this they must necessarily empathise with activists. They must laugh at the same jokes, regret the same setbacks, and celebrate the same 'victories'. Most of all, they must share the same beliefs. As they do so they might find that the activists 'have a point' and that stereotypes are misleading. It is easy to imagine how, under these circumstances, an undercover officer might form a bond with an attractive member of the group that matures into a sexual relationship. Certainly, rules, procedures and structures could not hope to prevent it. (Waddington, 2016)

Here, the author of *Liberty and Order* finds little danger to liberty, only to the operational success of the infiltration and the psychological impact on the undercover officers.

Beyond a few exceptions, the political deployment of undercover officers is an area that policing scholarship has frequently shied away from. This is understandable, as it is a field of inquiry cloaked in secrecy, denial and conspiracy theories. The obstacles for academics are all too obvious: much criminological research into policing is reliant on police–academic research partnerships, or at least on police willingness to offer access to academic researchers. Where the object of analysis is the surveillance state or 'secret' state practices, reliance on such insider knowledge is necessarily limited. While most academic research has an interest in rendering police practices 'visible' and transparent, the secret state maintains an interest in 'invisibility' and confidentiality.

To illustrate this point further, let me quote a lengthy passage written by Rob Reiner, from his foreword to an edited book entitled *Introduction to Policing Research: Taking Lessons from Practice*. Reiner (2016, p xiii) writes:

> Professor Jennifer Brown, a pioneer of cooperation between police and academic researchers, has usefully distinguished between four

possible roles in accessing policing for research. She contrasted the difficulties, ethical or other dilemmas, and opportunities facing what she called: inside insiders, outside insiders, inside outsiders and outside outsiders. Inside insiders were police officers themselves conducting research on policing; outside insiders were former officers who had become academics; inside outsiders were academics employed within police organisations for research; and outside outsiders were academics with no formal connection with the police seeking to research policing.

When I began research on a police force for my PhD nearly half a century ago, the few academics who ventured into this territory were all outside outsiders. In the heyday of student protest and counter-culture deviance there was more than a little mutual hostility and suspicion between the cops and the campuses …

This fascinating and invaluable collection of essays is testimony to the sea change since then. [The authors] all illustrate the intellectual and practical policy payoff of the cooperative and mutually beneficial relationship now established between the police and academe.

Reiner's description may well be a useful narrative of how policing studies has evolved, in Britain, over the past 50 years. But my intention is to complicate the picture a bit more and to advocate for a return – if indeed it ever existed – to the more cautious atmosphere between cops and campus that Reiner describes.

This raises methodological and political issues, especially if we consider the voices of outside insiders in policing research. One such outside-inside voice is that of Robert Lambert, a retired undercover and counter-terrorism officer in London's Metropolitan Police. In recent years, he resigned from academic positions in terrorism studies at the University of St Andrews and criminology at the John Grieve Centre for Policing and Community Safety at London Metropolitan University. His career profile as a police officer and researcher, meticulously pieced together by the Undercover Research Group (nd), is of particular interest here, not least because Lambert remains one of the most controversial figures at the centre of political undercover policing. The precise circumstances of the nature of Lambert's role is yet to be revealed. At the time of writing, the Undercover Policing Inquiry website simply provides the cover name 'Bob Robinson', the cipher HN10 and lists his groups of deployment as 'London Greenpeace/Animal Liberal Front' between 1984 and 1989. But activist accounts, information in the public domain and reports seen by investigative journalists suggest a degree of involvement beyond what is implied by these bare facts.

Lambert joined the Metropolitan Police in 1977, became an operative in Special Branch and was soon deployed by the SDS. In his role as a covert operative, he adopted the identity of 'Bob Robinson' as part of a controversial tactic to assume the names of dead children. The real Bob Robinson had died aged seven of a heart condition. Lambert was deployed to inform on animal rights activism. His covert role was underpinned by a relationship he struck up with an activist known as Jacqui, who was 22 years old – ten years younger than Lambert. Jacqui was unaware that Lambert was a police officer, or that he was married with children, when she became pregnant. Like other officers who targeted political campaigners, Lambert eventually disappeared from Jacqui's life and left her to support their son by herself. Jacqui only found out about Lambert's true identity when she discovered a grainy photograph of him alongside a newspaper article naming him as an undercover officer.

According to other activists involved in the animal rights group, Lambert encouraged the use of direct action which would ultimately bring them to the attention of the police. They also claim that he co-wrote a leaflet titled 'What is wrong with McDonalds?', infamous for sparking a libel suit by McDonalds which resulted in the longest libel trial in English legal history. In 1993, Lambert became a manager of SDS operations, apparently ordering intelligence gathering on a number of family justice campaigns and their supporters. Lambert was in charge of undercover officer (and now whistleblower) Peter Francis, who says that he was tasked with smearing the Stephen Lawrence justice campaign. Lambert eventually retired from the Metropolitan Police in 2006 and was awarded an MBE for his services to policing in 2008.

This is just a rough sketch of Lambert's deployment and his managerial responsibilities. Much of the detail remains hidden from public view, with activists taking responsibility for piecing together a fuller profile. Lubbers (2019) describes how the painstaking work of investigating and profiling former undercover deployments in social movements is crucial for activists whose lives were infiltrated. Working together with the activists concerned, journalists and researchers within and outside of the university have been able to expose a range of 'distasteful police practices', including 'stealing the identities of dead children, and tricking targets into intimate and even sexual relationships with agents – in some cases leading to the birth of children who were subsequently abandoned' (Lubbers, 2019, p 225).

Most of what we know about undercover agents placed into political campaigns by the British police has been brought to light by the persistence of activist investigations – perhaps a prime example of deviant knowledge. They helped reveal that the Bob Lambert deployment was just one of many, and while some of it stands out as particularly manipulative and harmful, it is also indicative of the wider policing strategies used to target and disrupt activist groups. Very little information has come from former police officers themselves, even when, as in the case of Lambert, their academic work is directly related to their former police role.

## Critical studies in counter-terrorism

'Moral ambiguity', as described by P.A.J. Waddington, hardly characterises Robert Lambert's role in Special Branch. As we saw earlier, in an unprecedented apology and out-of-court settlement with a number of women who were deceived into long-term manipulative relationships with undercover officers, the Metropolitan Police admitted to human rights violations and abuse of police powers. But what about Lambert's role as an academic? What about the research partnerships he was involved in? Here we have a different 'seductive milieu' (Waddington's words again), in which the former policeman encounters a critical and deliberative environment, in which his knowledge is actively sought out and where he finds recognition for his 'expertise'.

Lambert made his name as a left-leaning academic on the periphery of the Critical Terrorism Studies project. Critical Terrorism Studies was launched as a series of conversations, research networks and publications to offer a counter-narrative to the dominant, 'orthodox' understanding of terrorism (see Jackson, 2007; Jackson et al, 2009). At the core of this project are a set of political and ethical commitments to an appreciation that all terrorism knowledge is socially or culturally constructed and that the 'terrorism' label is therefore inherently contested. While broadly unified around a normative critique of state discourses on violent terror, the project itself is an umbrella term for diverse outlooks and scholarly interests. Some working within the framework adopted the centrally placed view that:

> [R]eal partnerships between researchers and counterterrorism police officers are possible, and arguably vital in the name of scholarly endeavour and the deconstruction of problematic hegemonies, but only when adequate safeguards are placed around any research relationships or that the relationships are alive to the inadequacies of [the] same. (Spalek and O'Rawe, 2014, p 152)

In an article published in the project's journal *Critical Studies on Terrorism* after the stories surrounding the political undercover units had come to light, Basia Spalek and Mary O'Rawe offer their perspective on the undercover operations that involved the infiltration of social justice and environmental activist communities. The researchers make two important disclaimers: first, there is no accepted definition of terrorism, and therefore counter-terrorism; and second, the policing field is steeped in the unique difficulty of research access with senior police managers acting as gatekeepers. It is, in their words, a field of research 'geared to keeping outsiders guessing and firmly out of the inside track' (Spalek and O'Rawe, 2014, p 152). Keeping these disclaimers in mind, it is highly surprising then that they insist on referring to the deployments of Special Branch undercover officers in a range of political groups as 'counter-terrorism work', or that they would come to the conclusion that the 'missing voices' in existing research are those of (former) undercover officers themselves.

Certainly, knowledge of undercover protest policing is hindered by a number of strategies of denial and cultural practices aimed at maintaining the invisibility of undercover units. Or, as Spalek and O'Rawe (2014, p 150) put it: 'it is important for researchers to understand that working within the counterterrorism field involves degrees and shades of risk in the service of trust-building, sensitivity and the empowerment of communities.' The possible gains from applying this particular lens of Critical Terrorism Studies to the infiltration of protest groups in recent times is therefore appealing. As police work continues to confuse political campaigning with domestic extremism and conflates civil disobedience with terrorism, we may also see further efforts to approach police infiltration of protest groups through the lens of terrorism prevention. However, I fundamentally reject the framing of the spycops scandal as belonging to the field of counter-terrorism, critical or not. Instead, I find that in their efforts to learn from policing failures and to improve current practice, analysts equally risk conflating the non-violent direct action repertoires of political protest groups with terrorism. This is true even where police operations are treated with critical scepticism. For example, Spalek and O'Rawe do not question the fact that counter-terrorist activity involves the infiltration of protest groups, although they concede that 'having sexual relationships, and indeed, on occasion, children, with women whilst undercover and of potentially working to entrap vulnerable individuals into planning terrorist acts', raises issues of 'trust, credibility [and] legitimacy' (2014, p 151).

Further, Spalek and O'Rawe cherish the possibility that academic researchers can benefit from working relationships with former counter-terror and undercover police officers. It is clear that the perspectives of former undercover officers can contribute to understanding of 'police knowledge'; that is the perceptions by police of the protest groups they are deployed to infiltrate, often revealing the persistence of stereotypes and exaggeration. But I contend that the evidence of undercover police hiding their true identity from British courts and juries, their refusal to answer questions regarding sexual infiltration practices and the Metropolitan Police's stance of 'neither confirming, nor denying' the existence of undercover police severely question the information gathered from closer working relationships. From my perspective, some researchers' insistence on bringing former police officers into research projects is of detriment to critical knowledge.

This is not to suggest that the information received from activists is not also selective, incomplete or misleading. However, the narratives told by activists give us an angle from which to consider the actual harm caused by infiltration. Groups that have sprung up following the spycops scandal, such as the Undercover Research Group, Police Spies Out of Lives or the Campaign Opposing Police Surveillance, are examples of collaborations between the affected political activists, and there have been arguments that bottom-up, activist-led research is critical in complementing or (in the absence of real progress in the official inquiries) upstaging top-down attempts at fact-finding (Lubbers, 2015). Together, activist researchers offer an important corrective to much of the protest policing literature that too rarely considers the views of protesters.

The reason for this conflation of terrorism and protest may lie in the nature of the relationship between the criminological profession and active and former police officers. Spalek and O'Rawe's intervention in the debate around undercover policing throws up important questions facing academic researchers, specifically those working within policy-facing disciplines. Key issues that arise include the possible impact of research on policy and police practice, the levels of trust that can be achieved vis-à-vis communities subjected to surveillance, the legitimacy and reliability of information provided by the police, and the obvious and operationally necessary lack of transparency regarding surveillance operations. Spalek and O'Rawe argue that it is indeed possible, and crucial, for working relationships between counter-terror police officers and academic researchers to be established apparently also where police work is better described as counter-protest activity. It is an opening gladly accepted (as in their earlier collaboration, see Spalek and Lambert, 2008) by Bob Lambert (2014), who finds in it the justification for his outside insider status as a former police officer within the academic research community. After all, his academic roles are due to 'his counter-terrorism experience', conveniently omitting the fact that this included his years of service in the SDS. Lambert, of course, does little (so far) to answer the allegations against him other than to point to ongoing criminal investigations.

Then consider the scepticism that Spalek and O'Rawe rightly display: 'Researchers can grow to like and trust the counter-terrorism police officers that they engage and do research with, but ultimately, there is no rational conclusion that can be reached as to whether or not researchers also are being manipulated' (Spalek and O'Rawe, 2014, p 159). Viewing the issues raised by the infiltration of campaign groups as an aspect of counter-terrorism or domestic extremism serves to accord a special status to former police infiltrators, some of whom have made the transition into academic careers themselves. It is hoped that academic research can benefit from 'police knowledge' and that 'any research relationships that are developed between researchers and counter-terrorism police officers serve as critical vehicles through which to hold officers to account' (Spalek and O'Rawe, 2014, p 159). I can see no evidence of this with regards to the undercover policing by the SDS and the NPOIU.

Unsurprisingly, the activists that were deceived by Lambert and other undercover officers working under his direction were also not convinced. They launched a campaign to put pressure on London Metropolitan University to sack him from his academic post as a criminology lecturer. The Islington Against Police Spies group picketed the campus in London and a group of prominent activists – George Monbiot, Lois Austin, Dave Smith and Helen Steel – wrote to the University of St Andrews demanding Lambert's resignation.

The universities stood by Lambert. Louise Richardson, the St Andrews' principal who went on to become vice-chancellor of Oxford University, reportedly told the local student newspaper that 'hiring people who have had real-world experience in an institution which is teaching counter-terrorism is entirely legitimate' (quoted in Evans, 2015b). It is unclear if she fully appreciated what that 'real-world experience' of infiltrating social movements and engaging in relationships with four women while undercover entailed or what it meant to the women thus deceived. In any case, she went on to state that in her position she could not 'get involved in what people do privately whoever they are, so I think the university were legitimate to hire him [Lambert] and I think it has been reasonable for us to keep him' (Evans, 2015b).

Contrary to Richardson's assertion, there was nothing private about the activities that Lambert engaged in while undercover or during his stint as SDS manager directing other deployments. He was in the employ of the Metropolitan Police and arguably built his later academic career precisely on his 'experiences' as a police officer. This was not lost on the activists campaigning for his sacking. A spokesperson for the campaign group stated:

> We're saying he's not a suitable person to be working here, supervising students, some of whom may be vulnerable, when he's shown evidence of having a very dubious attitude towards women and consent in the past. Can he be trusted not to abuse the power that he's abused in the past? I don't think he can. (Evans, 2015c)

And it was not just the usual suspects either. *The Observer* columnist Nick Cohen, a contrarian figure on the Left, argued that Lambert was 'uniquely unqualified' to be teaching potential future police recruits (Cohen, 2014). One can only imagine the faux uproar of those who revel in the idea of snowflake students and university cancel culture if such a campaign, however small, had been launched today.

There were other academics who came to Lambert's defence. Stefano Bonino, a counter-terrorism expert, argued that Lambert's academic expertise in the field was indispensable. Bonino asserted that a lecturer in terrorism studies brings vital knowledge in combating contemporary political violence. In a letter published in *Times Higher Education*, he reminded his readers of recent terrorist attacks and juxtaposed this to the campaign calling for Lambert to lose his university jobs. It is the experience of managing the SDS and its undercover deployments into 'far-Left and far-Right' groups that made Lambert stand out as a researcher, according to Bonino. Lambert and the SDS, in this view, 'helped to save lives' despite the 'murky' backstory (Bonino, 2015). The campaign to have Lambert sacked from his university roles failed to 'differentiate between academic expertise and morality' and could not appreciate the efforts of lecturers acting in 'the realm of a complex political world' (Bonino, 2015).

To be fair, Bonino was not the only one impressed in this way by Lambert's work. The former police officer had become a frequent speaker at progressive and anti-racist conferences, criticising the government's counter-terrorism strategy. Somewhat ironically, the 2011 launch for his book *Countering Al-Qaeda in London: Police and Muslims in Partnership* was hosted (just weeks before his SDS past was revealed) at the Houses of Parliament by the Islington MP Jeremy Corbyn. Corbyn had himself been put under Special Branch surveillance 'amid fears that he was attempting to undermine democracy' (Dixon and McCann, 2017).

While academic opinion of Bob Lambert remained contested for some time, there was no more space in London's progressive circles for him after his exposure. What the *Times Higher Education* letter failed to remember was that police officers-turned-academics are not the only ones inhabiting a 'complex political world'. Other academics, in fact, had lived the altogether involuntary experience of finding themselves as the targets of covert police surveillance. Some of those responded with a letter of their own, titled 'Who will police the police?', in the same publication (UCPI, 2017b). It was signed by leading climate scientist Simon Lewis and physicist Jonathan Oppenheim, as well as critical management scholars David Harvie and Keir Milburn. All had been politically active, notably in and around the Camp for Climate Action, and had thus been targeted by undercover policing deployments.[3] They defended the calls for Lambert's resignation 'precisely because morality is not divorced from the political world' and because 'ethics must be integral to teaching, and nowhere more so than in the tutoring of those who will have privileged power over the lives of citizens and the political movements essential to democratic society' (UCPI, 2017b, p 22).

Once again, the incompatibility of academic ethics and secret policing was brought into sharp focus. The URG, set up to shine a light on the murky world of police infiltration, reiterated the campaigners' objection:

> Should lecturers be made accountable for their non-academic past? Yes, … when a criminology lecturer devoted decades to abuse of citizens and the counter-democratic undermining of campaigns for seemingly

no reason other than they threaten established power, it demolishes their credibility and legitimacy. (Undercover Research Group, 2015)

Bob Lambert did resign from his academic posts, turning, as he announced, to independent scholarship. At the time of writing, he is still to appear in open session at the Undercover Policing Inquiry. He has, to my knowledge, no longer offered his 'expertise' on undercover policing either to academic discussion or to the women seeking answers about the deception they were subjected to. He retains his MBE for services to policing.

## Criminological knowledge from below

As a researcher, Bob Lambert was an outside insider – a former undercover cop who had become an academic criminologist. While his autonomy to conduct research from his perspective and with his background is not in question, his failure and unwillingness to outline this perspective and to account for his past in a transparent manner makes the working partnerships between him and outside outsiders manipulative.

In the case of political undercover policing, it is very questionable that academic research can benefit from a close and cosy relationship with retired and practising police officers who refuse to answer questions relating to their own involvement in political policing, who may be bound by the Official Secrets Act or by potential criminal proceedings against them, who are protected by the Regulation of Investigatory Powers Act, and who are taken out of the firing line by the police's Neither Confirm Nor Deny (NCND) strategy and the public inquiry's granting of anonymity for a significant number of undercover officers. There may be exceptions. But, in summary, as a police institution that has shown so much interest in maintaining secrecy about its own practices and policies, Special Branch simply does not make for a good research participant.

If accountability of police surveillance powers remains elusive to traditional research, where does this leave the potential for 'deviant knowledge', the kind of inquiry that was conceived by Reece Walters as a 'criminology of resistance'? The undercover policing scandal, although it did not rock the foundations of the Metropolitan Police's legitimacy in the same way as other critical issues, has been accompanied, and indeed brought to light, by sustained campaigns for truth and justice. As Phil Scraton noted in reference to Hillsborough, the existence of campaigns running alongside inquiries and inquests can be regarded as 'an alternative method for liberating truth, securing acknowledgement and pursuing justice' (Scraton 2013b, p 2). Or, as Joanna Gilmore and Waqas Tufail (2015, p 100) have suggested, 'in the absence of effective official mechanisms of holding police officers to account, vibrant community-led campaigns and radical independent police monitoring groups continue to play an essential role in seeking justice'. Indeed, individuals who have already found out that they were the victims of police infiltration have been at the forefront of speaking out against the abusive practices that appeared to be the tradecraft of the spycops units. It is clear from their determination of revealing the details of the police deployments into their private lives that they are not satisfied simply with the police's side of the story. Although this chapter's focus has been on the challenges for criminological knowledge of undercover policing, it has also hinted at some radical alternatives that would find academic criminologists more closely engaged with activist researchers.

The difficulties in accessing police-controlled data, however, persist. While deviant knowledge presents a hopeful alternative to relying on police permission and partnerships to break open the hidden world of political policing, yet another strategy is for researchers to treat the police's 'resistance to its own visibility as data' (Ullrich, 2019). The following chapters will do just that.

# 4

# The public inquiry as a site of struggle

## "We are not prepared to confirm or deny"

The culture of institutional misogyny running through the undercover units left its mark on the women deceived into relationships with officers. Among them, and a prominent voice in the campaign for transparency, is 'Alison' – her real name restricted by the Inquiry. Her continuous probing and an investigation by journalists at *The Guardian* established beyond doubt that her former partner, whom she knew as 'Mark Cassidy' and who had become a respected campaigner in groups around the Colin Roach Centre in London in the second half of the 1990s, was in fact the undercover officer Mark Jenner. After years of suspicions, he was outed by a trade union activist in 2011 and the story gained national attention two years later. Jenner had adopted the identity of a labour activist from Merseyside, new in Hackney, and looking for a political home. He found it in the Colin Roach Centre, a well-known community resource for union, community and anti-fascist organising. Within a short while, he was in a serious relationship with one of the centre's regulars. Protected by her pseudonym, Alison gave moving testimony to parliament's Home Affairs Committee in 2013, a couple of years after Jenner's outing: 'It has impacted seriously on my ability to trust, and that has impacted on my current relationship and other subsequent relationships', she said. 'It has also distorted my perceptions of love and my perceptions of sex' (Home Affairs Committee, 2013b).

Alison was 29 years old when she met Jenner and began a relationship with him. For several years during his deployment, apparently to monitor trade union and anti-fascist activities, they lived together in her flat. 'We lived together as what I would describe as man and wife', she told MPs (Home Affairs Committee, 2013b). He played an active part in her family life, attending birthdays and weddings using his police-issued cover identity. The man everyone knew as 'Mark Cassidy' was trusted, at first, by Alison's family, friends and political acquaintances. All the while, his wife – the woman who had married a police officer – hardly saw him and the Jenners are reported to have attended couples counselling. Alison is one of the authors of the book *Deep Deception* that tells the story of several women thus affected. As the book was published, almost a decade after the Select Committee invited her evidence in parliament, the public inquiry has still not asked Jenner to talk publicly about his deployment.

There were early signs that her boyfriend was not who he pretended to be. He would not commit to starting a family with Alison. 'It was the time when I wanted to have children, and for the last 18 months of our relationship he went to relationship counselling with me about the fact that I wanted children and he did not', she recalled (Home Affairs Committee, 2013b). After he disappeared, Alison spent more than ten years wondering and worrying about Jenner, even hiring a private detective in the hope of tracking him down. She was, in the words of the journalists who broke her story, 'heartbroken and paranoid, feeling that she was losing her mind' (Lewis and Evans, 2013). Meanwhile, Jenner worked just a few miles away at Scotland Yard after having disappeared from the activists' lives without an apparent trace. Eventually, they were able to track him down. But up until April 2018, when the Undercover Policing Inquiry finally confirmed that a Special Demonstration Squad (SDS) officer referred to by the cypher HN15 had used the cover name 'Mark Cassidy' (though the officer's real name was not published until much later),[1] Alison's requests for answers were stonewalled. In the intervening years, his police employer did not so much as to deny Jenner's identity; it flatly refused to comment on any information put to it by Alison and others. 'We are not prepared to confirm or deny the deployment of individuals on specific operations', the police force declared (Lewis and Evans, 2013).

The refusal to comment on Alison's suspicions and to confirm the surveillance operation that targeted her left Alison traumatised. Although her own investigations had revealed the true identity of the man she had loved as 'Mark Cassidy', the absence of an official acknowledgement represented a gaping hole in her life's history. The police response to 'neither confirm nor deny' Jenner's identity and his relationship with Alison not only denied her any answers but also left her in a Kafkaesque situation where her personal reality failed to find affirmation in the public sphere. To pick up again on the phrase used by Imran Khan on which the discussion in Chapter 1 was centred, Alison knew the truth – at least partially – but the police (non-)response denied her an 'acknowledged truth'. She explains herself in her co-authored book: 'despite the compensation, the apology and the ongoing inquiry, I still have no answers from Mark or his employers as to why, for five years, this officer was entwined in my most intimate and personal life. And I'm not sure I ever will' (Alison et al, 2022, p 361).

Answers to Alison's questions were supposed to come from the public inquiry, established by Theresa May in 2015 under the chairmanship of Sir Christopher Pitchford. As a statutory inquiry with its legislative framework provided by the 2005 Inquiries Act and the 2006 Inquiries Rules, the Chair had the power to request documents and to compel witnesses to give evidence in person and in public. The former SDS field officer and whistleblower

Peter Francis was quoted as being hopeful by the announcement: 'I have been calling for such an inquiry since October 2011', he said. 'When the full truth comes out about the police's work and activities, across the UK, against political campaigns and protests since 1968, I think they will be very shocked' (Francis, 2014). But what promised to be a process to lift the lid on undercover policing turned quickly into an exercise of denial.

Despite the early hopes for the Inquiry to establish the 'full truth', the disappointment felt by many with it now can come as no surprise to those studying accountability processes. Political science and policy studies have generated a huge body of literature on how institutions avoid blame when accused of wrongdoing. I can only touch on a tiny part of this work in looking at practices of denial in police organisations. For those informed by earlier work in the sociology of deviance, the first study that springs to mind might be Stanley Cohen's book *States of Denial: Knowing about Atrocities and Suffering*, first published in 2001. In it, Cohen placed the organised denial of responsibility for harm and crimes at the centre of sociological analysis. Denial involves both political and psychological processes. For Cohen, it combines structural and individual elements (Cohen, 2001). There is plenty of evidence of individual acts of derailment in the Undercover Police Inquiry: police officers telling untruths, lessening their role, their knowledge, their leadership. In one of the most egregious examples, Mark Kennedy briefly employed the public relations specialist Max Clifford to change his identity from one of a police spy to one of a victim of a police conspiracy against him.

But in this chapter, I will focus on institutional denial. I read the police organisation as a broader institution than normally assumed. It includes not just frontline officers (they take a backstage role in my analysis), but police managers, press officers and, crucially, their legal representatives. The chapter argues that the Undercover Policing Inquiry presents us with rich materials for a case study related to state-institutional denial. To pick up on the argument made in the introduction to this book, the chapter examines the centrality of truth claims and blame avoidance. We are treading in the footprints of recent work on secrecy in public inquiries, such as the secrecy scholar William Walters's assertion that public inquiries constitute 'a promising milieu for scholars interested in what we might call the partisan politics of secrecy and scandal' (Walters, 2021, p 95). On the official website of the Undercover Policing Inquiry, the tagline declares: 'Getting to the truth of undercover policing and providing recommendations for the future'. Sir Christopher Pitchford, the Inquiry's first Chair, made it clear in his opening remarks on 28 July 2015: 'The Inquiry's priority is to discover the truth. This is a public inquiry to which, as the name implies, the public will have access' (UCPI, 2015, p 6). More than eight years later, it is difficult to avoid the conclusion that the Inquiry has stood in the way of discovering the truth, rather than helping it.

Such a conclusion would, however, overlook considerable complexities. For one, the work that was undertaken by the Inquiry was enormous. In January 2022, for example, its website listed 248 core participants; 233 SDS and National Public Order Intelligence Unit (NPOIU) staff had been identified as potentially having relevant evidence to give; 222 directions, rulings and notes had been published; 69 officers from the SDS had had their cover names published; and 2,903 evidential documents and files had been published. By 2023, the whole exercise had cost some £60 million. The Inquiry was also some four years behind schedule and still stuck on assessing evidence from events half a century earlier. We will explore some of the reasons for the considerable delay in the proceedings in due course, but the police's reluctance to pass comment on the identities of undercover officers named in the media made for a formidable obstacle right from the start.

## Political accountability in public inquiries

The chapter advances two arguments. First, the police's *invention* of Neither Confirm Nor Deny (NCND) as an organisational doctrine caused harm to individuals justifiably awaiting answers and harm to the inquisitorial process of the public inquiry. It shaped the adversarial tone in the proceedings and highlighted the asymmetrical power relationships between policing bodies and non-police core participants. Second, the police's submission that it would not provide answers to the vast majority of enquiries about suspected deployments was untenable in the public inquiry context – clashing markedly with the assumption that a public inquiry would be 'public' – and it was sharply contested by the victims of police abuse. The Inquiry was therefore a 'zone of politics' (Walters, 2021, p 95), or in the words that I would choose instead, it presented itself as a *site of struggle*.

Stan Cohen's *States of Denial* analyses how the state's response can shift from outright denial to an acceptance of liability if put under pressure. Cohen (2001) argued that criminologists have helped to normalise state crimes which stand in a disproportionate relationship to the vast body of research carried out on relatively minor transgressions. Both criminology and state actors have found ways of denying or justifying atrocities on huge scales. Elsewhere, Cohen describes acts of denial as a 'spiral' (Cohen, 1993), where states first deny the existence of atrocities committed, or, upon exposure, engage in forms of partial denial to shift attention or blame. Scraton (1999), similarly, employs the Foucauldian notion of a 'regime of truth' to question the adequacy of police accountability in processes whereby the state seeks to reconstruct and suppress the truth. These are not literal denials. Rather, they issue public self-criticism embedded within discourse that 'implicates the rule of law, harnessing its processes and procedures to conduct a sophisticated "legal defense"' (Scraton, 1999, p 279; Cohen, 1996). Conceivably, various police actors and their oversight bodies are deeply embedded in a spiral of denial of their own. It is most clearly evident in the Metropolitan Police's 'policy' to NCND undercover deployments.

Non-disclosure and denial (or non-confirmation) were central features of the undercover policing scandal, but they provided different problems from those theorised by Stan Cohen. Rather than simply mechanisms to deflect the apportioning of blame for human rights abuses, strategic non-disclosure and the invention of a policy of NCND engaged questions of secrecy, openness and public interest in novel ways. A lot of this can be gleaned from submissions made by the barristers instructed on behalf of individual officers, the Metropolitan Police Service, the National Police Chiefs' Council (NPCC) and the National Crime Agency. Early on during the drawn-out preliminary phase, in 2016, the Metropolitan Police's legal team led by Jonathan Hall KC summed up the police perspective on disclosure and secrecy in a preliminary argument about the level of openness that the Inquiry should adopt throughout. Hall told the Inquiry that the public interest in protecting the police's secrets was 'very high indeed' and 'the circumstances where [the MPS] will not maintain NCND with respect to undercover deployments will be rare' (UCPI, 2016c, p 31). The force's lawyers submitted that the Inquiry could operate effectively even if the evidence is not made public, nor accessible to other core participants. As Hall put it pointedly: 'The question arises, if there are significant closed parts of a public inquiry, is it a public inquiry at all? The Metropolitan police submits the answer to that question is yes' (UCPI, 2016c, p 3).

In Britain, public inquiries are now favoured instruments to respond to crises in government and governance. Their quasi-independent status from both the executive and the legislature grants them a privileged role in establishing the facts of past events and learning the lessons of institutional failures, thereby seeking to restore public confidence and trust. Their seemingly transparent and public character is decisive for one of their central functions: providing a public response to 'the insistence that "something must be done"' (Burgess, 2011, p 3). Inquiries into major incidents and breakdowns of institutional management, in particular, gain high status within legal and administrative circles. They are typically chaired by senior members of the judiciary and granted a level of autonomy and, in some instances, statutory powers under the Inquiries Act 2005. Their symbolism is not lost on those observing public inquiries: unlike in the High Court their chairs do not wear wigs, their inquisitorial nature lends itself to a closer and more cosy relationship with the public, and their ways of working indicate openness, transparency and truth.

It is perhaps ironic, then, that the Undercover Policing Inquiry is tasked with breaking open one of the most invisible fields of public management and control – undercover policing. It is true that 'in an apolitical age characterised by public cynicism and mistrust, the relative authority that public inquiries enjoy, compared to fixed institutions, is striking' (Burgess, 2011, p 8). The proliferation of calls for public inquiries and inquests in Britain is perhaps symptomatic of declining reverence by both the public and the elites towards institutions. Despite this there are important criticisms that frequently accompany public inquiries, especially where they regard the investigation of serious institutional failures or wrongdoings. Their justification is, after all, based on 'a democratic pluralist position not without its critics' (Scraton, 2013a, p 48). Most importantly, inquiry teams are well aware that they will be scrutinised on the basis of identifying not just individual transgressions but on their ability to point to systemic breakdowns. Furthermore, the Inquiries Act 2005 has significantly reduced the independence of public inquiries by establishing a stronger framework for ministerial influence over the inquisitorial process.

For some, the establishment of a public inquiry as a tool of accountability and policy learning may therefore amount to little more than a ministerial move to increase the government's popularity at the expense of one or several of its public institutions (Sulitzeanu-Kenan, 2010). Similarly, in their now classic work on official discourse, Burton and Carlen consider them to be a 'routine political tactic directed towards the legitimacy of institutions' (Burton and Carlen, 1979, p 13). As some authors have noted, public inquiries into state crime, such as the collusion of state actors with non-state political violence in Northern Ireland, were 'essentially mechanisms for re-establishing the legitimacy of the authoritarian state' (McGovern, 2013, p 11; see also Rolston and Scraton, 2005; White, 2010; Gilligan, 2013). While this may be so, commissions of inquiry and other official reviews into state malpractice are able to work with some level of independence from governmental agendas and may contribute to establishing facts which challenge official denials of wrongdoing.

This, too, is recognised in some of the critical criminological literature, though it finds less acknowledgement in political science research. Let us take the following example. In 2022, the UK government introduced a so-called legacy bill to propose an offer of immunity from prosecution for perpetrators of historical crimes linked to the Northern Ireland Troubles who agree to cooperate with a truth-recovery body. At the same time, the legislation would effectively end the possibility of criminal sanction for state agents involved in serious violence and of further inquests into politically motivated killings. At the time of writing, the Northern Ireland Troubles (Legacy and Reconciliation) Bill is in the final stages of receiving amendments. It has been widely condemned by victim advocates and those seeking accountability for crimes committed by British army officials and informants. The sociologist Mark McGovern, for example, has characterised the legacy bill as an attempt to protect former British soldiers from having to answer for their actions in court and 'to enshrine impunity and deny accountability and truth' (McGovern, 2022, p 82). In contrast, the large body of evidence relating to collusion in the North of Ireland, resulting from both official and unofficial reviews or investigations, is being met with an ongoing culture of denial among British elites who seek to limit and control further avenues for accountability. This argument in part refutes the state narrative that legacy inquiries do not work.

There are echoes here of my own reading of public inquiries. This challenges a totalising view of secrecy, closure and concealment in public inquiries, which would itself conceal their contested processes. If we dismiss the institution of a public inquiry as a mere whitewash, where does this leave the many participants, those that pin their hopes on its outcomes and those who seek to shape its processes in their favour? My starting premise, therefore, is not that public inquiries act as cover-ups, but that they are *sites of struggle*. There is little in the academic literature that I can hook my understanding to, but one political interjection, by Stuart Hall, is noteworthy for its political reading of a pre-Inquiries Act public inquiry. Commenting on the strategic lessons that the political Left could draw from the Lord Scarman Report following the 1981 Brixton riot, Hall (1982) suggested that there is more to official recommendations for police reform than an attempt at foreclosing debate and legitimising existing practice. In fact, he contended, the appearance of cracks and differences within the established positions on law and order signalled a political opening that progressives would do well to engage with and exploit: 'internal contradictions', Hall wrote, 'are not random occurrences and we need to understand both why they occur and what they mean' (Hall, 1982, p 67).

Internal contradictions are all too obvious in the Undercover Policing Inquiry, which – following Hall's perspective – presents itself to us as a site of struggle. Whether the Inquiry provided for the kind of political openings that Hall detected in the Scarman Inquiry is another matter. Struggles over disclosure and openness were, in any case, at the heart of it.

## The limits of Neither Confirm Nor Deny

As policing gets drawn into the realm of politics, from which it usually, albeit unsuccessfully, seeks to distance itself, any inquiry into a key function of policing will present its participants with high stakes around reputation, accountability and legitimacy. For this reason, political strategies within such inquiries turn to questions of concealment, denial and truth-telling. Narrative and narrative form matter here. This is nowhere more the case than in the Undercover Policing Inquiry, where the very practice of policing via deceptive and secretive means is at stake. And although as a tactic of reputation management and neutralisation it appears blunt and lacking in credibility, it is perhaps of no great surprise that police organisations approached the public inquiry into its secretive and politically charged units with one simple dictum: 'we will neither confirm nor deny'.

Despite this, it is my aim in this chapter to show that, while as a strategy the response to NCND the existence of undercover deployments served to obfuscate, the principle itself was an invention that ultimately failed to conceal the extent of SDS and NPOIU infiltration. NCND responses are not entirely uncommon. They can be used by public authorities, for example in answering freedom of information requests where the information held would be exempt from the duty to disclose. The justification commonly given is that even a simple confirmation or denial that the requested information is held by the organisation may allow inferences to be made about the existence of sensitive or potentially damaging materials. In the world of intelligence, the NCND response gained particular application. In the United States, for example, where NCND is also known as the Glomar response – following a Cold War CIA reaction to media inquiries about covert plans to recover a Soviet submarine – the response has become semi-folkloric. When the CIA joined Twitter in 2014, its first Tweet read: 'we can neither confirm nor deny that this is our first tweet'. In the UK, the Information Commissioner's Office (ICO) sets out the exemptions that cover the duty placed upon public authorities to answer requests for information, including information held by the police and other law enforcement organisations for the purposes of criminal investigation. The ICO, in explaining the exemptions, explicitly refers to the example of police intelligence gained through covert surveillance:

> [A] police force may hold information regarding particular properties they have under surveillance – it is likely that if a request were made for information about the surveillance of a certain property, this information would be exempt … A public authority could therefore refuse to confirm or deny whether it holds information about a property under surveillance. (Information Commissioner's Office, nd, p 6)

A report by the human rights charity JUSTICE shows how NCND 'is most often used by public authorities in the national security and law enforcement contexts' but has also been abused to shield state-funded bodies from legitimate scrutiny, 'to avoid disclosing information that may reveal unlawful activity' (JUSTICE, 2017, p 6). JUSTICE argues that '[t]he use of NCND in this way weakens public trust in agencies and public authorities. Most crucially, it also risks undermining basic individual rights and the rule of law' (JUSTICE, 2017, p 8). Others who had followed the Metropolitan

Police's preparations for the public inquiry were in agreement. In a report for the Centre for Crime and Justice Studies, a London-based think tank, researcher Helen Mills also noted that NCND became the 'routine police response' (Mills, 2017, p 5) to queries by activists about the identity of suspected infiltrators: 'That the police were prepared to go to considerable lengths to maintain this response became clear once the activists presented evidence produced by their own research to the police. It included dropping a prosecution case rather than reveal the presence of an undercover officer' (Mills, 2017, p 5).

Alison's story of being denied the truth about 'her' undercover officer demonstrates the impact on the victims of the abusive deployments. But all of it brought to the fore the question of what NCND actually was. Was it a policy, a principle, a delaying tactic?

One early description of NCND as a policy came in the first report of Operation Herne, the police-internal investigation into the allegations surrounding the SDS and NPOIU. The report on the use of covert identities, led by Derbyshire Chief Constable Mick Creedon, stated:

> The policy of 'neither confirming nor denying' the use of or identity of an undercover police officer is a long established one used by UK policing. It is essential so as to provide for the necessary operational security and to ensure undercover officers are clear that their identity will never be disclosed by the organisation that asked them to carry out the covert activity. The duty of care owed to such officers is an absolute one and applies during their deployments, throughout their service and continues when they are retired. (Operation Herne, 2013, p 3)

Characterising this 'absolute' version of NCND as police doctrine, the chief constable inadvertently hit on a major source of embarrassment for the secretive police units in question: what if their undercover officers are arrested in the course of their deployments? What if these officers were charged and put on trial? Would they be instructed to maintain their cover even then?

These are not hypothetical questions. Spycops officers provided testimony to courts or went on trial for protest-related offences while still assuming their police-issued false identities. In this way, they potentially misled judges and juries and undermined the safety of convictions. It is one of the many issues that the Undercover Policing Inquiry is meant to examine in detail.

Some of these details are already known. In a Channel 4 interview, Bob Lambert admitted that he was arrested 'four or five times' (Davies, 2013) while undercover, and appeared in a magistrates court charged with a minor public order offence. Even though he appeared in court using his cover identity he had constructed from the death certificate of 'Bob Robinson', he declined to be drawn on the question whether he intentionally misled the court. Activists are dismayed by the fact that this admission was made in 2013 and a decade later Lambert has still not been asked to give public evidence to the Undercover Policing Inquiry. When the police's own investigation Operation Herne looked into the matter, it found that the need to maintain cover and to carry on in the deployment after activists had been charged and prosecuted was given as the justification to attend court in their covert identities. These were not acts of rogue officers. As the investigation found: 'Documentation has been identified which supports the premise that SDS management were aware of the practice' (Operation Herne, 2014b, p 5).

To take another example, Jim Boyling, using the name 'Jim Sutton', infiltrated the direct action group Reclaim the Streets in the late 1990s. Reclaim the Streets was known for organising mass, carnivalesque gatherings on public highways, protesting against car culture as a symbol of capitalist excess. He was arrested alongside other activists at a protest at the Transport for London office in 1996 and prosecuted giving a false name and occupation. The officer maintained the identity of a protester even as he was party to the discussions between the protesters and their defence lawyers. Boyling, posing as a co-defendant, was represented by the same law firm as the other activists (Evans and Lewis, 2011a). The case came to a trial in which Boyling appeared using his assumed name. As Rob Evans and Paul Lewis reported in *The Guardian* some years later, the officer 'maintained this fiction throughout the entire prosecution, even when he gave evidence under oath to barristers' (Evans and Lewis, 2011a). Boyling, alongside the other activists, was acquitted. Just one, John Jordan, was convicted. Jordan, after Boyling's role in the trial had been exposed in 2011, successfully appealed his conviction.

The undercover practices have prompted the non-police, non-state core participants to question the lawfulness of spycops tactics during their opening statements. Charlotte Kilroy KC, on behalf of the women who were deceived into intimate sexual relationships with undercover police officers, argued that the practice of lying to court revealed the spycops units' disregard for the rule of law and democracy: 'By their willingness to lie to courts', the barrister said, 'the police were attacking the very institutions which it was their duty to support' (UCPI, 2022e, p 90). Activists involved in the targeted groups did not mince their words either. They made it quite clear that they regarded undercover officers to be little more than state-sanctioned liars. 'Some spycops went all the way to court themselves', one wrote in a blog post. 'They would swear to tell the truth, the whole truth and nothing but the truth and, from the first question asking their name, they lied and lied and lied' (Badger, 2017). In short, any witness statements that they were to give in the Inquiry was already to be treated with a heavy dose of suspicion.

## *Disclosure failures in a major protest trial*

In most cases, the police were able to cover up the arrests and prosecutions of their undercover field officers and to keep them out of the courts altogether. But when Mark Kennedy, the officer with a seven-year record of infiltrating grassroots environmental movements, was arrested in a pre-emptive police raid on a group of activists in 2009, something had gone wrong. Kennedy was arrested, charged and prosecuted under his false identity of 'Mark Stone'. It was this prosecution, which dramatically collapsed, that was a key ingredient in the chain of events that would lead to the exposure of spycops units and their tactics. At the heart of it all were the failures by police to disclose their deployments in a criminal trial.

During the first decade of the 2000s, climate activists had stepped up their campaign against fossil fuel-based energy production. The first Camp for Climate Action in 2006, with Kennedy's involvement, pitched up not far from the Drax coal-fired power station in Yorkshire. Plans to build a new coal plant drew climate campers to Kingsnorth, in Kent, two years later. In April 2009, activists congregated at a school in Nottingham ahead of a plan to disrupt the operation of Ratcliffe-on-Soar power station. Again, Kennedy was among them. The protestors had history on their side: Ratcliffe is now one of just three remaining coal-fired plants in the UK and earmarked for closure. But the police, and the Crown Prosecution Service (CPS), saw things differently.

A dawn swoop by hundreds of police officers on the unsuspecting protesters in the school led to 114 arrests and charges for conspiracy to commit aggravated trespass, one of the largest ever pre-emptive arrests of protestors in Britain. All bar one of the protestors were represented by the experienced protest lawyer Mike Schwarz; Kennedy was one of the arrestees and one of those charged, yet the only one to opt out of legal representation. Twenty-six of the activists were eventually brought to court, in two groups. The first 20 were convicted of conspiracy to close down the coal plant after failing to convince a jury in Nottingham crown court that their planned actions were necessary to prevent immediate harm to life from climate catastrophe. The trial for the remaining six was to follow in early 2011. Yet on 7 January that year, their prosecution spectacularly collapsed when the CPS dropped the case because of 'previously unavailable material that undermines the prosecution's case' (cited in Evans and Lewis, 2011b). That material was the evidence that Mark Kennedy, who had infiltrated the group, took a role in planning the protest and made secret recordings of their meetings. Following Kennedy's exposure as a police officer a few months earlier, Schwarz and the defence team had sought disclosure of this evidence.

Who was to blame for the failure to disclose this evidence to the defence and the resulting collapse of the high-profile trial? The police and the

CPS, headed at the time by Keir Starmer, appeared to blame each other. At Starmer's request, the government's Chief Surveillance Commissioner, Sir Christopher Rose, was asked to look into the disclosure failures that led to the collapse and the subsequent quashing of convictions. Delivering his report in December 2011, Rose said: 'The crucial question at the heart of my inquiry is: why was it not disclosed?' (Rose, 2011, p 4). Rose's answer was essentially to point the finger at one individual, the CPS official Ian Cunningham. But more systemic failings, including a possible attempt to protect Kennedy as a police asset among the climate campaigners, were ruled out: 'Nothing I have seen or heard suggests that, at any stage of this prosecution, there was deliberate, still less dishonest, withholding of information which the holder believed was disclosable' (Rose, 2011, p 29). In the community of activists who had been arrested in the case, the report was branded as a whitewash. One of the defendants in the Ratcliffe-on-Soar trial is quoted in *The Guardian* (Evans, 2011), stating:

> The Ratcliffe case was one of the most sophisticated policing operations in recent history involving a four-month investigation culminating in the largest pre-emptive arrest in British legal history. For this report to claim that when the question of disclosure arose, every time, every person associated with the case suddenly became incompetent, but institutionally everything is fine is totally absurd. This report can be added to the great litany of British judicial whitewashes.

Keir Starmer went on the BBC's *Newsnight* programme to limit the damage to the CPS. Grilled by the programme's anchor Jeremy Paxman, he held firm to the view that there were no systemic non-disclosure issues at play. Paxman asked the then Director of Public Prosecutions repeatedly if he could be absolutely confident that there were no further unsafe convictions on the basis of undisclosed undercover police activity. Starmer did not directly answer the question. All he could commit to was that the CPS would look into any further allegations that co-defendants in trials were acting undercover if such cases were brought to his attention.

Starmer's proposition was an absurd one. How could anyone arrested and prosecuted for a protest-related offence, conceivably as far back as the SDS's founding year in 1968, alert the CPS of undercover police officers' involvement in their trials? How would they know? It appeared that Starmer pushed the ball back into the police's court – it was on them to disclose their own activities, something they were not prepared to do.

Non-disclosure of undercover police involvement in bringing evidence to the courts may have been a convenient way of maintaining the secrecy of the SDS and NPOIU, but the collapse of the Ratcliffe-on-Soar trial made it increasingly untenable and raised questions over the safety of potentially thousands of convictions for protest-related offences. What followed was a deep reach into the toolbox of neutralisation strategies. Rather than denying its secrets, the police re-deployed the principle of neither confirming nor denying the existence of undercover officers. What was intended to frustrate activist attempts to confirm the identities of suspected infiltrators also posed a formidable challenge to the workings of the public inquiry. In fact, it put into focus the very meaning of carrying out a public inquiry into secretive practices by an institution of the state.

## The Inquiry's legal approach to restriction orders

The police's stated intention to maintain the anonymity of the majority of undercover officers, their handlers and managers became the central issue with which the Inquiry had to grapple in its lengthy preliminary phase. Open hearings took place in March 2016 to aid the Chair in establishing the legal principles that would guide his decisions on Section 19 applications for restriction orders. His ruling, 85 pages long, followed on 3 May 2016. This was the crucial document that would identify the fault lines among core participants and seek to overcome them. Pitchford's starting point came down to a recognition of two competing public interests – openness and confidentiality. The ruling stated that 'the application of the legal principles identified will bite upon the separate interests of the police and non-police, non-state core participants' (UCPI, 2016b, p 4). In the interest of openness, no restriction order would be made, Pitchford asserted, unless it was necessary to do so in the opposing interest of protecting individual police officers and the wider policing function from harm.

The Chair's ruling sought to overcome this opposition of secrecy and transparency via, essentially, a tautological formulation. While Section 21 of the Inquiries Act 2005 gives him the statutory power to compel persons to provide evidence, produce documents or appear as witnesses, Section 22 outlines a number of exemptions. Most relevant here is the exemption for reasons of public interest immunity. In essence, this exemption could justify the non-disclosure of material if doing so (withholding the evidence) is in the public interest. And what are the grounds for public interest immunity? Pitchford's answer, and this is the linchpin of his approach, boils down to a circular fudge: there is a public interest in secrecy whenever secrecy is in the public interest!

Pitchford was unwilling to rule about the legal approach to anonymity and other restrictions at a general level. The case for restriction orders was to be made with the specific concerns of each deployment in mind. This decision to take an 'incremental route' through case-by-case decisions on restriction orders and anonymity remained largely non-committal towards the issue of disclosure. In the view of many transparency campaigners, it also failed to address the central question of how the Inquiry would 'get to the truth'. However, the ruling did give some reassurance to the non-police, non-state core participants in saying that the police's NCND position cannot amount to a blanket ban on disclosure. As the accompanying press note read:

> The Ruling states that there will be no blanket solution in respect of restriction orders and that that the practice of 'neither confirm nor deny' will not, by itself, be a reason to make a restriction order, although it may be a consideration as part of the balancing act the Chairman will undertake when applying the legal principles and in weighing up competing public interests. (UCPI, 2016e)

This explicit rejection of blanket anonymity for former police officers essentially ended the police's NCND policy in the public inquiry. At the same time, however, it opened up the route for long delays and protracted processes in assessing restriction order applications and risk assessments.

For some observers, the Chair's arguments underpinning his ruling on the legal approach to restriction orders were not entirely unreasonable. His case-by-case approach finds support, for example, in the perspective taken by the ethics and policing scholar Katerina Hadjimatheou (2017). Hadjimatheou summarises it in her examination of the secrecy/openness debate in the Undercover Policing Inquiry:

> [P]olice continue to be obliged by considerations of the just balance between secrecy and accountability, to undertake risk assessments for each case in which disclosure is requested. This conclusion does not exclude the possibility that *in practice* all risk assessments end up favoring an NCND response to the request. (2017, pp 285–6, emphasis in the original)

Such qualified support for the Chair's ruling did include, therefore, an important caveat. The confidentiality principle upon which the police relied had itself not been questioned. Although Pitchford ruled out that he would issue blanket anonymity orders, his incremental approach might still have the effect of severely limiting public access to the evidence. In practice, as we will see, later rulings on risk assessments and applications for restrictions, particularly those guaranteeing anonymity for former or serving police officers, only heightened the sense that the Inquiry had come down firmly on the side of secrecy.

How did we get to this point? For the police, the value of maintaining secrecy had been demonstrated in some unexpected legal precursors. One such case was tested before the Freedom of Information Tribunal, the place to appeal the denial of requests by the Information Commissioner's Office. In *Marriott v Information Commissioner* (2011), the Tribunal found that the historical files relating to the Jack the Ripper murders were exempted from Freedom of Information requests. It also found that the public interest in maintaining this exemption outweighed the public interest in disclosure. That ruling, in 2011, came in response to the case brought by a lay historian before the Tribunal that concerned the nineteenth-century murders committed by Jack the Ripper. The researcher, Trevor Marriott, had requested access to historic files contained in the Special Branch archives that would reveal details about paid informants in 1880s London. Marriott believed that access to the information would allow him to follow a lead on the unsolved murders in East London (Barrett, 2011; Higgerson, 2011). The Information Commissioner had overruled a Metropolitan Police denial to release the files, but agreed that the names of informants could be redacted. This followed the police's wish to conceal details of its network of informants, even as it existed more than a century earlier. And the reasoning? In the Metropolitan Police's submission, its current approaches to members of the public to act as police informants could be undermined if the force could not guarantee total and 'eternal' anonymity. Essentially, opening the files on the historic Jack the Ripper case would cause harm to policing today, some 120 years later. The Metropolitan Police rehearsed similar arguments again in its bid to prevent the publication of details about its undercover operations into political groups from 1968 onwards. Even as campaigners and investigative journalists began to shine some light into the role played by the SDS and the NPOIU in monitoring and suppressing political protest, they encountered a rapid closing of ranks within the Metropolitan Police and other forces.

## The mosaic effect

In a short statement on the issue of anonymity and restriction orders, the NPCC submitted to the Inquiry that further 'established general principles' existed. Among them were that 'the public interest in protecting the identity of undercover officers is very strong' and that 'the risk of a seemingly innocuous piece of information being part of a "mosaic effect" leading to the identification of an officer is real' (UCPI, 2016a). By employing the jargon of 'mosaicking', the police submissions were able to shift the narrative away from the intentional search for truth in the Inquiry towards that of the risks posed by an unintentional revelation of information. From the perspective of *confidentiality*, the idea that a full mosaic picture of the political undercover police could crystallise was of concern. The Inquiry's question should not be, accordingly, how best to learn what happened, but how best to protect police-held data.

For campaigners, however, the combining of small jigsaw pieces to arrive at a more complete understanding of the deployments should precisely be the Inquiry's objective. On the mosaic effect, the Inquiry was addressed by Ben Emmerson KC, representing Peter Francis. Francis had questioned why the assumed cover names of undercover officers could not be disclosed. The identities had, after all, been designed exactly for the purpose of protecting the true identity of the officers. So how could a cover name now be seen as leading to the exposure of someone's real persona? In Ben Emmerson, Francis had enlisted one of the country's most famous human rights lawyers who acted as the United Nations' special rapporteur on human rights and counter-terrorism. The barrister had counted among his clients Katharine Gunn, the GCHQ whistleblower who had been prosecuted for breaking the Official Secrets Act in the run-up to the 2003 Iraq war. For Francis, the possibility of being prosecuted under the same Act was a constant obstacle to revealing further information about the SDS. In a public hearing on 23 March 2016, Emmerson put Francis's concerns to the Chair:

> First of all, the mosaic principle. We would ask you, Sir, to look critically at assertions that there are risks of mosaic identification and not simply to accept at face value that the disclosure of an identity – which after all was intended to protect the individual from disclosure and from their true identity being known – that the disclosure that a particular individual was an undercover officer by the name of John Bloggs, that that is something which would imperil the safety – and I put it that way because, although privacy is in the balance, in a sense one's focal point in the first instance is on safety of the undercover officers themselves or of their families. (UCPI, 2016d, p 95)

The argument surrounding the mosaic effect stretched further than the safety of the (former) officers. From the police's perspective, identification would not just pose harm to the person, but *harm to policing*. To prove that revealing the cover names of officers who infiltrated progressive social movements would harm investigations of terrorism or serious organised crime, the police had to dig deep. One particular document, eventually released in redacted form by the Inquiry, did a lot of the heavy lifting – yet it must also be one of the most bizarre police reports in the Inquiry's possession. The 40-page paper on the mosaic effect seeks to explain 'how the incremental release of information can be used to identify' former undercover officers (UCPI, 2017c, p 2). The identities of its authors, two Metropolitan Police risk assessors going by the curious codenames Jaipur and Karachi, are themselves kept concealed and the publication is itself redacted in various places.

The report summarises the Metropolitan Police's concern around the possibility that the safety of officers could be compromised if the force had to depart from its NCND policy during the course of the Inquiry. The report cited 'aggravating factors' that made it 'almost impossible' to judge whether the release of a particular part of information could lead to further exposures and put former undercover officers at risk. As officers in the SDS and NPOIU were deployed as covert human intelligence sources, the report admits that they were required 'to form close friendships with activists ... and spend considerable time with them over the course of many months and years' (UCPI, 2017c, p 3). The anonymous authors assume that officers themselves may have inadvertently disclosed policing secrets over the lengths of their deployments. While NCND is the answer to the risk of mosaic exposure, Jaipur and Karachi are careful not to paint the public inquiry as the problem. The level of scrutiny of undercover policing that could arise within this forum is welcomed, yet they make the argument that its public nature could be exploited by 'active criminals' (UCPI, 2017c, p 4).

Having accepted the role of a statutory inquiry into its own practices, the Metropolitan Police's report looks for risks to its operations elsewhere: most of the blame rested with 'the concerted effort by activists and others' (UCPI, 2017c, p 2) to understand the deployments and in some cases to reveal true identities. In the report, it is the Undercover Research Group (URG) that is constructed as the main risk to officers. A large part of the report simply reproduces information from the URG's website and its statements made to support its application to become a core participant in the Inquiry. One of the URG researchers, Dónal O'Discroll, has been granted core participant status (on account of his close friendship and working relationship with Mark Kennedy in a range of environmental, social and animal rights campaigns) and this is noted as 'of concern' by the police report. The application by the URG, founded after Kennedy's exposure, to assist the Inquiry as a core participant had been rejected by Sir Christopher Pitchford as early as October 2015.

It may be that the Metropolitan Police was surprised that the activists calling for accountability appeared skilled and better informed than they thought: 'Their work is professional and meticulously researched', the report laments, a fact it ascribed to the involvement of Eveline Lubbers, author of a book on corporate and police spying on activists (Lubbers, 2012). Bizarrely, there is also a particular focus on the internet in the report, which apparently makes it easier for activists to share their personal recollection of suspicions and details of infiltrators. The internet is seen as the 'primary enabler' of the mosaic effect, as it allows activists 'to compile information about suspected UCOs and compare details ... of meetings and protests and highlight common themes and inconsistencies' (UCPI, 2017c, p 3). As much as Jaipur and Karachi, the report's authors, may have wished for a time when transparency campaigners could not send emails or set up Facebook groups, they were powerless in avoiding the 'risks' of independent researchers doing their own probing into police infiltration.

The issue of the mosaic effect was accepted by all as the crucial matter by which the NCND strategy would become operational. This was not just a matter of requiring the police to disclose their operations in their entirety. In effect, all Inquiry participants accepted that to guarantee the safety of (former) undercover officers, there may well be situations where their 'real' identities would be concealed. They could, for example, be allowed to give evidence to the Inquiry in their cover identities. For the police this was not enough, but for the Chair this was the point of balance between security and disclosure that his ruling had to address. In an exchange with Ben Emmerson (UCPI, 2016d, p 103), that binary was maintained:

| | |
|---|---|
| Chair: | Then comes the question of mosaic identification, which is a matter of fact I will have to consider. |
| Emmerson: | Yes. |
| Chair: | In the end, if there is evidence that the true identity would be revealed merely by disclosing the undercover name of a police officer, I will have to make the balance in that knowledge. |
| Emmerson: | Yes. And will I submit, if I may say so, formidably difficult judgments ahead. |
| Chair: | How nice of you to sympathise. |

The difficulty is here expressed as striking the right balance between disclosure and security. Certainly, the issue can be seen in this way. The more that police concealment of its methods is maintained, the safer these methods are. But these arguments were not heard in a court; they were heard in the inquisitorial context of a public inquiry.

This regulation of disclosure through a balance of competing public interests is itself problematic. In a study of Britain's Iraq war secrets, Thomas (2020, p 77) argues that it presents 'no balance at all ... because security only features on one side'. The fact that the argument in favour of secrecy revolves around the claim that openness is harmful to security obscures the fact that security can be undermined by excessive secrecy, too. As Thomas expresses the critique of legal discourse that rests on the balance metaphor in public inquiries and in Freedom of Information law:

> This one-sided emphasis on harm unravels the pretence that the public interest test 'balances' arguments for and against disclosure. 'Balance' implies that two opposing objects can be quantified like two objects on a set of scales, giving speakers on both sides of a dispute an *equal* chance of winning the debate, subject to the strength of their evidence.

However, this balance is unequal because the opposing public interests are not quantified in the same terms. (Thomas, 2020, p 85, emphasis in the original)

In this vein, Peter Francis's barrister took the opportunity to remind the Chair of his responsibilities towards those who were seeking answers about the police operations in which they had been targeted:

> On the other side of that balance, self-evidently, not knowing the fact that a particular individual with whom one was associated ... not knowing that that person was in fact an undercover officer renders the participation of the target in these proceedings effectively pointless. It is going to be, in practical terms, impossible if that information is not made available ... Indeed it [confidentiality] would have such a detrimental effect on the conduct of the Inquiry, it would be difficult to see how that could easily be overcome. (UCPI, 2016d, pp 95–6)

Public inquiries, by their statutory framework, allow for a level of participation. If participation, however, hinges on at least a minimum amount of disclosure, different questions arise: what if disclosure is so minimal that it undermines effective participation in the public inquiry? Or in other words, how public does a public inquiry have to be to qualify as a public inquiry (see Ireton, 2018)? As we have seen, the Metropolitan Police submission was clear on this point. The Chair should resist calls for maximum disclosure because the Inquiries Act allows him to hear evidence in secret. But for Emmerson, the matter was not closed:

> Well, if there must be some degree of effective participation, then there must be an irreducible minimum duty of disclosure. The two go hand in hand ... if those behind me and to my left are not able to know if there was infiltration of their constituency offices, their organisations, their homes, their beds, by undercover police officers, they are not going to be able to participate in any effective way at all. So to that extent the core irreducible minimum must be – and this is the issue – the identity, the undercover identity, of the officers concerned. (UCPI, 2016d, pp 116–17)

If, for the non-police, non-state participants, the possibility of a public inquiry worthy of its name was the disclosure of the cover identities used by undercover officers, the police submissions cited legal precedents, which, in their view, should sway the Chair's balancing act in favour of secrecy. The NPCC, for example, supported the Metropolitan Police in asserting the importance of the NCND 'principle' (UCPI, 2016f). In its submission to the preliminary hearings in early 2016, the NPCC argued that the NCND response was born from the requirement to protect the public interest (in fighting organised crime). It stated that in cases of informants working for the British state in Northern Ireland, the public interest amounts to revealing as little as possible about the existence (or not) of these assets. This, the NPCC said, had been a long-established principle. But the police lawyers also argued that it had found its legal footing – in the striking case of the British spy codenamed 'Stakeknife'.

## The Scappaticci problem

There have been few cases of British intelligence sources that have received as much speculation as that of the informant going by the codename 'Stakeknife'. The spy was the jewel in the crown of British army intelligence, allegedly recruited as a volunteer from Belfast and employed by the secret Force Research Unit of the British Army to infiltrate the Provisional Irish Republican Army (IRA) in the late 1970s and during the 1980s. It is thought that Stakeknife reported on the IRA for over 25 years, but there have also been reported accusations that the asset acted as a double agent. In any case, it is alleged that he was one of the IRA's heads of internal security, sometimes referred to as the 'nutting squad', and therefore centrally involved in the murder and torture of suspected informants within the organisation (see, for example, Leahy, 2020).

In the early 2000s, media outlets began speculating that Stakeknife was the identity of Freddie Scappaticci, an IRA man who had been interned by the British alongside Sinn Féin president Gerry Adams in the 1970s. Charged with identifying and interrogating potential informants within the organisation, Scappaticci was both 'chief rat and rat catcher-in-chief' (Harkin, 2020). Scappaticci denied the accusations but was eventually arrested in 2018 by officers from Operation Kenova and died in 2023.

The Scappaticci case highlighted the use of NCND by the British security apparatus. As Scappaticci denied the accusations against him when they first emerged, he sought a judicial review against the decision by the Northern Ireland Office to 'neither confirm nor deny' any allegations. He argued that the British government infringed on his Article 2 rights (the right to life) by not confirming his own denial as he had received death threats upon the accusation that he had worked for the British Army as a spy in the IRA. However, his application for judicial review was refused. In the 2003 High Court of Northern Ireland judgment, Lord Chief Justice Carswell reasoned that there were 'powerful reasons for maintaining the strict NCND policy', namely:

> To state that a person is an agent would be likely to place him in immediate danger from terrorist organisations. To deny that he is an

agent may in some cases endanger another person, who may be under suspicion from terrorists. Most significant, once the Government confirms in the case of one person that he is not an agent, a refusal to comment in the case of another person would then give rise to an immediate suspicion that the latter was in fact an agent, so possibly placing his life in grave danger ... There is in my judgment substantial force in these propositions and they form powerful reasons for maintaining the strict NCND policy. (NIQB, 2003, p 3)

The judgment has made itself felt way beyond terrorism-related cases. Arguably, 'none of the North's post-conflict cases is more central to these arguments, and for bringing together a "neither confirm nor deny" stance with the state's human rights-based justification for secrecy, than the case of Freddie Scappaticci' (McGovern, 2016, p 6). It was, then, heavily relied on by police lawyers in the Undercover Policing Inquiry.

However, relying on the Scappaticci ruling to insist on the consistent application of NCND responses to 'the vast majority' of all undercover operations left the Metropolitan Police and the NPCC in an awkward place. Simply put, there was absolutely nothing to suggest that the confirmation or denial that undercover officers, working for the SDS or NPOIU in England and Wales, who had exposed themselves or had been exposed by activists, would put the life of other agents 'in grave danger'. The police infiltration of progressive social movements on the mainland was simply not comparable to the presence of British intelligence agents in Northern Ireland.

## The Princess Diana exception

Another problem for the Metropolitan Police was that the rejected judicial review application in the Scappaticci case left room for exceptions to the 'policy'. Pitchford recognised as much when he noted that 'there have been occasions when either the holder of the information or the court or tribunal adjudicating upon it has found that the public interest in disclosure should prevail' (UCPI, 2016b, pp 47–8). There were a number of such exceptions found in case law, several of which proved that the interest in national security could quickly be trumped if the reputation of institutions of the state was concerned. One notable case regarded the circumstances of the deaths of Princess Diana and Dodi Fayed in 1997, which led to what we could call the *Princess Diana exception*. In 2004, a police investigation was launched into the widespread conspiracy theories that the security service MI6, under the orders of the royal family, had deliberately caused the car accident that killed the Princess of Wales and her lover in a Parisian tunnel. The wide-ranging investigation found that the allegations were without foundation and that the car crash was accidental. However, the conspiracy theories, fuelled by

Dodi's father Mohamed al-Fayed, refused to go away. It came to a head in the 2008 inquest into the deaths.

The contemporaneous head of the Secret Intelligence Service, Sir Richard Dearlove, gave evidence – in apparent contravention of the NCND policy – to officially deny that MI6 had been implicated in the deaths. Asked whether his denial was an obvious departure from the NCND response, Dearlove answered:

> When matters of, let's say, grave public concern arise, rare exceptions of policy are made, and obviously, in this particular instance in this court, I think one can understand why an exception is being made … There are various occasions when there is a strong demand for a public statement, and in the particular context, whether it might be a Parliamentary inquiry or let's say a court of law, an exception is made, but making an exception does not indicate an abandonment of the principle, which I think has been very valuable in, as it were, defending the integrity and the interests of the intelligence and security community. (Cited in UCPI, 2016b, p 50)

The former head of MI6 had to engage in some rhetorical acrobatics here to justify the denial issued by the security service. Exceptions to the NCND rule are 'rare', he was at pains to point out, and they are the result of 'grave public concern' and 'a strong demand' for an official comment. The exception, however, confirms the rule and the public interest in national security remains paramount. The fact that the reputation of MI6 and other intelligence bodies was at stake is not alluded to, yet it is clear that the abandonment of the policy in this instance was used to weaken the speculation around the car accident and answer Mr al-Fayed's accusations.

The Princess Diana exception revealed some of the holes in the police's case that there was overriding public interest in maintaining its principle of 'neither confirming nor denying' any reports of undercover deployments. But it took the intervention of one non-police, non-state core participant to reveal the extent to which the 'principle' itself was an invention.

## Contesting Neither Confirm Nor Deny

There is no question that the contestation around NCND was the defining moment in the preliminary hearings of the Undercover Policing Inquiry. During a hearing chaired by Sir Christopher Pitchford, which was concerned with the issues of disclosure and secrecy, the core participant Helen Steel was allowed to address the Inquiry directly. In Steel, the Chair heard from a formidable campaigner for environmental and social justice causes who had gained more than her fair share of experience of the legal system.

In Chapter 2, I explained that Steel is a core participant in the Inquiry without a designated legal representative and that her real name is known to allow her to represent herself. For two years in the early 1990s, Steel was in a relationship with a man she knew as 'John Barker'. 'Barker', the cover identity created for the undercover officer John Dines, was deployed to gather intelligence on the small social justice group London Greenpeace. The group was set up in the 1970s by London-based environmentalists with anarchist politics, first in opposition to nuclear testing programmes and later encompassing wider anti-corporate and anti-capitalist messaging. A particular focus in the 1980s was a campaign to highlight abusive labour practices by the fast food chain McDonald's and to draw attention to its business model that, the activists said, was built upon animal abuse and environmental destruction. As a lively campaign with connections to other community groups in the capital, London Greenpeace had already come into the focus of SDS operations before Dines infiltrated it. The undercover officer Bob Lambert, going by the name of 'Bob Robinson', began spying on the activists from 1984 (Lambert's role in London Greenpeace and his relationship with Jacqui is discussed in Chapter 3). Three years later, Dines joined the group and infiltrated associated campaigns around the London anarchist and squatter scene. According to Steel, Dines then deceived her into a relationship from 1990 onwards before his deployment was brought to a sudden end in 1992.

This was a tumultuous time for Steel, as she describes in her co-authored book *Deep Deception* (Alison et al, 2022). The infiltration by Bob Lambert had boosted London Greenpeace and pushed its agenda forward, clearly getting under the skin of McDonald's advertising strategists. For some time, the global corporation sent no fewer than seven private investigators to spy on the small activist group in London (Lubbers, 2012), further increasing its numbers. But when a six-page pamphlet, written in part by Lambert using his undercover persona, was handed out by the group outside its fast food outlets, McDonald's issued libel writs in an attempt to stop Steel and others from distributing the leaflet. The libel threat failed on Helen Steel and on another activist, Dave Morris. Defending themselves, they took on the corporation in a classic David and Goliath story that became the subject of England's longest ever libel trial and is chronicled in Franny Armstrong's 1997 documentary *McLibel*, featuring Keir Starmer as the barrister representing the activists.

In the midst of this, Dines suddenly left the field and abandoned Steel using a well-rehearsed cover story of burnout and deteriorating mental health. In reality, his deployment as an undercover officer in London's direct action circles had come to an end. But it was not the end for Steel. For years, she investigated Dines's background and whereabouts. Her investigation eventually took her to Australia, where she tracked her former partner down and confronted him. 'You owe me an apology', Steel said (Alison et al, 2022, p 354) when she spotted him at Sydney airport. He did apologise, as she explains in her recollections of the moment, but appeared to suggest that the relationship was simply a police prop to make his cover identity of a committed activist more probable. While Steel had known for certain that Dines was a spy in the London Greenpeace group, she had still no official acknowledgement of the fact.

Steel's experiences of police abuse and trauma, but also her tenacity as an effective campaigner negotiating the quagmire of the legal system, were apparent when she was given the chance to puncture the legalistic screen that covered the preliminary hearings of the Undercover Policing Inquiry. Her speech was one of the few times when the exchanges between lawyers and the Inquiry team were interrupted by an interjection from one of the core participants themselves. It had everyone in the public gallery on the edge of their seats.

What Steel had to say displayed an acute understanding of what the NCND policy would mean in practice. The Metropolitan Police's legal team that acted on behalf of the force in the public inquiry had previously sought to thwart the common law claims brought by her and other women deceived into long relationships with undercover policemen. The claims included deceit, misfeasance in public office and breaches of the Data Protection Act (alongside claims under the Human Rights Act), in *AKJ and others v Commissioner of the Police of the Metropolis and others* [2013] EWHC 32 (QB). The Metropolitan Police's legal strategy that aimed for the women's case to be inadmissible in court rested on an absurd and wilfully offensive argument. As *The Observer* newspaper reported at the time (Boffey, 2014), the force's lawyers argued that to hear the case in open court would be grossly unfair because – wait for it – as its client could not deviate from its own NCND policy, it was unable to defend itself against the women's accusations. It was a particularly jarring strategy as it coincided with public statements made by the Metropolitan Police's most senior officers that the force would commit itself to transparency and honesty in the face of the revelations. NCND was not a straightforward denial and therefore was much more advantageous to the police leadership. By arguing that it *would not* defend itself, the force could claim that it *could not* defend itself. The argument failed to convince the judge and just days later the Home Secretary announced that a public inquiry would be forthcoming. The police's insistence of keeping the women's cases out of the courts was no longer sustainable (Alison et al, 2022, p 323). Yet, the force was still not moved to confirm the identities of its spies.

The case thus returned to court in 2014. In a High Court ruling, *DIL and others v Commissioner of the Police of the Metropolis* [2014] EWHC 2184 (QB), the presiding judge found that the Metropolitan Police's NCND position had become 'simply unsustainable' with respect to Bob Lambert and another former officer, Jim Boyling. Both men had been exposed, then self-disclosed and were named in the media and in public reports. But the force was not ordered to admit to the deployment of John Dines (Evans, 2014), although the judge recognised that this 'may only postpone the day of reckoning'. In addressing the Chair on this matter, Steel hoped that she was one step closer to the day that her former partner's true identity would be confirmed.

The presence of a core participant who spoke during this phase of the Inquiry disrupted the otherwise legalistic proceedings. With microphones only available to the teams of lawyers assembled in the hearing room, space had to be found to enable this instance of public participation. The Chair called out: 'Is Helen Steel here? Would you like to come forward, please? We will make you a place' (UCPI, 2016d, p 143). When a place was found among the lawyers representing the non-police, non-state core participants, Steel began: 'I just wanted to start by saying that throughout all the legal proceedings that I have been involved with where the police have asserted Neither Confirm Nor Deny they have never offered any documentary evidence of this so-called policy' (UCPI, 2016d, p 143). Steel reminded the courtroom of the wider context of the Undercover Policing Inquiry. This was not an inquiry into undercover policing in the abstract, she said; it had a specific political dimension. In short, it was a public inquiry into *political* undercover policing because it deals with the infiltration of political campaign groups and potential human rights abuses of political activists, their friends and families. The distinction was important. For Steel, this subject matter was different from undercover operations to investigate organised crime:

> [T]he intention is not to obtain evidence for prosecution; it is to obtain intelligence on political movements. The result of that is that while general undercover operations are subject to a certain amount of outside legal scrutiny as a result of the requirements for due process and fair trials, political undercover policing has never been subjected to outside scrutiny until now. (UCPI, 2016d, p 144)

For political campaigners and targets of spycops deployments, the Undercover Policing Inquiry was thus an unprecedented opportunity; not just in the sense that victims of police abuse could be heard in a public forum, but also in that it opened up a route of accountability for an abuse of power. This accountability, however, necessitated a level of openness that was not forthcoming. Steel summed up her submission as such:

> The reason for wanting maximum transparency and disclosure is a political one. Without the names of undercover officers who targeted each group it is impossible to start to assess the whole impact of

their surveillance or the extent of the abuses committed. Without full disclosure we won't get the full truth and we can't ensure that preventative measures are put in place to stop these abuses happening again. These were very, very serious human rights abuses committed by this unit ... We want to stop them happening again. That is our purpose in taking part in this Inquiry and that is the real public interest that requires that there must be openness and transparency. (UCPI, 2016d, pp 158–9)

When Steel finished, my field notes from the day recorded: 'spontaneous round of applause in the public gallery. Pitchford does not look best pleased.' It was as if a huge pressure had been lifted from those activists in attendance. They had finally been heard in the public inquiry.

## A brick wall of silence

The ruling on the legal approach to restriction orders was Sir Christopher Pitchford's legacy to the Undercover Policing Inquiry. In November 2016, he was diagnosed as suffering from motor neurone disease and in May the following year, Sir John Mitting took over as the Inquiry's new Chair. The case-by-case approach to deciding on anonymity and other restrictions may have undermined the police's NCND policy, but it did not necessarily lead to greater transparency.

On the face of it, the new Chair was committed to implementing Pitchford's ruling. At his first oral hearing, he gave assurances that he would not tolerate the police's use of NCND in the public inquiry: 'the reality is that Neither Confirm Nor Deny has no part at all to play in Special Demonstration Squad deployments ... [It is] a pointless exercise' (UCPI, 2017d, p 14). However, pressed on what this would mean in practice, the new Chair was quick to qualify the statement:

> Forgive me, just so my words are not misunderstood. I can conceive of circumstances, in particular in relation to recent, still more in relation to current deployments, that the Neither Confirm Nor Deny policy might have a part to play. It is actually rather more likely that nothing at all will be said in public about, let's say, a current deployment and that it will be neither confirmed nor denied that it is being undertaken. (UCPI, 2017e, p 15)

By the time Sir John Mitting held his second hearing, he had issued a series of 'minded-to' notices that indicated how he would opt to restrict a host of police documents from publication and grant anonymity to a large number of officers. The non-police, non-state core participants saw his stance towards them hardening. At the earliest opportunity, their legal representative, Philippa Kaufmann, sounded the alarm:

> Can I just start by saying at the outset, on behalf of my clients, that we are extremely disappointed that what looked so promising at the last hearing in terms of disclosure and the bases of the risk assessment has turned out for us to be so alarming. We feel we are in no better position now than we were before the last hearing. On the contrary, we feel the situation has got worse. (UCPI, 2018d, p 7)

Kaufmann suggested that the Inquiry, under Mitting's chairmanship, was taking a 'wrong turn' (UCPI, 2018d, p 7). NCND had not gone away, she argued. Rather its continuation as a policy was the effect of the way that anonymity decisions were made on the basis of closed representations by police officers. In short, the non-police, non-state participants and the public were not only prevented from learning about the identity of the officers, but also were not permitted to see the reasons behind the anonymity orders. Kaufmann thought that the intelligence jargon of the mosaic effect had swayed the Chair's opinion and she masterfully exposed its Kafkaesque logic (UCPI, 2018d, pp 21–2):

Kaufmann: To put it shortly ... a Neither Confirm Nor Deny approach is effectively being taken in relation to disclosure of the mosaic effect. That is we can't say anything in cases where we can say anything because that might lead in cases where we can't say something to the identification of matters that would then lead to the revelation of that particular individual's identity. I see that you look puzzled, but that's kind of how Neither Confirm Nor Deny works.
Chair: I was wondering how you got to the end of the sentence as coherently as you did.
Kaufmann: Being very familiar with Neither Confirm Nor Deny, Sir, you will know exactly what I mean.

Mitting knew exactly what the non-police, non-state participants were saying, yet he was not going to move. When Kaufmann cited the example of an officer whose anonymity order was justified on the basis of a risk assessment, which itself had been redacted, Mitting observed: 'With respect it is not a Neither Confirm Nor Deny approach. It is stronger than that. It is a flat refusal to say anything about the deployment in open.' The Chair's case for secrecy was straightforward. This officer and others were 'examples of deployments where you are going to meet a brick wall of silence' (UCPI,

2018d, p 36). If nothing else, it was at least an honest retort to the insistence by the non-police, non-state core participants that their effective participation would hinge on the level of disclosure they were to receive by the Inquiry. In those cases where Mitting was committed to maximum secrecy, it represented the end of the road for participation in the process. As Kaufmann finally conceded: 'there really is nothing we can say in relation to [these officers] if we are meeting a brick wall' (UCPI, 2018d, p 37).

The 'brick wall of silence' metaphor left its mark on those in attendance at the Royal Courts of Justice. The phrase eventually made its way onto a protest banner, displayed outside the Inquiry venue and it became a metaphor for the way that the police interest in secrecy was maintained by the Chair citing what he perceived to be the public interest.

The police invention of NCND as a policy not only aided concealment, it produced and reproduced asymmetric relationships in the search for truth. Knowledge in itself is not enough. Alison and Helen Steel had knowledge of the fact that their lives had been infiltrated, interrupted, manipulated by police spies. Yet, the key to official acknowledgement lay with the police. NCND produced a ritual by which secrets were not simply hidden and denied. Access to truth, not the truth itself, became the linchpin of the undercover policing scandal.

In the preliminary proceedings of the public inquiry, this played out as a crucial balancing act between competing public interests. At times, the public interest in national security conflicted with the public interest in alleviating the concern over the wrongs of undercover policing. At other times, the conflict was better expressed as one between effective participation of designated core participants in the public inquiry and the police's stated policy of 'neither confirming nor denying' that specific deployments had taken place. Eventually, the NCND 'principle' upon which the police's engagement with the public inquiry rested came under intense pressure and fell apart following critical scrutiny. Yet, its power and simplicity were such that it held sway over much of the proceedings.

# 5

# Dirty data and devices of dis/closure

## Secrecy, security, disclosure

Sir John Mitting's comments that campaigners inquiring into the identity of former undercover officers who had been granted anonymity were to meet a 'brick wall of silence' drew the ire of non-police, non-state core participants. But his comments were made in a specific context of protecting a select few deployments from any scrutiny whatsoever. The questions over the level of disclosure and privacy accorded to the police were more complex than that. This chapter turns to the questions of how the public inquiry produced novel arrangements for the disclosure of police secrets and how these remained shaped by unequal power relations. If I say that these arrangements, aiming as they were to balance competing interpretations of the public interest, were characterised by complexity, this is not to take away from the fact that the Inquiry largely failed to satisfy the campaigners' desire for answers and explanations; indeed, the logic of secrecy dominated the Inquiry's approach to its work. Instead, I am reminded of the Foucauldian perspectives that are so prevalent in the academic study of surveillance. In *Discipline and Punish*, Foucault wrote:

> We must cease once and for all to describe the effects of power in negative terms: it 'excludes', it 'represses', it 'censors', it 'abstracts', it 'masks', it 'conceals'. In fact, power produces; it produces reality; it produces domains of objects and rituals of truth. The individual and the knowledge that may be gained of him belong to this production. (Foucault, 1991, p 194)

By now it should be clear that I am not quite ready to drop 'once and for all' the language of repression and concealment. Too often have the Chair's rulings erred on the side of non-disclosure. But Foucault's imperative nonetheless illuminates the way that the public inquiry has turned secrecy into a 'ritual of truth'. The opposition between denial and disclosure has taken centre stage; yet presented as a binary logic (openness versus secrecy), we would fail to appreciate the tensions that continue to play out in this arena. To elaborate on the argument about secrecy and denial that I have made so far, this chapter thus takes inspiration from the recent contributions made by William Walters to the emerging field of secrecy research. For Walters

(2021), in his work on the 9/11 Commission held after the 2001 Al-Qaeda bombings of the Twin Towers in New York City as well as other targets, these are best conceived as dis/closure. Thinking of the NCND strategy in this way allows us to interrogate the 'covert imaginary', or in other words the public understanding of secrets. When we think of state secrets, we can easily be drawn into a binary conception of transparency and secrecy, one which assumes that a fundamental truth is concealed in a totalising manner by the maintenance of state secrets. What the previous chapter has shown is that the dialectic of transparency and secrecy rests on more complex ways of managing information held by public institutions. In this present chapter I am concerned with the extent to which the Undercover Policing Inquiry became a data holder itself.

## From secrecy to dis/closure

The unavoidable contradiction blighting the Undercover Policing Inquiry is that it is tasked with a public investigation into normally secret policing practices. It is precisely for this reason that it offers such rich material for an analysis of the tension between accountability and secrecy. It sets the Undercover Policing Inquiry apart from many others. But it is not the only one where matters of disclosure, security and secrecy came to the forefront. In another context, William Walters has made the argument that there is merit in looking at public inquiries as 'promising avenues to pursue secrecy research in the domain of national security' (2021, p 88). Walters argues that public inquiries come with the promise and possibility of 'enhanced powers'. In the UK, statutory inquiries can compel witnesses to give evidence in public and force them to disclose materials held in their possessions. For Walters, this suggests that inquiries may be bestowed with 'a combination of enhanced moral, political and legal authority enabling them to look into areas that might otherwise remain opaque to the publics and parliaments' (Walters, 2021, p 97). They then appear as fundamental instruments in the pursuit of democratic accountability, especially where state secrecy is concerned.

While Sir Christopher Pitchford tried to set a standard for decisions on anonymity and redactions, his incremental, case-by-case approach only raised more questions than it could answer. How should we calculate risks of harm to police officers? Were risks of exposure ever entirely avoidable? Some field officers led double lives, deeply embedded in political networks and close-knit affinity groups, over multiple years – did they all expect that their covers could be maintained ad infinitum? Many brought exactly this argument to the Inquiry: they had been guaranteed anonymity for life. I contrast this argument with an approach I have adapted from Walters's book *State Secrecy and Security*, in which he proposes the concept of 'devices of dis/closure' to read the work of public inquiries. By the term devices of dis/closure,

Walters means 'an account in which classifying, redacting, anonymizing and other practices are grasped as part of the economy of producing and circulating knowledge under securitized conditions' (Walters, 2021, p 91). State secrecy can then be thought of not as absolute, but as managed and contradictory. Public inquiries act in such contradictory ways in relation to state secrecy too. They do not simply conceal – although they can! – but they also produce new ways of navigating competing pressures of disclosure and secrecy. The way that this plays out remains specific to national contexts, legislative frameworks and the subject matters under investigation.

Walters approaches the question of state secrecy by noting that secrecy has remained relatively marginal in academic scholarship on security: 'For all the attention that security and securitization have received in recent years … a focus on practices, discourses and technologies of secrecy have been a secondary concern for most scholars' (Walters, 2021, p 144). This is beginning to change, Walters notes, as 'we are seeing a growing scholarly interest in questions of concealment, obfuscation, conspiracy, deception and exposure' (Walters, 2021, p 144). The public inquiry, in many jurisdictions and in all sorts of disguises, can here become a privileged site of scholarly interest. In fact, the inquiry, with its ambition to 'establish the facts' or 'uncover the truth', shifts to the centre of attention. My own interest in the conduct of the Undercover Policing Inquiry has followed such a path. For my purposes, therefore, inquiries and their associated phenomena such as the political disagreements over information disclosure, redactions and restrictions are not black boxes that produce lengthy reports based on the available evidence. It is the contestation within public inquiries that interests me most. Walters articulates this pointedly:

> And it means we no longer see them in purely instrumental terms – as means to the end of making or breaking secrets and revealing truths. They are no longer merely the back-drop, props or supporting cast in the drama that has the secret as the head-line act. Instead, they all become equally significant and meaningful foci for secrecy research. (Walters, 2021, p 145)

By advancing the public inquiry as a place of relative transparency, it can become an important site of research into secrecy and national security. Nonetheless, Walters also emphasises the contested politics within public inquiries that may seek to limit transparency. In order to do justice to both the potential of transparency and the logics of security, he proposes that inquiries employ 'devices of dis/closure' (Walters, 2021, p 99). He writes:

> Seen from the angle of dis/closure … public inquiries operate in ways that are not dissimilar to the methods of investigative journalists or

scholars who probe sensitive topics. In order to make public, or to investigate issues *in the name of the public*, they must at the same time enact certain operations of closure, concealment and confidentiality. (Walters, 2021, p 99, emphasis in the original)

All of this is true for the Undercover Policing Inquiry, though previous chapters have made it clear that the Inquiry has erred on the side of maintaining police confidentiality. Walters focuses on the 9/11 Commission which was appointed by the US Congress as an investigatory commission in 2002, following the terror attacks in New York City and the Pentagon a year earlier. An early political dispute arose when Henry Kissinger, Nixon's polarising former Secretary of State, was appointed to chair the investigation. When the politician-turned-consultant was pressed to disclose his client list to dissociate himself from any potential conflicts of interest, he stepped down from the role. With a new leadership, the bi-partisan Commission delivered its final report in 2004. To gain access and analyse classified security documents, the Commission had to establish a securitised infrastructure to enable its work: secure offices and digital environments, clearances for staff and so on. These measures permitted, so the argument went, a thorough investigation without releasing all documentation into the public domain.

We begin, now, to get a clearer view of how devices of dis/closure work – politically, morally and technically. I will reflect on these three domains (the political, the moral and the technical) in the following pages.

## Devices of political mediation

Devices of dis/closure are conceptualised by Walters as *political* because they often arise out of contestation and may mediate between conflicting demands and interests (Walters, 2021, p 91). Conflicting demands in the Undercover Policing Inquiry are all too obvious and I have expressed them as the competing perspectives of openness and confidentiality. Non-police, non-state core participants – including the victims and targets of undercover policing and those sharing their interest in openness such as researchers and journalists – have continually put across their view that the Inquiry should aim for maximum disclosure. The police and other state core participants, on the other hand, have sought to limit the extent to which the Inquiry discloses details of undercover deployments. However, the juxtaposition of these irreconcilable interests only scratches the surface of how secrecy manifests itself. Understood as political mediators, devices of dis/closure have played structuring roles in the Undercover Policing Inquiry. For example, documentation bundles prepared in advance of evidence hearings are released selectively to groups of core participants, with restrictions on discussing their contents with outside parties. This has led to absurd situations. In her opening statement, one woman complained that disclosure she received about a relationship she was deceived into with an undercover policeman was restricted to her and her lawyer. She was thus not permitted to discuss what she had learned about her personal life even with her husband (UCPI, 2021b). The secrecy shrouding the contents of her Special Branch files was such that it took a heavy emotional toll on her and her family, even with the deception having occurred decades earlier in the 1970s. Eventually, the Chair was moved to loosen the restrictions placed on the documents disclosed to her. But for other core participants, the ability to discuss the contents of intelligence files contained in the Inquiry's hearing bundles remains severely limited, even among victims of undercover policing who were given access to the same files.

In the Undercover Policing Inquiry, the personal is political and the political is personal. Decisions about disclosure or restriction made their impact felt on the activist communities seeking answers. Yet, cases where Sir John Mitting could be persuaded of the public and personal interest in openness were rare. Take one example: in 2017, Mitting announced that he would restrict the identity of officer HN297. The Metropolitan Police had applied for a restriction order to protect the real name of HN297 but did not seek an order to prevent the publication of the cover name he used in the field, which was already in the public domain. This approach, the Metropolitan Police argued, would meet the balance between the public interest in disclosure and non-disclosure (UCPI, 2017f). The accompanying risk assessment produced by the police listed HN297's pseudonym as that of 'Rick Gibson', who had infiltrated the Troops Out Movement and the revolutionary socialist group Big Flame. The officer had assumed the identity of a deceased child and activists were eventually able to expose him as an undercover officer when they found the real Rick Gibson's death certificate. He was withdrawn from the field upon exposure in 1976 and has since died. There was, therefore, no risk to HN297 from his former activist associates. The risk assessment noted that the probability of the media seeking out the officer's family if his true name was publicly confirmed was low and that its impact would be minor (UCPI, 2017g). And yet, pre-empting his ruling on the application on behalf of HN297, Sir John Mitting insisted that the real name could not be published, as 'it would likely interfere with the right of his widow to respect for her private life under Article 8 of the European Convention' (UCPI, 2017h). A reasonably minor risk that media attention could extend to the surviving family of a deceased officer whose deployment came to an end in the 1970s was sufficient for the Chair to see the privacy rights engaged here.

This, and similar, indications that Mitting was minded to grant anonymity even to deceased police officers appeared to depart quite substantially from Pitchford's restriction orders protocol. It drew sharp criticisms from a number of core participants. Guardian News and Media, publisher of *The Guardian* and *The Observer*, argued that it contravened the open justice principle and limited the ability of a free press to report on the proceedings (UCPI, 2017i). Submissions made on behalf of the non-police, non-state core participants warned that such wide-ranging anonymity for former police officers would lead to 'a one-sided Inquiry that is largely limited to the police's own account' (UCPI, 2017j, p 2). Shortly afterwards, the Chair was confronted with a more urgent and unforeseen challenge. The publication of HN297's cover name, 'Richard Gibson', had prompted an investigation by researchers in the Undercover Research Group (URG). Eveline Lubbers found that HN297, in his cover identity, had befriended several women and potentially deceived more than one into entering a sexual relationship with him. Their evidence suggested that the spycops tactic of sexual infiltration could have been used as early as the 1970s. Despite their findings rocking the foundations of the HN297 anonymity order, the Chair could not be persuaded to lift the restriction order preventing the publication of 'Richard Gibson's' real name just yet. He would, however, feel obliged to do so if the victims' lawyers were to provide him with 'plausible statements' from the women mentioned (UCPI, 2017f, p 147).

This, they did. The URG researchers had been able to track down a woman – herself now known by the pseudonym 'Mary' – who said that she had been in a relationship with 'Gibson'. She said that they were sexually intimate for a short period of time and that he became a frequent visitor to her shared flat while she was active in student politics at Goldsmiths College. Mary's statement quickly changed the Inquiry's approach. She was granted the status of a core participant, her own identity protected via a restriction order and the real name of HN297, Richard Clark, was communicated to her in May 2018. There were now public interest grounds, in the Chair's view, that permitted the infringement of the rights to privacy otherwise enjoyed by HN297's family. Yet, the whole episode was a further indictment, if any was needed, of the Inquiry's privileging of the police narrative and its reluctance to work with the non-police, non-state core participants.

## Devices for appeals to morality

Walters describes devices of dis/closure in this sense as mediators, as they would potentially allow for a resolution to competing interests in secrecy and transparency. The Gibson/Clark affair is also instructive because, following Walters's conceptualisation, they equally have a *moral* dimension, or in other words, 'they raise questions of trust' (Walters, 2021, p 91). The victims of police spying frequently made clear that they lacked or had lost trust in the Inquiry to discharge its duties, especially after the appointment of Sir John

Mitting as its Chair. Could the Inquiry be trusted to handle the personal data it was a recipient of responsibly and with care?

Mitting, too, recognised that as Chair his decisions were not only bound by law but by their moral implications. He stated that women deceived into relationships with undercover officers had a 'moral right' (UCPI, 2017k, p 146) to learn the true identities of the officers. But although there were some indications that this moral right would be extended to mean a public right to know, at first the Inquiry only communicated HN297's identity to 'Mary', but refrained from publishing it. As the Chair told a preliminary hearing on Special Demonstration Squad (SDS) anonymity:

> My current intention is that the real name of HN297 should be communicated by the Inquiry to Mary. We have her address and we have her witness statement signed in her real name. As a piece of private information, it would then be for her to decide what she wished to do with it. There would be no restriction order made and therefore no obligation upon her to deal with it in any particular manner. (UCPI, 2018d, p 108)

This in itself created discontent among the wider group of non-police, non-state core participants. In effect, the Chair's stated moral obligation towards the women deceived by male officers, and therefore also the denial of the right to know for other targets of police infiltration, created a distinct class of core participant. Lubbers, writing for the URG, expressed the problem: 'With this approach, the Chair effectively creates a special category of "deserving victims", by making it a personal, rather than political right to know the real names of the spies who targeted them' (Lubbers, 2018). The non-police, non-state core participants pointed to Sir John Mitting's strictly conservative views of morality; many considered him an entrenched member of the judicial establishment, who had described himself as a 'pedantic English lawyer' and had openly admitted that his views on marriage and extra-marital affairs may stand him accused of being 'a little naive and old-fashioned' (UCPI, 2018d, p 119).

The question of morality further arose when Sir John Mitting considered an application for anonymity by officer HN104. 'Carlo Neri' had spied on trade unionists and anti-racist activists in and around the Socialist Party. His application for a restriction order to protect his real name was made because he feared retaliatory violence from the activists he had targeted, against himself and his family. Mitting, in granting the order, found that this fear was 'not irrational'.

The fear of violence against his family jarred markedly with the manner of 'Neri's' exposure by campaigners and those targeted by his deployment. In a blog post on the URG website, the group's founders Dónal O'Driscoll and Eveline Lubbers detailed how they were able to expose him. Crucially, the researchers had already identified 'Neri's' real name and that of his family but chose not to publish it. That, they said, should be the role of the public inquiry: 'Yet again, the people affected by undercovers in their lives had to go through the painful process of uncovering the truth. Something that could have been avoided if the Pitchford Inquiry would release the list of cover names of undercovers from the Special Demonstration Squad' (O'Driscoll and Lubbers, 2016).

'Carlo Neri', the policeman, had shown himself less than concerned with protecting his family, when – according to his long-term activist partner Andrea – he used their real first names and photographs in the development of his cover legend. Andrea and the URG were more careful; they regarded 'Neri's' family as another victim in the undercover police's web of lies. O'Driscoll's account provides some clues as to the URG's working methods:

> The surname was an unusual one so we were able to track down his family, and it started to emerge that this Carlo had family members with the same first names that Neri had used when talking about his family. There were some differences, but it soon became apparent that he had simply taken middle names instead, giving us confidence we were on the right track. We found that his sister ran a delicatessen in North London and other aspects fell into place as well. Added up, the stories matched, surprisingly so. I spoke to Andrea, and sent her websites of members of the family. She rang back – she recognised the people who appeared on those websites from photos that Carlo Neri had out on a shelve [sic] in her house when he lived with her. The hunch had paid off and it seemed that we had found our man. (O'Driscoll and Lubbers, 2016)

Their approach to exposing the undercover officer was driven fundamentally by the ethical belief that those deceived into personal friendships and intimate relationships deserved to know. That, for them, did not necessitate total disclosure outside of a formal process of accountability:

> There is a lot more to the Carlo story which we have not revealed. Carlo intruded into people's lives and it is not our desire to expose more than is necessary. We feel deep sympathy not just with those taken in by his lies, but also with his real family. They are also victims in this. (O'Driscoll and Lubbers, 2016)

However, accountability did require that the police officer should be named. Only he was able to answer crucial questions: who knew? Who authorised the deployments? Who else was monitored? The campaigners at Police Spies

Out of Lives, who offer support to many of the affected women, spelled out the ramifications of such an abdication of responsibility on the part of the Chair: 'We have been placed in an extremely difficult and distressing position by Mitting's approach, which was to use emotional blackmail to silence us. We believe the Inquiry should have named him' (Police Spies Out of Lives, 2019). The group draws attention, once more, to the political dimension of the undercover policing scandal, which could not be divorced from a moral one. The relationships were not initiated by rogue officers, its statement says, but by a state-sanctioned policing tactic that objectifies women's lives for the purposes of intelligence. They echoed the sentiments expressed by the URG in the Gibson/Clark case:

> Sir John Mitting promised ... that if during the course of the Inquiry a woman discovered she had a relationship with an undercover police officer she had a right to know the officer's real name, and the Inquiry would inform her of it. He then went on to state that it would be her decision whether or not to publish the real name in the public domain. In doing this, Mitting has misrepresented it to be a personal and moral issue. We believe that this is a deeply unfair burden for any woman who has been deceived into an abusive relationship to have to carry. And it is not merely a personal issue – these inhumane and degrading relationships were state-sanctioned. This is part of a shocking anti-democratic scandal and should be viewed in this context, as a political issue. (Police Spies Out of Lives, 2019)

Mitting disagreed in principle; he had decided to restrict the real identity of the officer from publication.

Yet, the restriction order only prevented the publication of 'Neri's' real name if this was discovered from documentation or evidence given during the course of the Inquiry. It could not prevent anyone from naming 'Neri' in public if they knew his name independently from it. In his anonymity ruling, Mitting had shown awareness of its limitations. Multiple campaigners as well as media outlets knew the real name but had so far refrained from using it in public. 'There is nothing I can do', admitted the Chair, 'to prevent any of them from publishing his real name' (UCPI, 2018e, p 1). But it was his responsibilisation of the activists and affected women that drew the sharpest criticism. Despite the allegations made against 'Carlo Neri' and the human rights abuses committed by undercover officers, he appealed to the campaigners' 'humanity' and their judgment (UCPI, 2018e, p 1) to keep the real name to themselves. Mitting could have hardly done more than this to be accused of gaslighting the women deceived by the police officer. Perhaps inevitably, HN104's real name did make it into the public domain. The journalist and author Michael Gillard published the name

Carlo Soracchi on Twitter, apparently without first consulting the affected women or the Inquiry.

These and other cases remind us that devices of dis/closure 'do not offer automatic fixes for political conflicts' (Walters, 2021, p 92). Instead, new arenas for contestation emerge, centred on the proper management of securely held data.

## Devices for technical data management

As a third characteristic, Walters thinks of devices of dis/closure as *technical* in that they rely on a material infrastructure for their management. In the case of the Undercover Policing Inquiry, the process of intelligence file redaction was not just a moral or political one, but one of basic organisation and professional diligence. Mark Ellison KC had criticised the Metropolitan Police's record keeping in his Stephen Lawrence Independent Review, deeming it 'chaotic'. Asked to consider whether a statutory public inquiry was needed to further investigate the allegations of corruption surrounding the police investigation into Stephen Lawrence's murder, he hesitated. Despite the statutory powers afforded to a public inquiry under the Inquiries Act, Ellison thought that its potential to discover more than he had was 'limited'. His reasoning was damning: 'Fundamentally this is because of the chaotic state of the historical records held by the MPS [Metropolitan Police Service]', he wrote (Ellison, 2014, p 16).

Operation FileSafe, launched in 2014 as part of the Metropolitan Police's wider response to the Ellison report and the announcement of the public inquiry, is a review of the Metropolitan Police's document handling and record management, including an assessment of any physical materials held by the force that may be of relevance to the Inquiry. It is overseen by an Assistant Commissioner's public inquiry team. It is clear that the team had its work cut out. The Metropolitan Police has no integrated information management system and during the lifetime of the undercover units data has been filed away in multiple physical and digital locations, not all of which were indexed or searchable. Much of the relevant documentation had simply been left in local police archives or dotted around offices, instead of being logged in the force's General Register (UCPI, 2017l). It became clear that improvements to record keeping had to be made quickly, if the Metropolitan Police was to fulfil its duty to assist the Undercover Policing Inquiry.

Though Operation FileSafe may look like a technological exercise – the Metropolitan Police's overarching IT improvement strategy was the grandiose and dystopian-sounding 'Total Technology' – it was also politically charged. In UK policing, record keeping has frequently been a sensitive issue that has fuelled allegations of corruption and cover-ups. Too often, the political sensitivity of good record keeping and the importance of transparency for public trust appear to be lost even on the most senior officers. Police in Scotland perhaps led the way when they ordered that sensitive documents belonging to an undercover investigative unit were to be 'torched in a garden incinerator' (McDonald, 2019). An experienced undercover officer seconded to the special operations unit at the now-defunct Scottish Crime and Drug Enforcement Agency – described in the press as a sort of Scottish FBI or MacFBI – had found unaccounted-for cash, bank cards and phone bills in a covert location used for operational matters. The officer reported the abnormalities to her superiors who investigated – and had her discoveries burned in their headquarters' car park (BBC, 2019; see Brian, 2020).

Of course, bad file keeping was not a privilege of police organisations. As the Inquiry's Terms of Reference extend to the question of what the UK government knew about the undercover operations into political activity, the role of the Home Office has been moved into sharp focus. Before the Undercover Policing Inquiry was formally established, there had been more question marks about inadequate record keeping and the concealment of contemporaneous documentation in the department. In 2014, the department's then permanent secretary commissioned the former Director at the Audit Commission, Stephen Taylor, to investigate the extent of the Home Office's awareness of the SDS and its methods. By and large, Taylor's report absolved the Home Office of any responsibility for what went on within the undercover unit. There was 'no evidence', Taylor said, that employees in the government department knew of the 'controversial' tactics used to infiltrate political groups (Taylor, 2015, p 23). He found that only a few officials knew of the SDS and would have received its annual reports.

While he was not able to prove any malpractice, Taylor could barely conceal his disbelief that records pertaining to the SDS were absent in the Home Office data systems. He could find no evidence at all of any meetings or correspondence between the department and the SDS covering the whole 40-year period between 1968 and 2008. In fact, there was no mention of the police unit anywhere and remarkably this included the development files for the Regulation of Investigatory Powers Act (2000). Had such wide-ranging legislation been drafted without acknowledgement that Special Branch operated a political undercover police unit? The only exceptions were 24 letters dealing with funding authorisations and obtained via the police investigation Operation Herne. There was more. The absence of any surviving records was conspicuous because the files would have been marked as Secret or Top Secret, with strict procedures covering their removal or destruction. In fact, Taylor did find a trace. His searches brought up a 'consistent file reference' to a record in the Queen's Peace Series 66 1/8/5, which he believed to be the SDS file. His report states that 'there is no record to show where this file is or when it may have been destroyed' (Taylor, 2015, p 3). He must have at least considered the possibility that the

Home Office had something to hide, because he goes on to say: 'It is not possible to conclude whether this is human error or deliberate concealment' (Taylor, 2015, p 8). If there is anything to learn from that, it is that the need for secrecy also characterised the Home Office's decision to keep the SDS running. Some of the 24 letters identified by Taylor were annual requests for continued funding of the unit from senior managers in Special Branch. The Home Office reply typically emphasised that finances could be made available under the condition that the arrangement remained secret. It appeared to be a case of the Home Office saying to the police that they could continue to operate a secret political unit tasked to spy on left-wing activists, as long as they would not be found out. Secrecy reinforces itself in this way.

While the Taylor report would not rule out deliberate concealment in the Home Office, this became the accusation against one of the SDS successor organisations, the National Domestic Extremism and Disorder Intelligence Unit (NDEDIU), a specialist operations unit once overseen by the National Police Chief's Council before its control was subsumed under the Metropolitan Police's Counter-Terrorism Command. The claims were made by a whistleblower who was employed at the NDEDIU. The officer, a sergeant, reported that members of the unit may have shredded files that could have revealed the extent of the police monitoring on the political activities of a senior Green Party politician and London Assembly member, Baroness Jenny Jones. Baroness Jones had found herself on the Metropolitan Police database monitoring 'domestic extremists', even while she was a member of the Metropolitan Police Authority, which was set up to scrutinise the force. She had issued the force with a Subject Access Request, under data protection legislation, exercising her rights to receive a copy of the personal data that the organisation held on her. Fearing that information about her had been collected from intelligence reports by undercover officers, Baroness Jones applied to be a core participant at the Undercover Policing Inquiry. However, alongside other high-profile campaigners, such as the human rights activist Peter Tatchell, her application was not granted. In 2014, Jones received a four-page letter purportedly from an officer within the domestic extremism unit who said that he had witnessed three colleagues shred a stack of papers that he believed contained information about her. As reported by Rob Evans for *The Guardian* newspaper in January 2016 (Evans, 2016), the whistleblower told her that he had 'not become a police officer to monitor politicians or political parties' and that he had reported his allegations to the Metropolitan Police's Directorate of Professional Standards. Apparently, no action was taken by the internal standards unit and Baroness Jones was not told of its conclusions. Inaction, however, could not silence the tenacious peer and the scandal went all the way to the top. *The Telegraph* was prompted to use the headline 'Sir Bernard Hogan-Howe under fire', as Jones questioned the integrity of the then Metropolitan Police Commissioner and asked the Independent Office for Police Conduct (IOPC) to investigate. The IOPC investigation into the claims, published as the 'Baroness Jenny Jones report' (IOPC, 2019a), did not find evidence that any shredding of materials had been related to Baroness Jones's access request or done in an effort to frustrate her attempts to see her personal files held on the domestic extremism database. But the episode put the intelligence work of police units monitoring political activity in Britain into the spotlight again and left a sour taste in the mouths of campaigners whose own subject access requests were not responded to.

In at least one other case, an allegation surfaced that files pertaining to political undercover policing had purposefully been shredded in the NDEDIU, even after the public inquiry had instructed their safekeeping. When investigators from Operation Herne, the police-internal review of the SDS, visited the NDEDIU, an officer in the department informed them that he had seen a staff member prepare files for shredding, which he believed to be in scope for the upcoming public inquiry. The allegations were passed on to the Metropolitan Police's Department for Professional Standards, which took no further action but eventually passed the information on to the IOPC. The watchdog carried out an investigation, named Operation Hibiscus (IOPC, 2019b), between 2016 and 2019. As with its Jenny Jones investigation, the IOPC review could not establish for certain whether materials relevant to the Undercover Policing Inquiry were accidentally or deliberately destroyed. All it could do was to identify an email trail that made reference to a 'crate' of materials with a possible connection to the former National Public Order Intelligence Unit (NPOIU) officer Mark Kennedy. The crate could no longer be found and Operation Hibiscus left no doubt that vital documents had been destroyed.

The IOPC report suggested that 'a reasonable disciplinary tribunal properly directed would conclude on the balance of probabilities that material relevant to the UCPI had been shredded by MPS personnel after a command circulation stating that material relevant to the UCPI should not be destroyed' (IOPC, 2020, p 2). One former officer would have had a case to answer for gross misconduct over the destroyed files, yet they had since left the force. The report also criticised the Metropolitan Police's anticipation of its duties to aid the Undercover Policing Inquiry. The force had not sufficiently made clear to its officers which material was likely to be of interest to the Inquiry and the NDEDIU – though a national unit – had failed to set up a clear process for auditing previously destroyed materials. Again, the police's intransigence and non-cooperation was underlined:

> It is extremely unfortunate that a number of those managers have refused to engage with this investigation to provide evidence about what steps, if any, were taken in this regard. As set out above the

investigation had no power to compel them to do so, although the inquiry may do if it considers their evidence on these issues may be relevant. (IOPC, 2020, p 2)

Operation Hibiscus reported in 2019, a few months after the Jenny Jones report. It will not come as a surprise that the Inquiry has not (yet) demanded witness statements from NDEDIU managers at the time of writing this in 2022.

I have found this conceptualisation around the political, moral and technical dimensions of disclosure useful for thinking through the practices of information management in the Undercover Policing Inquiry. For this reason, it is worth citing Walters's argument again in length:

> [T]his focus on devices moves analysis beyond the dichotomies of the covert imaginary, which shape the way we often perceive the public inquiry form. It moves us beyond a naïvely optimistic view of public inquiries that sees them as unveiling exercises – as though they draw back the curtain and reveal to the public a previously secret world … A focus on devices of dis/closure also avoids the other extreme: it challenges the overly cynical, and sometimes conspiratorial view of public inquiries, the one that dismisses them as little more than political theatre designed to cover up rather than reveal the truth. (Walters, 2021, p 92)

I broadly share this view, which seeks to complicate the frequent simplification of the public inquiry's function. Nonetheless, that the relationship between secrecy and disclosure in the Undercover Policing Inquiry could not lead to a straightforward conclusion of a 'cover-up' should not take away from the fact that the power relations between state and non-state participants were deeply asymmetrical.

## Dirty and hidden data

What does it mean to say that the public inquiry is a site of struggle over the disclosure and protection of data? I propose to proceed with this question by using the conceptualisation by the surveillance scholar Gary Marx, with whom we can think of the intelligence generated by covert surveillance as 'dirty and hidden data'. This is defined by Marx (1984, p 79) as 'information which is kept secret and whose revelation would be discrediting or costly in terms of various types of sanctioning'. Despite the relative absence of dirty data from social research, it has underpinned some innovative methodological approaches in surveillance studies (see Hameed and Monaghan, 2012; Walby and Monaghan, 2011).

The personal details of political activists that were collected by covert human intelligence sources working for the SDS or the NPOIU constitute dirty data in this way. Revealing any information about the undercover deployments could see the units accused of moral wrongdoing and unlawful practices. A report for the Centre for Crime and Justice Studies, authored by Helen Mills, shows the difficulties that people encountered when they tried to find out what information the police had gathered about them. Mills writes:

> In the course [of] asking questions about undercover police operations, a number of avenues to getting more information had been explored by those interviewed, including asking for a copy of their police record (a subject access request under the Data Protection Act 1998). Under an exemption from disclosure for the purpose of safeguarding national security, access to police records was either denied or the personal files received were so heavily censored they were rendered useless. (Mills, 2017, p 4)

Over the past few years, I have talked to or interviewed many activists who were left similarly frustrated in their efforts to access their personal data. Many of them had attempted to find out about the extent to which they had been placed under surveillance, sometimes after learning, through media reporting or directly through the work of the URG, that people they had been close to had been exposed as undercover police officers. All of them felt that conventional mechanisms for accessing data that was held about them, for example in police intelligence reports, had failed. Data remained hidden to them.

Dirty and hidden data may also be useless data. This has indeed been a returning theme of the witness statements provided by activists to the Inquiry's evidence phase. They were surprised not simply by the level of infiltration into their lives, but by the apparently pointless nature of reporting. Their evidence attests to the fact that the data held by the police and passed on to the Inquiry would be mistakenly characterised as related to 'national security' or generated by 'high policing'. So much is even admitted by its conservative Chair, who had previously presided over national security cases as a High Court judge.[1] In fact, criminologists have argued that the rise of covert policing in the 'security state' is rarely seen as exceptional, but rather as 'unremarkable and mundane' (Loftus, 2019, p 2080). It consists of everyday and ordinary interactions – even though to the targets of policing it is highly personal and potentially makes them vulnerable. This mundane nature of intelligence gathering, with little regard for personal privacy or the viability of a civil society, was noted as soon as snippets of evidence were released by the Inquiry. A statement to the Inquiry made on behalf of

Lindsay German, the veteran socialist politician who had been a founding member of the Stop the War coalition and a long-standing member of the Socialist Workers Party's central committee, spelled out how far the net of undercover surveillance had been cast. The officers who had infiltrated the Socialist Workers Party, German's legal representative said, appeared to be preoccupied with the same minutiae of people's personal and professional lives as other officers deployed during this time: 'Their indexes contain more reports on personal details, such as the physical appearances and relationship statuses of female activists, than anything remotely disorder related … the real focus is on members' employment details and trade union affiliations' (UCPI, 2022e, p 35).

The spying operations, having taken a life of their own, needed to be seen in the light of anti-democratic statecraft and divorced from the narrative of public order policing. In German's submission: 'Increasingly, the Squad's focus shifted away from anything that could genuinely be described as "police work"' (UCPI, 2022e, p 5). This glimpse of the routine nature of the information collected by undercover officers then gives rise to a further thought: what does the Inquiry *do* with all this data? Being in receipt of police files has not necessarily been conducive to the Inquiry's work. It may well be that the volume of materials passed on to it by the state bodies is simply too large. As early as 2017, the Inquiry stated that it had received over one million pages of evidence from the Metropolitan Police alone (UCPI, 2017m). It may have been interpreted as the police's eagerness to aid the investigation and to be transparent. But a footnote elaborated:

> Not all of the documents provided are relevant. For example, on one drive … nearly 120,000 documents were provided of which over 90,000 comprise non-user generated files such as executable and help files for standard applications, printer drivers and manuals and other similar 'documents' which are very unlikely to advance the Inquiry's investigation. (UCPI, 2017m, p 7)

It may have been a deliberate tactic, which, as the independent researcher Connor Woodman has suggested, means that the Inquiry team has to spend time and effort to trawl through these irrelevant files. 'The Met's tactics', Woodman writes, 'may well be to drown the Inquiry team in mostly-useless documents in the hope that important fragments will escape their notice' (Woodman, 2018).

What appears useless to some, however, can be of interest to others. In April 2019, Sir John Mitting published a document (UCPI, 2019b) that set out the course the Inquiry sought to adopt in considering how and whether to publish the materials it would receive during its evidence gathering phase.

He announced his intention to amend the Inquiry's restriction orders protocol to incorporate the proposed evidence gathering process. Setting out how documents in possession of the Inquiry would be disclosed to the public, and therefore to observers who were not granted the status of core participants, the Chair wrote that 'it is the intention of the Inquiry to publish and include in the Open Hearing Bundle only a selection, sufficient to demonstrate the nature of the deployment and the activities carried on during it and the principal issues raised by it' (UCPI, 2019b, p 6). There were obvious implications that the Chair had to consider. Not only do the files held by the Inquiry contain personal information, and therefore raise questions about data protection, but they would also be subject to a variety of restriction orders and necessary redaction. Clearly, as the Chair signalled in a later statement, 'the nature and scale of the task needs to be understood' (UCPI, 2019c, p 1).

## Academic access to the evidence

How should the Inquiry decide which selection of documentation would fulfil its ambition to show to the public the nature of the deployments and the impact on society? As a researcher with an interest in social movements and political activity, I was concerned. Was the Chair and the Inquiry's team best placed to make these decisions? I believed not, and so did several of my colleagues. We articulated our reservations about the approach directly to the Chair, in a letter co-signed by several senior researchers working at British universities. In it, we urged the Chair to amend his intention to disclose the full files for each hearing only to the core participants and their lawyers. The general public and interested observers would gain access only to Open Hearing Bundles, already redacted, with a selection of files 'handpicked' for relevance and representativeness by the Inquiry team.

We argued that the subject matter of the Inquiry was an important aspect of academic research, some of it funded by government, and restricting access to the research community had to be grounded in real concerns over the materials to be disclosed, rather than on the Chair's judgment of what would be of interest to the public. We wrote:

> The matters with which the Undercover Policing Inquiry is concerned are of vital interest to academic researchers in a number of disciplines. This submission asks the Chair of the Inquiry to consider that a successful Inquiry is inherently bound up with the ability of academic researchers to access data and contribute to practical and theoretical knowledge production. We believe that the Inquiry's intention regarding its evidence gathering process ... stands in potential conflict with the interests of the research community. (UCPI, 2019d)

In the Chair's reply to our letter, he acknowledges the importance of preserving the Inquiry's record for the purposes of academic research. Yet, he points to the 'administrative burden' on the Inquiry in processing materials for publication and the need to avoid unnecessary costs, which are such that in his judgment the 'degree to which it is reasonable to publish material to permit effective understanding' of the Inquiry is met. Further, the reply suggested that data held by the Inquiry was subject to the restrictions under the Inquiries Act and that, upon completion of the Inquiry, all documentation would be preserved as part of the record of the Inquiry. It was then down to academic researchers to request access to these records (UCPI, 2019e).

It was an unsurprising answer, but also an unsatisfactory one. An anecdote told by Roger Stone, a panel member in the Stephen Lawrence Inquiry which was chaired by Sir William Macpherson, in his book *Hidden Voices* (Stone, 2015), reveals the patchy nature of archiving public inquiry materials. Stone explains how in February 2014 he had been in a conversation with Mark Ellison, the barrister who at that time was still putting the final touches to the Stephen Lawrence Independent Review, which investigated the claims that the Lawrence family's campaign for justice had been placed under surveillance by undercover officers. He discovered to his surprise that the Stephen Lawrence Inquiry files had been split up into multiple locations and that neither he nor Ellison had been aware that they were both only given partial access. Stone describes the revelation as a 'bombshell' (Stone, 2015, p 143). In June 2014, Stone made a complaint to the Home Secretary that senior officials in the department may have undermined the Inquiry, including now in the way that they had split up its archives and kept one part of it private. The answer he received, from the permanent secretary, confirmed that the evidence files remained in the Home Office as they contained 'information which should not be in the public domain' (cited in Stone, 2015, p 144), while the police investigation into the murder continued. Stone comments:

> It seems bizarre that the Home Office should guard any papers of a live police investigation, in particular such a high profile case … In the interests of transparency and open government, archives of public inquiries are public material. They should be publicly available as soon as possible after the end of the inquiry concerned. (Stone, 2015, p 144)

Upon conclusion of a public inquiry, it effectively ceases to exist. All materials in its possessions become the property of the sponsoring government department. In the case of the Undercover Policing Inquiry, this is the Home Office. But will the Home Office make the archives public? With what level of redaction? Richard Stone's personal recollections of handing his files over to the Home Office at the end of the Lawrence Inquiry, and his subsequent difficulties of finding his own personal notes in the archives, suggest that this will not be a straightforward matter. The archives of the Undercover Policing Inquiry may not suffer the same fate as that of the Lawrence Inquiry. The latter had to deal with paper copies; the materials in the former are available in digital format. These, too, will need to be redacted as they contain sensitive and personal data and could conceivably become the subject of legal dispute over disclosure again.

Stone is absolutely right to indicate that public access and full transparency are important and they certainly were in the Lawrence case. In his opinion, any delays or difficulties in getting hold of documentation can feed conspiracy theories and undermine trust in public inquiries. As he expresses it: 'If we believe, as we are told, that the reasons for the unavailability of the materials are not sinister but are merely administrative, the outcome of the delay and diversion is the same' (Stone, 2015, p 91). Interestingly, Stone goes further, and his argument chimes with those of us as academic researchers who wrote to the Chair of Undercover Policing Inquiry. He writes: 'Not having access to an inquiry archive does more than feed conspiracies: analysis by academics and journalists is prevented; informed comment is not possible' (Stone, 2015, p 91). This was at the heart of our concern around the way that the Undercover Policing Inquiry would disclose material to the wider public and it will remain the concern going forward.

## The problem of self-incrimination

The fact that the data might be useless should also not conceal Gary Marx's point that 'dirty' data are potentially embarrassing or harmful to the data holder. Evidence held by the police as well as by non-police participants in the Inquiry may be incriminating. This is a well-recognised problem for public inquiries. Giving evidence about personal or political matters in public is potentially embarrassing for the witness or could lead to self-incrimination and later criminal sanctions. The problem may be addressed by the Chair of a public inquiry by seeking an undertaking from the Attorney General that evidence given to said inquiry would not be used in any future prosecution for potential offences. The trade-off here is clear: such an undertaking would increase the likelihood of full cooperation by all witnesses with the inquiry, yet would complicate any criminal investigations that may arise independently. We can think of such undertakings as devices of dis/closure, insofar as they provide a regulatory framework to increase the likelihood of the disclosure of hidden data. Like other such devices, they remain contested and can foreground the asymmetry in the proceedings.

On the question of whether the Undercover Policing Inquiry should seek an undertaking from the Attorney General, the non-police, non-state core participants put forward their view in a submission to the Chair. In brief, they argued that asymmetry in the proceedings should be recognised and put front and centre. After all, the public concern giving grounds to the Inquiry was over the wrongdoings and failures in the various police and state parties. A preliminary hearing on the nature of the undertaking to be sought was held on 27 April 2016. For the Chair, Sir Christopher Pitchford, the reason for such an undertaking was that 'the Inquiry obviously wants to receive the best evidence it can from witnesses who are frank and truthful. If a witness is asked a question whose answer may implicate them in a criminal offence, they are entitled to decline to answer it' (UCPI, 2016i, p 2). An undertaking from the Attorney General would thus have the effect of enabling witnesses to disclose potentially self-incriminating evidence without fearing prosecution.

Not surprisingly, for those who saw the Inquiry as a part of the official acknowledgement that their human rights had been infringed by unjustifiable police intrusion into their lives, this was not good enough. A simple undertaking of this nature would potentially shield former police officers and their superiors from further accountability in the courts and deny their victims an avenue to seek redress. And although non-police witnesses would also receive such assurances, those who did not give evidence (for example, other activists and friends of the non-police, non-state core participants) would not. What they proposed instead was to base the undertaking to be sought on the recognition that their participation in the Inquiry rested on unequal footings. Police officers, they argued, should not receive protection by such a measure: 'an undertaking should be sought to ensure that evidence given to the Inquiry ... could not be used in criminal proceedings or investigations against anyone *other than police officers and state officials or employees*' (UCPI, 2016g, p 1, emphasis added)

Their submission pointed to the Inquiry's Terms of Reference, which set it up as an investigation into undercover police operations, *not* into the activities of political activists. 'It necessarily means', the lawyers argued, 'that it is inherent in the purpose of the Inquiry that the NPNSCPs [non-police, non-state core participants] be considered and treated as *victims*' (UCPI, 2016g, p 4, emphasis in the original). Counsel to the Inquiry recognised the essence of the argument in so far as they noted that there are 'those who participate in the Inquiry either as confirmed victims or as arguable victims of undercover policing which contravened their rights under the European Convention on Human Rights' (UCPI, 2016h, p 5).

The Chair published his ruling on the matter on 26 May 2016 (UCPI, 2016j). The undertaking he was to seek from the Attorney General would be equally applicable to all witnesses giving evidence to the Inquiry. It would make no distinction between the activities of victims of undercover policing and those individuals and state institutions accused of wrongdoing.

And it would also not be so extensive in scope as to encompass any potential criminal offences committed by activists other than those giving evidence to the Inquiry. By implication, therefore, the non-police witnesses could not be certain that by cooperating fully with the Inquiry, they would not bring about future police investigations into their friends' protest activities. The non-police, non-state core participants were less than impressed. It appeared to them that police witnesses had been favoured by the ruling and that their own status as victims in the proceedings had not been recognised.

The Undercover Policing Inquiry was not the first one to deal with the problem of self-incrimination in its approach to evidence gathering. Similar undertakings have become commonplace in UK statutory inquiries. The Brook House Inquiry into the mistreatment of detainees in an immigration removal centre, for example, sought an undertaking from the Attorney General that would protect immigration detainees from further immigration enforcement action solely on the basis of the evidence they provided to the Inquiry. However, custody officers were similarly protected from criminal prosecution on the basis of their witness statements (Schlembach and Hart, 2022). By contrast, in the Sheku Bayoh Inquiry in Scotland, an undertaking to seek protection from self-incrimination by witnesses was rejected by the Solicitor General. In the Inquiry's view, the undertaking was necessary in discharging its obligation to 'ascertain the truth' and to pre-empt the possibility that police officers would rely on 'the right to silence' (McKerrell, 2022: 45). However, it would have limited the possibility of criminal proceedings taken against the officers. To the relief of the family, and in agreement with the family's lawyer Aamer Anwar, the sought undertaking was not granted.

In the Grenfell Tower Inquiry, corporate witnesses made an early application to the Chair of the Inquiry, Sir Martin Moore-Bick, and his panel, to persuade them to seek an undertaking from the Attorney General that no evidence given to the inquiry would be used in any potential criminal prosecution of these witnesses. The application made it clear that corporate participants would claim the privilege against self-incrimination during the proceedings and effectively refuse to answer vital questions. The application was interpreted as a threat. Unless an undertaking was sought and granted, those involved, for example with the refurnishing of the tower, would ensure that the inquiry failed on its terms to find the truth about the disaster. The proposed undertaking was forcefully opposed by a core participant group of those bereaved and survivors of the Grenfell disaster, represented by the well-known socialist barrister Michael Mansfield. He argued, not unreasonably, that the timing of the application by the corporate participants had been designed to disrupt and delay – or 'sabotage', in his words – the inquiry's work. Mansfield accused the applicants of leading the inquiry and those affected by the fire to believe that the refurbishment companies and the local council would be transparent and cooperative in assisting the inquiry. Yet at the earliest opportunity to frustrate any progress, they had threatened to stonewall vital avenues of the investigation. Here, as in the Undercover Policing Inquiry, the proposed undertaking acted as a politically contested device of dis/closure to get to the truth. During a preliminary hearing, Mansfield made sure that he would be understood on this point.

> Mansfield: In fact, I'm going to go one stage further and say were it to be granted, given the climate of denial and the buck-passing which we have already seen … the granting of an undertaking in this case will be tantamount, I fear, to a licence to lie.
> Chair: Well, Mr Mansfield, that might be going a bit far, mightn't it? (Grenfell Tower Inquiry, 2020a, p 13)

In his ruling on the application to seek an undertaking, however, the Chair showed some sympathy for Mansfield's argument:

> It is very regrettable, in our view, that the position likely to be adopted by the witnesses was not made clear months ago when the consequences could have been debated without the disruption to the timetable that has now inevitably occurred, but now that it has been raised, we have no option but to deal with it. (Grenfell Tower Inquiry, 2020b, paragraph 11)

In this way, asymmetric distributions of power in the inquisitorial arena came to the fore also here. Those who, in litigation or criminal investigation, would stand as the accused parties could find ways of taking charge of significant aspects of the public inquiry. It was a point not lost, again, on the Chair:

> Mr Mansfield asked indignantly why the witnesses should be allowed to dictate the terms on which they answer questions. We can well understand why those whom he represents should see the question in that light, but the reality is that it is the law which gives them the right not to incriminate themselves and, to the extent that it can be invoked, allows them a measure of control over the course of events (Grenfell Tower Inquiry, 2020b, paragraph 25).

Sir Martin Moore-Bick's ruling on the matter thus disappointed the bereaved and survivors. Not only did he seek the undertaking to protect witnesses from prosecution – though it does not, to be clear, amount to immunity in any future civil or criminal proceedings – he also extended it to both natural and legal persons, thereby shielding companies themselves from the charge of corporate manslaughter.

## Obstruction and obfuscation

Where Mansfield saw an act of sabotage in the Grenfell Tower Inquiry, the victims and other non-state participants in the Undercover Policing Inquiry tended to see the heavy dose of adversarialism they encountered as resulting from deliberate police obstruction and obfuscation. To be sure, this view was never accepted by the Metropolitan Police. Despite the sensitive nature of the material under investigation, it declared itself to be committed to data transparency. In its written opening statement to the Inquiry, dated 22 October 2020, the force's lawyer said: 'From the outset the MPS has been committed, from the Commissioner down, to openness and transparency with the Inquiry' (UCPI, 2020g, p 3). Among continuous criticism that the huge delay experienced by the Inquiry was in most part due to the police's intransigence and obstruction, however, this was a difficult line to maintain.

The police's legal representative, Peter Skelton, was now forced to defend the position at the opening of the evidence hearings in November 2020:

> Sir, having read the submissions of some of the non-state core participants, I wish to be absolutely clear: the MPS has not and will not obstruct or otherwise undermine your public inquiry into undercover policing. The MPS has not and will not improperly delay the work of the Inquiry. On the contrary, the MPS has a strong interest in helping the Inquiry to complete its valuable work as effectively and swiftly as possible. (UCPI, 2020h, pp 4–5)

There was too much evidence to the contrary for any observer to accept this reasoning. Yet, rather than addressing its shortcomings, the Metropolitan Police line was reinforced through repetition. In a letter to the Inquiry, dated 8 January 2021 and written by Steven Bramley, the Director of Legal Services for the Metropolitan Police, the force made its position clear again:

> The continuing misconception that the Inquiry is and has been obstructed by the MPS may be understandable given the contentious nature of the issues under investigation, but it is incorrect and it is damaging … it takes time to declassify and ensure formerly secret documents can be published as openly as possible. (UCPI, 2021c)

The letter accepted that a reason for the huge delay in hearing evidence in the Inquiry had been the difficulties of identifying and disclosing secret police intelligence material, yet it deflected all responsibility. Not content with the irony that the mass of intelligence files on members of the public collected by Special Branch made for the complexity of the task in redacting them, the force's legal advisor pointed to external factors. His letter continued: 'The process has also been slowed by complexities in obtaining documents held by the Security Service; and by limits on that agency's capacity to review those documents for publication. More recently, the pandemic has understandably affected the rate of work' (UCPI, 2021c). Moreover, the Director of Legal Services shows himself directly concerned with the perception of the Inquiry in the public sphere and the police's reputation:

> The misconception about the nature of the MPS's participation in the Inquiry is highly damaging for the Inquiry and its work as it foments distrust and cynicism, and erodes public confidence in the Inquiry's ability to reach independent, fair and truthful conclusions. The misconception is also damaging for the MPS, for which it is important to acknowledge the mistakes of the past and to learn from them, not evade them. (UCPI, 2021c)

And he went further. It was, in the MPS's submission, an 'essential component' of police participation in the Inquiry that the public could be assured it was doing so in 'good faith'. For that, the force now requested Sir John Mitting's assistance. The Chair should make clear, Bramley wrote, that there was 'no basis for the allegation that the Inquiry's work has been or is being obstructed by the MPS' (UCPI, 2021c). Mitting obliged. Following a first round of oral evidence, he convened a Directions hearing to determine the arrangements for a second phase of evidence sessions amidst continuing uncertainties during the COVID-19 pandemic. Before inviting submissions, the Chair took the opportunity to address the meeting, fundamentally agreeing with the police's legal letter:

> So the Metropolitan Police has been in the position of the recipient of documents, just as everybody else has, and it has, as you know and I know, the task and the duty of ensuring that documents which are put into the public domain do not contain material that would damage the public interest. That is what has taken the great bulk of the time which we have all taken to get here. (UCPI, 2021d, p 4)

It was an extraordinary reinterpretation of the facts. Mitting accorded the police the role of data recipients in the same line as those who had been targeted by its operations and omitted its role in producing the intelligence files in the first place. And he referred back to his earlier assumption that the public interest role of the Inquiry is to serve the public interest in secrecy and redactions. The Chair's confidence in the police's dedication to transparency appeared stronger than ever:

> I entirely accept that those instructed by the Metropolitan Police Commissioner ... have done their level best to cooperate with the Inquiry, and the idea that they have deliberately instructed [sic, obstructed] it is simply erroneous. Nevertheless they, like the Inquiry and everybody else, face difficulties which have to be surmounted, and they are manifold. They are not easy to surmount, and they inevitably create difficulty and delay. But the idea that the difficulties that we have experienced can be put down to deliberate obstruction is wrong. (UCPI, 2021d, p 4)

The accusation of deliberate obstruction was not as far-fetched as Mitting suggested here. And it spoke to the uncomfortable asymmetry that remained unaddressed by the Inquiry's Chair. While he defended the police legal strategy, the requests for more openness by the non-police, non-state core participants were denied. It appeared that Mitting knew that the 'success' of his Inquiry rested on his ability to gain access to police-held documentation. The experiences and contributions of police targets and victims came only as secondary considerations. If those non-police, non-state core participants had few grounds to expect anything else from the police's legal strategy, the Chair's remarks only served to further cement in them the belief that he had little understanding of their position.

## "Give us our files!"

> The notion that I can get to the bottom of every conceivable issue that arises from these deployments and determine precisely what happened in every instance is fanciful. This is an exercise in historical analysis and like all exercises in historical analysis it cannot achieve perfection. (Sir John Mitting – UCPI, 2019f, p 32)

There was nothing 'historical' about the experiences of deception and manipulation felt by the victims of abusive undercover policing tactics. The difficulties of receiving disclosure from the police as well as from the Inquiry were all too real and reopened wounds of deception and manipulation. From their perspective, if the task of publishing redacted documents from police intelligence sources was so complex, then this only proved that the surveillance operations had been vast and indiscriminate. It only underlined the need for a meaningful search for answers and explanations. Those who already knew that they had been targeted by undercover officers answered the Inquiry's intransigence and the police's obfuscation with one demand: "Give us our files!"

Throughout the drawn-out preliminary phase, the police's defence of secrecy was as forceful as the Inquiry's insistence that its approach to disclosure was the right one. Yet, they served little to persuade the non-police, non-state core participants that their voices mattered. Finally, in November 2020, more than five years after the Home Secretary had set its Terms of Reference, the Inquiry proceeded to hold its first evidence hearings – virtually and conducted remotely due to the continuing social distancing measures in place at the time. The hearings began with opening statements and allowed some of the victims' voices to be raised. One of the most uncompromising criticisms of the Inquiry's approach to disclosure was made in Dónal O'Driscoll's opening statement. O'Driscoll is a core participant on account of his close relationship with Mark Kennedy during the latter's deployment in the climate action movement. He became a founding member of the URG and a formidable advocate for transparency in the Inquiry. O'Driscoll spoke for many of the non-police, non-state core participants when he accused Sir John Mitting of siding with the police interest in secrecy. He is one of the few core participants who represent themselves in the Inquiry and could thus address the Chair directly, rather than through a legal representative. This he did with sharp-witted clarity:

> I have been left with the impression that the Inquiry believes it can do its work without the non-state non-police core participants if needed. That it can learn the truth adequately enough from material provided by the police. That it can interpret the events we lived through, the moments and movements we were part of, without our help. That the truth can be obtained from the words and documents of units whose core training was to lie to people and was willing to pervert the course of justice. It is precisely the opposite. Without the understanding and knowledge we bring, there is no hope to penetrate the half-truths, the outright lies and the self-justification we know is in the police files. (Undercover Research Group, 2020)

The statement gave voice to the victimisation that many of those targeted by police intrusion had felt during the preliminary stages of the Inquiry. Rather than finding acknowledgement, answers and explanations, they had found themselves in a quasi-legal labyrinth with the odds stacked firmly against their call for transparency. O'Driscoll continued:

> My experience representing myself is that this attitude towards us permeates everywhere; the bias is visible in many of its decisions. Time and time again we have come up against it, either being stonewalled or finding the ground shift beneath us, or just being denied basic consideration around disclosure. The constant prioritising of police

needs over ours, exacerbates the pain we all feel. (Undercover Research Group, 2020)

O'Driscoll was followed by Ruth Brander, instructed by the lawyers for the largest group of non-police, non-state core participants and several of the women who were deceived into relationships by undercover officers. Like O'Driscoll, she did not hold back but expressed the victims' frustrations and pointed out the Inquiry's key failings in their eyes. While the objective of 'discovering the truth' remained at the forefront of the Inquiry's self-representation, she noted, the widespread sense was that any progress had stalled: 'Unfortunately, sir, nearly every decision taken since then has reduced his prospect of doing so. The central problem is the over-reliance on the police to voluntarily give themselves up to scrutiny, notwithstanding their appalling record in that regard' (UCPI, 2020i, p 51). Brander argued that instead of bending to the police's will, the Inquiry would do well to rethink its approach and to treat the non-police, non-state core participants as a 'significant resource for the Inquiry in its search for the truth, not just as a source of information about their own individual cases but in uncovering the deeper underlying themes of relevance to the Inquiry's terms of reference' (UCPI, 2020, p 55). If the widespread use of restriction orders to protect former officers from being identified meant that members of the public who had been spied on were effectively denied their chance to give evidence to the Inquiry, the approaches to disclosure and evidence gathering only compounded the sense that those on the non-state side were not equal participants.

Brander, O'Driscoll and others who spoke at the start of the first evidence hearings of the Undercover Policing Inquiry ultimately failed to move the Chair's position. Barely a year later, they found out that the Inquiry had allowed several police officers to give evidence in secret, including two officers who had admitted to sexual relationships while undercover (Evans, 2021). Although the Chair's reasons for the closed evidence sessions remained largely opaque, in some cases he reasoned that asking the officers to give evidence in open session, even under their false identities, would contravene their human rights to a private life. This conundrum – that an investigation into human rights abuses would have to remain human rights law compliant itself – is the issue that I want to turn to in the following chapter.

# 6

# Human rights and data protection

## The spy's right to privacy

What are human rights, anyway? So far, we have considered the attempts by campaigners, lawyers, journalists and researchers to access hidden data and to gain the concession, from state actors, of an acknowledged truth. Some, though not all, of their strategies have been rights-based. That is predictable, considering their engagement in a state-sponsored inquisitorial process with a distinctly adversarial twist. What was less foreseeable was the reliance by the police and other state institutions on human rights. What I want to do in this chapter is to critically think through some of the implications of police legal arguments that shift the discursive terrain from one of institutional failure to one of individual harm. In what follows, my argument rests on a close reading and analysis of documents published by the Undercover Policing Inquiry – primarily applications for restriction orders, risk assessments and transcripts from oral hearings. The analysis highlights that rights-based legal discourse, especially as it pertains to the European Convention on Human Rights (ECHR), has been the centre-point around which the state's official strategy in the Inquiry revolves. Most cynically, this has meant that the Convention's Article 8, 'the right to privacy and family life', has become the foundation of the police's efforts to maintain secrecy and avoid accountability.

I do not want to delve too deeply into the legal debate around the Convention's uses and abuses, promises and limitations. My approach shall remain sociological in nature. But there is a body of law scholarship that allows us to clarify what we mean when we talk about human rights. Marie-Bénédicte Dembour's 'four schools of thought' model has been influential in disentangling some competing ways of thinking about rights. It distinguishes between 'natural scholars', 'deliberative scholars', 'protest scholars' and 'discourse scholars'. Dembour argues that, despite the common conception of human rights as 'unambiguous and uncontroversial', the academic literature is in fact characterised by 'a lack of agreement about what human rights are' (Dembour, 2010, p 2). The natural school of thought conceives of human rights as absolute and universal rights possessed by every human being. For the deliberative school of thought, human rights come into existence only through a social contract, the continuous process of agreement and disagreement that offers the promise of a universally accepted and rights-based polity. The protest school of thought regards human rights as the foundation of advocacy. It simultaneously believes in the promise of redress for injustice and criticises the way that powerful elite groups have skewed human rights law in their favour. Finally, the discourse school of thought critiques the language of human rights and its de-politicising effects. It identifies rights-based language as part of a hegemonic liberalism that subjugates other forms of claims-making, protection and emancipation.

In previous chapters, I explained how some activists hesitated to apply for core participant status in the public inquiry. In many ways, they rehearsed the kind of arguments that we would expect to find in Dembour's last two schools of thought, protest and discourse. These arguments conceptualise a particular relationship of rights to power. On the one hand, rights-based claims can offer an effective challenge to oppression, especially if oppression is thought of as a lack of protection of minority groups from majority interests. On the other hand, they can also manoeuvre emancipatory politics into a cul-de-sac position, whereby an international legal system that enshrines enduring privilege and inequality *by design* is granted legitimacy through the recognition by its adversaries.

It is a paradox to which many of the affected activists were alert to. Yet, it remains unresolved. Wendy Brown illuminates the paradoxical circumstances at play in her reflections on the use of legal rights within and by feminist movements. Legal claim-making, she argues, may lead to formal justice but rarely addresses the structural conditions in which injustice had been allowed to exist in the first place. For those seeking liberation from oppression, it is especially important to grapple with this context 'given the transposition of venue, from the streets to the courtroom, of many social movements over the last two decades … what are the perils and possibilities of this dwelling?' (Brown, 2000, p 230). In the courtroom, the language of rights creates a formal equality between the claimant and the defendant, which contrasts with the actual asymmetry in power and access to resources. In many ways, Brown's account is not unfamiliar to the discussions within social and political movements and her image of rights as a paradox continues to hold much sway two decades later. It may also help us to account for the prominence of the language of rights in support of police efforts to limit the public deliberation of its covert surveillance methodologies, past and present.

In this chapter, what emerges from an analysis of the relevant transcripts, and associated rulings, is that rights-based claims on the part of state parties have increasingly been incorporated into their legal strategy. But rather than producing a paradox of the kind outlined by Wendy Brown, we are here confronted with a paradox of a different kind: an inquisitorial process that was expected to revolve around the human rights claims of non-state actors, that is, primarily those who were targeted for potentially unlawful infiltration by police, has been turned into a validation of human rights for actors of the state. Police leaders, backroom staff and field officers, as well as their families, have all made claims that constructed the public inquiry as potentially undermining the rights of its state protagonists. As we will see, the ECHR and the UK Data Protection Act took centre stage in those legal arguments.

## Human rights, a different kind of paradox

The adversarial conduct that has characterised the public inquiry was quickly laid bare from when the first Chair, Sir Christopher Pitchford, held oral hearings on preliminary matters that would set the Inquiry on its course. I observed the adversarial nature of the proceedings in the Royal Courts of Justice. Lawyers for the police and other state institutions populated the rows of seats in front of the Inquiry team and Chair, while those targeted by undercover operations were seated in a small gallery space at the back, behind just a handful of their own legal representatives. When this was full, a spill-over room was made available, where observers could view the proceedings via a video link. The divisions were clear to see. But they were equally apparent when just reading the hearing transcripts or analysing the submissions made by the legal representatives acting on behalf of the different state and non-state parties. In its first five years, the Undercover Policing Inquiry invited submissions on a range of matters, held a series of oral hearings on emerging preliminary issues and produced transcripts of each of them. There is no doubt that those preliminary discussions and arguments that resulted in the restriction orders protocol – Sir Christopher's answer to the question of police officer anonymity – were the most significant ones with far-reaching consequences.

Let us briefly recall: Under section 19 of the Inquiries Act 2005, the Chair has the power to restrict public access to the Inquiry, by limiting attendance to its hearings or by placing restrictions on the disclosure of evidence and other documentation. Under section 21 of the same Act, the Chair can compel members of the public to produce documents held in their possession and to appear before the Inquiry to give evidence. Section 22 allows for exemptions from this requirement to provide evidence, notably on the grounds of public interest immunity. In early 2016, Sir Christopher Pitchford invited submissions and held two days of preliminary hearings to establish the legal principles upon which the Inquiry should act in making decisions upon applications for restriction orders. This would concern issues of anonymity and the extent to which evidence about undercover police officers or the private lives of those targeted by undercover operations should be withheld from disclosure. The Chair issued his 'Legal Principles and Approach' ruling on restriction orders in May 2016. The ruling set out that the Inquiry would pursue an 'incremental route' towards considering applications for restrictions. It effectively ended the police's argument that the Inquiry should conduct its affairs according to a presumption of non-disclosure (Neither Confirm Nor Deny [NCND]). It also severely curtailed the argument brought by the non-police, non-state core participants that the Inquiry should act according to a presumption of openness. In its effect, the approach further prepared the route for long delays and protracted processes assessing restriction order applications and risk assessments.

Some of the initial delay was put down to either the unpreparedness or the under-resourcing within the Metropolitan Police team tasked to support the applications for anonymity by its former officers. Despite warnings to the contrary, the Metropolitan Police's leadership embarked on a lengthy process to guarantee anonymity for its two main risk assessors, codenamed Cairo and Jaipur, despite both of them also being responsible for the security and welfare of the officers. It led to accusations that their risk assessments lacked objectivity and independence and eventually their withdrawal from the role.

Where Pitchford was clearly exasperated by what he called police 'failings', the non-police, non-state core participants tried to push him to accept that this was a deliberate police tactic. They had dealt with the Metropolitan Police's lawyers in the courts before and had learned that delays and obfuscation were systemic in their legal approach. The Chair remained resolute; he would not ascribe any intent to the police's struggles to get things moving. In an exchange with Kate Wilson, a core participant who had been part of the legal action against the police over an intimate relationship she had been deceived into, the Chair defended the police organisation:

Chair: [Y]ou must remember that the Inquiry has been dealing with the Metropolitan Police behind the scenes for the whole of the last year and I will repeat to you … there is a great difference between what you are saying is deliberate sabotage and incompetence, failure to plan, and foresight as to what would be required of them when the crunch came. Now, in March of last year we were told that the Metropolitan Police were expert at risk assessment. Well, they are not – not in the sense that you and I were led to believe at that time. So I am quite prepared to accept that there have been failings, but I want you to distinguish between deliberate actions …
Wilson: [*Interrupting*] Such as the destruction of documents.
Chair: That is nothing to do with what we are discussing today. (UCPI, 2017n, p 135)

Despite the apparent failings, risk assessments as well as independent medical reports remained critical to the endeavour of deciding on restriction order applications. Section 19 of the Inquiries Act requires the Chair to consider whether any harm or damage can be avoided or reduced by the issuing of a restriction order. This would necessitate, he said, consideration of Articles 2, 3 and 8 under the ECHR. He would therefore consider whether applications for anonymity or non-disclosure of documents, for example, could avoid or reduce the likelihood of death or (physical or psychological) injury or the infringement on a person's private and family life.

At this point, it appeared to be quite clear to Sir Christopher Pitchford that the risks of infringing on the human rights of (former) police officers needed to be evidenced and could not entirely rely on partial police self-assessments. In a note to core participants, he wrote: 'I do not intend to convey the impression that I expect the risk assessments necessarily to be supportive of the restriction order sought. I expect the assessment to be expert, critical and objective' (UCPI, 2016k, p 2). In his ruling, he further noted:

> I accept the invitation by the police services and the Home Office to treat with due respect the risk assessments made by those who are expert in policing and the risks attendant on the exposure of identities and police operations. However, this acceptance does not mean that I shall accept every expression of opinion offered to me, particularly when the opinion is offered at the level of generality. In the end I have the responsibility of assessing the public interest balance for and against restriction. That will involve critical assessment of evidence. (UCPI, 2016b, p 60)

The approach taken by the Chair has, more than any other issue, revealed the entrenched and opposing positions that structure the Inquiry process.[1] The separate interests are clearly identified in his ruling as those of public interests in disclosure and secrecy. To reiterate my earlier point, it establishes the notion, which runs through much of the Inquiry's legal dispute, that the arguments brought by the police and other state participants belong to the domain of human rights, whereas the human rights of non-police participants are not invoked.

## Protecting the anonymity of police officers

For the police, the matters of Article 8 protections were raised by Oliver Sanders KC, who acts on behalf of more than 100 former Metropolitan Police Service members of the Special Demonstration Squad (SDS) and the National Public Order Intelligence Unit (NPOIU). Sanders set out that although Article 8 was a qualified right, it could be relied on by former police officers. The expectation of confidentiality that his clients had from their time in the undercover units may not be absolute, but in the context of the Undercover Policing Inquiry they were, he said, 'bound up with the package of rights and interests that undercover officers, former undercover officers, have as a matter of article 8' (UCPI, 2017k, p 33). His reasoning hinged on an interpretation of Sir Christopher Pitchford's restriction orders ruling. Pitchford's decision, Sanders argued, had not ruled out that the qualified privacy rights that undercover officers enjoyed under the ECHR could be relied on in the process of deciding on anonymity. In fact, so the argument went, the possible infringements on these rights by disclosure should be a key plank of the decision-making process. Human rights, he argued, 'are very much in the mix and in my submission they have a very powerful in-built weight on the other side of the scales to the openness' (UCPI, 2017k, p 33).

Not only should Article 8 rights sway the Inquiry's public interest test in favour of maintaining secrecy, but as servants of the state who had expected a high level of confidentiality about the roles they undertook, the privacy of undercover officers should now be protected in a government-sponsored, statutory inquiry. If former officers had been loyal to the state and had done so with integrity and professionalism, that loyalty should now be returned to them: 'In my submission, for the state now to say – "well, we are going to have a public inquiry about that and that's all changed, sorry" – isn't acceptable unless there is some credible allegation of misconduct or wrongdoing' (UCPI, 2017k, p 36). More than that, the police submissions argued that any accusation of 'wrongdoing' needed to be assessed against the standards of practice *at the time*. Misconduct committed in the 1970s, say, should be considered with reference to acceptable behaviour and the organisational culture of the contemporaneous SDS.

Such general submissions weighed heavily on the individual anonymity decisions for SDS officers that followed and they had the effect of changing the wider narrative in the Inquiry. The privacy rights of officers, staff and their families became the basis upon which the new Chair, Sir John Mitting, decided upon anonymity and disclosure. Where non-police, non-state core participants had believed it to be an investigation into the breaches of their protected rights, they now saw it turn into a question of protecting the rights of state participants. Campaigners, already exasperated by the Inquiry's unwillingness to bring their testimony forward and the legal wrangling over the police's use of the NCND 'policy', expressed their disbelief. An Inquiry that they had invested much hope into, which was ostensibly set up to investigate the human rights abuses they suffered in relation to the spying on their political activities, was now invested in protecting the human rights of the police officers.

The Campaign Opposing Police Surveillance, for example, insisted that the restriction orders in respect to former officers' identities could essentially permit the Metropolitan Police to rely on its NCND response by the back door. 'Effectively', the group argued, 'Mitting is saying the rights of violators are more important than the rights of the violated' (Campaign Opposing Police Surveillance, 2018). The non-police, non-state core participants were faced with an insurmountable barrier: the metaphorical 'brick wall of silence' that Sir John Mitting had alluded to. Not only did they see decision after decision taken in favour of police anonymity, they were also granted only very limited insight into the grounds on which these decisions were based. They were, in this respect, mere bystanders rather than participants in the Inquiry. While they found the risk assessments and medical evidence presented in support of the cases of police officers' privacy gisted[2] or redacted, they knew full well that the officers and their employers had access to 'their' intelligence files. The power differentials were all too obvious.

For many, this lopsidedness was experienced as cognitive dissonance or cruel irony. No one could express it better than Helen Steel, who had been deceived into a relationship by the policeman John Dines and who years after his disappearance from her life was able to 'track him down' and confront him in Australia. Her account of the confrontation is genuinely harrowing and shows the complex emotions that informed her decision to find him (Alison et al, 2022, pp 350–7). That this desperate urge to find answers, driven also by care and worry about her former partner, was now spun by the police lawyers to be a matter of intrusion and harassment was, in Steel's words, 'insulting and distressing' (UCPI, 2017k, p 196). If the attempts by the women who were deceived in such similar fashion to find the men they considered 'abusers', to speak to them, to demand answers and accountability, were now re-interpreted as infringements of the former officers' human rights, what did these men tell the Inquiry in private? What did they say to their risk assessors, behind the gisting and redactions? Why were their narratives to be trusted when their police work had rested on carefully constructing falsehoods? Given the chance to address the Chair on the risk assessments she had seen, Steel tried to explain:

Steel: I wanted to draw your attention to the fact that there are numerous inaccuracies within a lot of these documents, and some of them relate to me personally and I find it quite insulting ... to see and read them and know that the police are being funded to promote these inaccuracies.
Chair: Yes.
Steel: And I think it is important that you know that from my perspective and the perspective of many of the women, we have seen the lies that these undercover officers are capable of, and just how convincing they are. They are professional liars. (UCPI, 2017k, p 194)

The point, she maintained, was not that everything that police officers were saying should be treated as falsehoods, but that the glimpses that she and others had seen of risk assessments and psychological evaluations were littered with inaccuracies. Much was hidden behind redactions and so the non-police, non-state core participants could not be given the opportunity to correct them. Yet, the inaccuracies pointed to exaggerations to the risk of harm posed by activists to police officers. And where infringement of privacy rights did occur, such as in the cases of John Dines or Bob Lambert, they should be seen as entirely justified in the knowledge that these men had committed the kinds of wrongdoings for which the Metropolitan Police had publicly apologised.

## Contesting the risk assessments

Helen Steel and other activists who were spied on by undercover officers could point to inaccuracies in the open risk assessments commissioned by the police. But they remained in the dark over the content of their closed or redacted sections. The confidentiality of some of the documents that supported undercover officers' anonymity applications made it near impossible for the non-police, non-state core participants to spot mistakes or exaggerations and to challenge them. This problem moved into the centre of the controversy when it transpired that risk assessments, though restricted from public view, could entail details of criminal convictions of those targeted by undercover police deployments. It seemed that such details would be included to promote the argument that a threat of physical harm may exist to the officers if their identities were made public. Some feared that the Metropolitan Police's chosen risk assessors were trying to present a picture to the Chair of individuals with long-past criminal convictions out to take revenge on former spycops.

In some cases, the convictions that the police disclosed to the Inquiry through its risk assessments were *spent* convictions as defined by the Rehabilitation of Offenders Act (ROA) 1974. Under the Act and its later amendments, persons who have become rehabilitated in respect of previous convictions should be treated as if they had not been convicted of the offence. After a rehabilitation period that varies with the offence, there is no duty on the formerly convicted person to disclose the conviction or the circumstances that led to it, such as in routine disclosure checks for professional employment. Subject to exceptions, evidence relating to spent convictions is also inadmissible in any proceedings 'before a judicial authority'. The ROA therefore provides for important safeguards against the misuse of personal data and against the invasion of an individual's privacy.

The issue left the Inquiry in a bit of a muddle. How, if at all, could spent convictions be considered as evidence in the proceedings of the Inquiry?

The Chair invited submissions from core participants and then held a preliminary meeting on the matter. There was little agreement as to how to proceed or even as to how the information about spent convictions processed by the police risk assessors might relate to the ROA. In the police's submissions, the Inquiry's duty of fairness to former officers necessitated that spent convictions could be raised in risk assessments. In a position statement, the Metropolitan Police said that 'it would be unfair and inaccurate for the Inquiry not to take into account evidence of the relevant previous spent convictions of those that pose or may pose a risk' to former officers applying for anonymity (UCPI, 2017o, p 3). The force's lawyers also argued that considerations of successful criminal prosecutions of activists would be required to demonstrate the effectiveness of undercover policing tactics. As the Inquiry's scope stretched to SDS operations as far back as 1968, the police submission considered it unavoidable that spent convictions should be admissible as evidence.

It was clear to all that without considering past criminal convictions, including for the purpose of testing their safety, the Inquiry could not fulfil its function. The central issue therefore became whether those targeted in undercover operations, whose criminal convictions underpinned risk assessments (and which in turn underpinned the applications for officer anonymity), should be told about the use of their data and whether they would have the right to make their own representations about the circumstances of their convictions. The police insisted that letting political campaigners know that their convictions had been brought up would be time-consuming and costly. Furthermore, it might lead them to suspect and possibly identify former activist friends as police officers. It would, in their view, undermine the very purpose of the restriction orders and the risk assessments on which some of them were based (UCPI, 2017p, p 2).

The non-police, non-state core participants argued that activists with spent convictions were granted protections and rights under the ROA, including the right to know when and where information about them was being used. In particular, by denying those activists the chance to make representations to the Chair, their criminal convictions would be taken as safe and fail-proof. Just as Sir Christopher Pitchford had ruled out a blanket approach to granting restriction orders, Sir John Mitting should now rule out a blanket approach to admitting past convictions into evidence (UCPI, 2017q). Where a criminal conviction, spent or unspent, had arisen out of a situation in which an apparent offence had been committed *during the course of an undercover deployment*, questions should be asked about the safety of these convictions in the first place. Otherwise, an Inquiry set up to, in part, investigate miscarriages of justice resulting from undercover police deployments would effectively admit evidence without critically interrogating its origins.

The dilemma was not easily overcome. Both 'sides' argued that the Inquiry had a duty of fairness towards them, resulting from their Article 8 privacy rights, the Inquiries Act 2005 and the ROA. Should the Chair take confidence in the safety of past criminal convictions and in the risk assessors' assertion that they could be taken as clues towards possible harms that would be incurred by named officers? Or should the Chair take a critical attitude towards the convictions of activists that had been targeted by undercover deployments, considering the extent of miscarriages of justice that had already been unearthed? Mitting concluded that a public inquiry, despite it not constituting a criminal trial, is to be regarded as a proceeding before a judicial authority. Therefore, the exemptions set out in the ROA would apply and give the Chair of an inquiry the exceptional power to admit evidence of and permit questioning about spent convictions. For this, however, he needed good grounds and these were not easily established. To justify the interference with the rights of rehabilitated persons would require a considerable amount of work, including the necessity to investigate whether the convictions admitted into evidence are 'safe' or might result from miscarriages of justice.

If this was the framework of rights upon which he had to decide, Mitting was trapped in a Catch-22 situation. The decision on whether to consider spent convictions would be premised on first testing their safety. In order to test their safety, the Chair would have to allow the convictions to be disclosed and discussed. There was only one escape route available to Mitting: a change in the law.

At the end of 2017, Sir John Mitting asked the Justice Secretary to lay before parliament an amendment to the ROA. The law should now include an exemption for statutory inquiries held under the Inquiries Act 2005 from the provisions that protect those with spent convictions. All such public inquiries would be able to consider the spent convictions of rehabilitated persons if this was deemed necessary to fulfil their Terms of Reference. The Secretary of State obliged and the ensuing secondary legislation was approved by parliament in 2019. With regards to the Undercover Policing Inquiry, the public inquiry exemption in the legislation now permits the police to disclose as evidence the spent convictions of political activists in justifying the use of covert tactics and in its applications for officer anonymity. The Chair, however, decided that he would not alert core participants in the Inquiry if their convictions were disclosed in risk assessments, nor would he allow them to make representations about them. 'Essentially', wrote the campaigner and researcher Dónal O'Driscoll (2017), 'a police officer can have falsely labelled an activist as a violent villain and now use that label to avoid accountability'. The actual effect of the change in law in protecting the identities of undercover officers, however, remains difficult to determine.

## Anonymity in numbers

By July 2022, the Undercover Policing Inquiry had held its first in-person evidence hearings and was preparing an interim report for Tranche 1. It planned to start Tranche 2 evidence hearings by Spring 2024. In an update (UCPI, 2022f), the Inquiry informed us that the process for determining restriction order applications that would guarantee anonymity to (former) police officers was substantially complete as far as the SDS was concerned. In total, the Inquiry ruled on applications made by 165 SDS officers, 51 of whom were back-office staff or managers, and it also confirmed the identities of a further four officers whose names were already in the public domain.

Anonymity rulings were not always in favour of maximum secrecy. The Inquiry released 70 cover names used by SDS officers and listed 102 political campaign groups into which they had been deployed. There was significantly more protection of officers' real names, with just 36 published on the Inquiry's website at the time. While the Inquiry stated that the publication of these details should 'enable members of the public to determine whether they have been affected by undercover policing and come forward with evidence' (UCPI, 2022a, p 10), there was no concerted effort to reach those who had been targeted by covert intelligence gathering and the level of restrictions imposed prevented just that in many cases. Still, the relative openness about SDS deployments contrasted with the secrecy clouding the more recent deployments of NPOIU officers. The Inquiry stated that applications for restriction orders were made by a total of 67 NPOIU officers, with 45 of them being management staff. A further four officers from the unit did not ask for a restriction to the publication of their cover names – 'Marco Jacobs', 'Lynn Watson', 'Rod Richardson' and 'Edward David Jones' had already been outed by campaigners. Only Mark Kennedy had his real name confirmed on the Inquiry's website.

Further information made available showed the relative success of former undercover officers to have their details kept confidential. Of 55 applications to have the cover names of SDS officers restricted from publication, 38 were granted and just 17 refused. While a significant proportion of all SDS staff, such as managers, chose not to ask for anonymity, in 107 cases the Chair was asked to rule on anonymity applications for the officers' real names. In one hundred of those, the ruling went in the police's favour. For the NPOIU, the Chair took decisions in 16 cases where field officers sought to restrict the publication of their cover names. He granted the police applications in 13 of those and only refused three. The three refusals concerned officers known by the cyphers EN35, EN37 and EN508, yet the full reasons for the Chair's decisions were set out only in a 'closed note'. Furthermore, even though the decision would mean the publication of the cover names, this was not immediately forthcoming. Scrutiny of the NPOIU was reserved for an unspecified date in the future, during Tranche 4 of the Inquiry's work, and publication was not deemed to be necessary until that time. This meant that even though the ruling regarding those officers' cover names was, in the first two cases, made in 2018, the political activists who were targeted by these officers might have to wait until the second half of the 2020s to learn of this fact. It may not come as a surprise now that in the majority of anonymity applications to keep the real names of NPOIU staff confidential, the Chair ruled in the police's favour. In 36 final decisions, 29 applications were granted.

The fact that these decisions were reached not usually on national security grounds, but on human rights considerations, does need further exploration.

## Anonymity, risk and harm

Most of the rights that find protection under the ECHR are encoded in UK law through the Human Rights Act 1998. This includes Article 8 of the Convention, the right to respect for private and family life. Before the Human Rights Act came into force, there was no statutory right to privacy in the UK. Article 8 is made up of two components and reads:

1. Everyone has the right to respect for his private and family life, his home and his correspondence.
2. There shall be no interference by a public authority with the exercise of this right except such as is in accordance with the law and is necessary in a democratic society in the interests of national security, public safety or the economic well-being of the country, for the prevention of disorder or crime, for the protection of health or morals, or for the protection of the rights and freedoms of others.

The rights thus protected are qualified (as opposed to absolute) rights. Infringements on Article 8 protections can be justified if they are lawful, 'necessary in a democratic society' and necessary to meet the aims set out in the Convention text. In practice, Article 8 has allowed for a broad interpretation of privacy rights and has been applied widely. In the Undercover Policing Inquiry, the rights enjoyed by former undercover officers and their families – including their safety, health and wellbeing – became a prominent factor in the determination of anonymity applications.[3]

A good example of this is EN108, the head of the NPOIU for two years. In January 2022, Mitting suggested that he was minded to restrict the publication of EN108's real identity (UCPI, 2022h), and his justifications for granting anonymity to this senior police figure are telling. The former officer is said to have joined the NPOIU first as the operational lead of its covert functions and then rose to the position of the unit's head between 2007 and 2008. He would have had managerial responsibility for the central years of the Mark Kennedy deployment as well as others during that time. It is clear that accountability for this deployment, including by hearing public evidence, is in the public interest. Yet Mitting was persuaded otherwise by the medical evidence that EN108 submitted as part of his anonymity application. Here is how the Chair summarised it:

> After leaving the NPOIU EN108 sustained injuries of at least moderate severity in the course of his police duties. They included head injuries which have had both an immediate and lasting impact on him. For reasons of medical confidentiality, and to avoid identification, they are more fully described in the closed note which accompanies this note … In the opinion of [a senior consultant psychiatrist], he has residual symptoms of post concussional syndrome and chronic post traumatic stress disorder and depression which have been, and may continue to be, susceptible to treatment. If administered, all three conditions will reduce, if properly treated. However, the disclosure of his real identity 'will have a very high negative impact on his mental health recovery, and may prevent him from recovering fully even if the treatment recommendations … are implemented.' (UCPI, 2022c, pp 3–4)

This medical history persuaded Mitting that the real name of EN108 should be restricted from publication. While he will be asked to provide evidence in public, this will be done under a cypher and with other protective measures that will prevent his identification.

The Chair's 'minded-to' note gives us some insight into the rationalisations for anonymity, even for the most senior officers with overall strategic responsibility in the undercover units. But it also leaves questions unanswered. The anonymity of the one-time 'head of the NPOIU' is justified, according to Mitting, because his Article 8 rights would be infringed upon were he named and asked to provide evidence under his real name. Infringement of his right to a private and family life may be justified if it is in the public interest. But here the balancing exercise of weighing out two different claims to public interest – one to accountability for human rights violations that happened under EN108's watch, and the other one to respect for his 'health and wellbeing' – falls in favour of anonymity. One could question the sense of this decision: can the medical conditions that are here described to be the result of a head injury sustained while on duty really provide the substantial grounds for granting anonymity to such a crucial witness? We cannot fully know, because the full details of the conditions are not publicly available. But we are told that they are treatable. Could the witness be named at a later stage, if the conditions were to improve? There appeared to be no such considerations.

## The Inquiry's reach abroad

Former officers and police managers were granted protective measures by the Chair for medical reasons. But the Inquiry also faced problems due to its limited statutory reach. Its power to compel evidence and to request attendance of witnesses at hearings only extends to the jurisdiction of the United Kingdom. Some of the former officers who were seconded to the undercover units now live abroad. Their cooperation with the Inquiry would therefore be entirely voluntary. In some cases, the Chair issued restriction orders preventing the publication of real and cover names of former officers, in recognition that they may otherwise refuse to give evidence.

One example is that of officer HN101, who infiltrated the Socialist Workers Party in the 1990s. The Chair recognises that there is no immediate threat to his safety and that the evidence HN101 could provide is of material interest. As well as medical considerations, the Chair's 'minded-to' note says this:

> [B]ecause HN101 lives permanently abroad, the Inquiry has no means of compelling him to provide or give evidence. The only means of obtaining worthwhile evidence from HN101 is to make the restriction orders sought and to permit HN101 to provide evidence, by way of a witness statement. Members of the group into which HN101 was deployed will be able to provide evidence about its activities, even if not about HN101 personally. (UCPI, 2018f, p 6)

Inadvertently, the Chair's opinion accepts as given the fact that former police officers may not cooperate with the Inquiry unless they can be compelled to do so, or given special protection. Despite this, the candour with which these witnesses are to supply the Inquiry with evidence is not put into question.

## Posthumous rights

In a different 'minded-to' note (UCPI, 2022g), Sir John Mitting reasoned that an interference with the privacy rights of former officers would only be justified if the publication of their real names served to produce new evidence about their deployments. To some surprise among observers of the Inquiry, this would extend to cases of officers who had since died.

In the case of HN80, who had assumed the name 'Colin Clark' to infiltrate the Socialist Workers Party and the Anti-Nazi League in the late 1970s, the

Chair cited a letter that he had received from the deceased officer's daughter. Mitting wrote:

> It provided a detailed account of her history and that of her family which I accept to be true. To protect their privacy and right to respect for private and family life under Article 8 of the European Convention on Human Rights ('ECHR'), no part of the letter will be made public. It sets out concerns about the possible impact of publication of her late father's real name on her well-being and on that of her family which I accept to be genuinely held. Although the chance that the events which concern her would occur is not great, it cannot be excluded. (UCPI, 2022g, p 1)

The Chair does not grant public access to the letter that convinced him to restrict the publication of HN80's real name. We are not told what 'events' are feared by the officer's family some 45 years after his deployment. But their 'genuinely held' concern means that interference with their right to privacy cannot be justified by the public concern over the undercover operation.

The possible, though unlikely, interference with the private life of another officer's former wife was again cited as the reason for not disclosing the identity of HN106. He had used the name and date of birth of a deceased child to create the cover identity of 'Barry Tomkins' and infiltrated socialist groups and the Blair Peach justice campaign in the early 1980s. HN106's deployment was of particular interest as he had appeared to launch his own political group only to then feed his employers information about it. He was also accused of having been in a relationship with a woman in his target group. None of this was enough to persuade the Chair of the public interest in revealing who HN106 really was and what career path he had taken after his SDS deployment. He reasoned:

> None of the members of the groups infiltrated or reported on by HN106 pose any threat to surviving members of his family. I have, however, been persuaded by a letter from one of his surviving sons that disclosure of his real name might lead to unwelcome interest in the whereabouts and circumstances of his surviving former wife [and their mother] which would, in any event, be likely to cause her concern. (UCPI, 2022g, p 1)

As before, the concern of a deceased officer's former wife that she could be confronted with 'unwelcome' interest was enough to tip the balance in favour of anonymity, we are told.

There are further illustrative examples. HN303 was an officer who used the name 'Peter Collins' to infiltrate the Workers Revolutionary Party

(WRP). Curiously, he ended up as a 'double agent' as the WRP sought to embed him as one of their own in the far Right and to spy on the National Front. Although HN303 is no longer alive, the possible infringement on the rights of his surviving family was cited by Mitting in defence of his anonymity order:

> A letter written on behalf of members of his surviving family has expressed what I accept to be a genuine concern about the possible impact of publication of the real name on one of them. Although the chance that harm would result is very small, it cannot be wholly discounted. Further, and in any event, that person would experience genuine anxiety, sufficient to interfere with the ordinary conduct of life, if the chance were to be taken. (UCPI, 2022b, p 2)

Mitting's balancing exercise between competing public interests which may qualify the privacy rights enjoyed by this deceased officer's family members now became a matter of speculation. The acknowledged 'public concern' about the undercover deployments and their methods could not justify, in the Chair's view, the interference with the privacy rights enjoyed by surviving family members, which were founded on the 'genuine concern' that there was a 'very small' chance of harm to them.

We can draw several conclusions from such reasoning. First, the threshold of Article 8 violations having a bearing on the Chair's decisions to restrict the publication of real names and identifying materials was extremely low and even applied in cases where adverse effects on individuals from disclosure were very unlikely. This substantially undermined the sense that officers and managers could be held to account and gave many observers the impression that the Inquiry saw its role as that of a keeper of secrets. Second, even where officers were reportedly involved in the kind of wrongdoing that had sparked the public concern around the undercover units, their privacy and that of their immediate family trumped the public interest in accountability. It appeared that disclosure was seen as a route to evidence – but nothing more.

Anonymity for former officers on the grounds of their privacy rights, or those of their surviving family members, does not tell the whole story. We have seen that anonymity was not granted to all police witnesses. There were rare occasions on which the Chair refused the applications of NPOIU officers to have their anonymity protected. One case was that of EN107, a senior officer with managerial responsibility for some of the unit's deployments in the mid-2000s. Mitting stated:

> The evidence of EN107 is likely to attract unwelcome interest from both traditional and non-traditional media and so cause some

interference with the right of EN107 to respect for private life. There is a small risk of other interference, but no real risk to safety. In those circumstances, such interference would be justified by giving effect to the public interest in EN107 accounting in the real name of EN107 for management of the undercover unit and the two deployments referred to. (UCPI, 2022h, p 3)

Here the Chair accepts the possibility that media interest may interfere with the Article 8 rights of the officer, but he is willing to justify the infringements on the basis of the public interest.

Where decisions went against them, or to further give weight to their applications for anonymity, some former officers indicated to the Chair that they would only be prepared to aid the Inquiry on their own terms. This, it must be said, did not go down well. For example, in a statement that he was minded to restrict publication of the real name of officer EN59 – who was seconded as a senior manager to the NPOIU between 2003 and 2005 – but not the name by which he may have been known to other officers in the unit, he said:

EN59 has sought to lay down strict and detailed conditions upon which he is 'prepared to engage further with the Inquiry'. The Inquiry will, of course, discuss with his legal representatives the measures which are required, when he provides and gives evidence, to protect his safety and welfare and that of those with whom he is associated; but he should be aware that the provision of evidence to the Inquiry is not, in the end, voluntary or subject to conditions imposed unilaterally by an individual within the jurisdiction. I will, if necessary, make use of the powers given to me ... to obtain his evidence. (UCPI, 2022c, p 2)

This is a much more forceful response to a former officer's reluctance to provide evidence in public and one which at least recognises that not all former police officers are willing participants in the Inquiry.

The case of HN332 is also an interesting one to note. In October 2022, the Chair revoked a restriction order he had previously made in regards to the former officer's real name (UCPI, 2022i). The restriction order had been made on medical grounds – the poor health of a now elderly man could be worsened if he found himself facing public scrutiny, an interference with his privacy rights that Mitting found was not justified. Upon the former officer's death, before he could be asked to give evidence, Mitting ruled that the grounds for his anonymity order were no longer present. Despite HN332's family plea to respect the wish to remain anonymous posthumously, the Chair decided that identification of the officer, in due course, would be justified in the pursuit of public scrutiny.

## Privacy and data protection

In this chapter, I have so far focused on the uses of human rights discourse and law in the process of anonymisation. These discourses found their basis in the ECHR and their inscription into UK law through the Human Rights Act. But the discourse of rights did not stop there. Indeed, as the avenue of human rights protection appeared to be increasingly populated by police claims to *their* right to privacy under Article 8 of the Convention, the non-police, non-state core participants in the Inquiry looked for a different route to openness.

The twist was provided by the introduction of the European Union's General Data Protection Regulation (GDPR), which was implemented in the UK through the Data Protection Act 2018. In theory, GDPR gives individuals far greater control and rights over their personal data in several ways, including consent, the power to access their personal data or to erase information held about them. Part of the rights outlined by GDPR is the right for citizens to obtain confirmation from the data controller – in most cases a private company or a public authority – as to whether or not personal data concerning them is being processed, where and for what purpose. Significantly, the controller has to provide a copy of the personal data, for free and within 30 days, in an electronic format. There are wide ranging exemptions. Courts and law enforcement, including the police, are outside the scope of GDPR in the UK and receive exemptions in certain circumstances under the Data Protection Act 2018. Data subjects, as defined by the legislation, cannot simply go to the intelligence branch of their local or national police force and demand access to the files containing personal data about them. Nonetheless, many have seen the regulation as a step change in the direction of data transparency and the empowerment of those whose data is collected and stored.

At the start of 2018, a central question arose in the Undercover Policing Inquiry, which led to renewed legal argument between the team of lawyers acting on behalf of the non-police, non-state core participants and the Chair. If the impact of the UK's implementation of GDPR through the new Data Protection Act in 2018 was indeed the empowerment of data subjects, could this also apply to data collected by undercover police officers? The non-police, non-state core participants thought that it might. Regardless of the common exemption of police-held data, personal information about thousands of political activists was now in the possession of the Undercover Policing Inquiry. As data subjects, they had rights protected in law and they sought to exercise those rights.

To the police lawyers, the updated Data Protection Act appeared to come as something of a surprise. At a hearing called to discuss the progress of the Inquiry following the publication of a strategic review in 2018, the lead counsel for the Metropolitan Police Service, Jonathan Hall, tried to reopen the issue of the restriction order approach:

Hall: Sir, the next topic is to ask the Inquiry to ask hard questions of itself about the process for restriction order applications on the basis of privacy. I assume – I don't know – that that model [case-by-case decisions on anonymity] is going to be pursued. But that clearly has enormous resource and time implications.
Chair: It does. If you read the [restriction orders] protocol carefully, I think you can see that there are permissible ways around, provided that we comply with the General Data Protection Regulation.
Hall: Yes. Gosh. Is that a serious road block? (UCPI, 2018g, pp 28–9)

It was indeed a serious road block, though one that the Chair was determined to sweep away. For the purposes of investigating undercover policing, the Metropolitan Police had handed over millions of pages of documents to the Undercover Policing Inquiry. The files, including personal and sensitive information about the individuals who were placed under police surveillance, were now in the hands of a public inquiry, which could *not* (or at least not necessarily) rely on the same exemptions from its GDPR obligations as those provided to law enforcement. In theory, every one of the thousands of people named in the intelligence reports would be entitled to make a request for access to personal data under Article 15 of GDPR, to which the Inquiry would be required to respond by providing a copy of the data.

The issue appeared to send the Inquiry into panic-mode. The Chair quickly convened another preliminary hearing, and then a further one, as he sought to seek clarity as to the public inquiry's responsibilities. Hearings took place on 31 January 2019 and 25 March 2019 and some of the submissions demonstrated how badly the issue of data protection rights was understood on the police side. Sir Robert Francis, a senior barrister who had chaired, among others, the public inquiry into the Stafford Hospital scandal and who represented the National Police Chief's Council, appeared to suggest that the Undercover Policing Inquiry should simply dispose of documents in its possession that were not immediately relevant to its Terms of Reference. Sir John Mitting quickly put this idea to bed. Responding to Francis's insinuation, he said: 'If that means we should shred or burn the documents, I doubt that that would be a useful exercise. It may not even be permissible' (UCPI, 2019f, pp 34–5).

Oliver Sanders KC, on behalf of former undercover officers, wanted to rely on the exemptions to subject access rights granted to courts:

Sanders: In our submission hearing evidence ... doesn't involve processing of personal data for the purposes of General Data Protection Regulations, if it is not done wholly or partly by automated means. That is an exercise which doesn't engage 'the data protection legislation'.

Chair: I can see that. But ordinarily this problem doesn't arise because of the court exemption. The courts do not face this problem at all. But the Inquiry is not a court, at least as I'm presently advised. I know it is being suggested that I am sitting in the judicial capacity. I doubt that, but I will hear submissions about that in due course. (UCPI, 2019f, p 203)

Sanders insisted that only data processed through some form of automation would fall under the remit of GDPR. As is the case in a court of law, the legislation would not apply to oral evidence hearings in the Inquiry:

Sanders: [A]s I speak to you and you speak to me, we are not processing personal data because our brains are not automated.

Chair: Oddly, if I hand you a document to read, I'm processing it, you reading it might not be.

Sanders: A paper document, no. If you email it to me, yes, but not a paper document. (UCPI, 2019f, p 204)

Referring to the non-police, non-state core participant's barrister Gerry Facenna, Mitting appeared to stop in his tracks:

Chair: There is a shaking of a head from a source [Facenna] which I suspect knows better than you or me what the answer is.

Sanders: Well, the data protection legislation obviously when one follows it down ... it bites on automated processing.

Chair: I am afraid you are attracting almost universal dissent. (UCPI, 2019f, p 204)

The Chair's exclamations captured the way that he and the police lawyer were stuck. Apparently, they had both lost themselves in the legislation. It fell to Gerry Facenna KC, acting on behalf of the non-police, non-state core participants, to intervene and put them right. Invited to do so by the Chair, Facenna interjected:

> Shall I just – before we dig the hole any deeper, the definition of processing in the General Data Protection Regulations ...: 'Any operation or set of operations which is performed on personal data or on sets of personal data, whether *or not* [my emphasis] by automated

means such as collection, recording, organisation and everything else.' So it is a red herring. (UCPI, 2019f, pp 204–5)

Facenna seemed to have put to bed the police lawyer's argument and signalled that that GDPR should indeed apply to the data that was now in possession of and processed by the Undercover Policing Inquiry. But he now met the resolve of the Chair to proceed with his Inquiry as he intended. The exchange between Sir John Mitting and Gerry Facenna is instructive. What, the Chair asked, would result from the application of GDPR to the work of the Inquiry? Would it not render impossible 'the proper discharge of the functions of the Inquiry' (UCPI, 2019g, p 21)? Facenna, one of the country's leading barristers in data protection, had met another expression of the brick wall, it seemed:

Facenna: But, sir, it plainly doesn't.
Chair: Forgive me, it does.

Facenna tried to explain his position as clearly as possible. The current approach to disclosure pursued by the Inquiry did not comply with Article 14 of GDPR:

Facenna: Let's assume you receive [a data subject access request under Article 14 of GDPR] from Ms Steel, if she doesn't mind me using her as an example, or Mr O'Driscoll, or another core participant who is already involved with the Inquiry. First of all, if you are processing their data, do you need to notify them? Pretty obviously yes, under Article 14. To suggest that doing so is either impossible or would substantially prejudice the work of the Inquiry seems unsustainable.
Chair: But that is a submission that is not founded on fact. The plain fact is that for the Inquiry to notify every data subject that it had personal data and special category personal data about that subject, and then to provide a copy of that data to them, would be completely impossible.
Facenna: But, sir …
Chair: It would ruin the functioning of the Inquiry.
Facenna: What would be the difference if the Home Office were to say that? If they were to say we don't currently have any processes for dealing with data protection, it would take us years and lots of money and would be incredibly disruptive to have to do that, or indeed any public authority or business. (UCPI, 2019g, pp 21–3)

Mitting would not be put on the spot like that. He retorted that he could not answer for the Home Office. What was on his mind was to find a way to discharge the Terms of Reference he had been given as Chair of the public inquiry and the resources currently available to him. These latter were constrained, he said, to about 60 staff and limited IT capacity. If he was now asked to divert resources to answer subject access requests under GDPR, it would 'scupper the work of the Inquiry' (UCPI, 2019g, p 23). The conflict between Gerry Facenna, on behalf of the non-police, non-state core participants, and the Chair was one of law versus one of 'fact', as Mitting expressed it. If core participants did indeed have enhanced data protection rights under the new legislation, there was nothing that the Inquiry could do to meet them. The 'facts' spoke for themselves and left little room for 'rights'.

## A 'weapon of last resort'

In statements following the submissions at the oral hearings and in writing, Mitting maintained that calls by non-police, non-state core participants for early and full access to documents containing their personal data would not be met. He cited two main arguments against their claims to subject access rights. First, the Inquiry had to maintain the privacy of all those who were spied on by the undercover units and because there are usually several names or identifiers on each intelligence report, giving people their files would also contravene GDPR. And second, if the Inquiry had to go through the millions of pages of conversations, recordings, meeting reports and trivia that the police had collected, to redact them and make them GDPR compliant, it would be so much work that it would effectively shut the Inquiry down. As the Chair put it:

> In the absence of a statutory exemption, every one of the thousands of data subjects named in the intelligence reports would be entitled to make a request for access to personal data under article 15 of the GDPR, to which the Inquiry would be required to respond by providing a copy of the data undergoing processing ... It would not be possible for the Inquiry to discharge this obligation. If it were to use its legal team and IT and administrative resources to do so, the substantive work of the Inquiry would come to a halt. (UCPI, 2019c, p 3)

In a nutshell, Mitting admitted that the Inquiry could not be lawful and exist; and its existence had to trump its lawfulness.

The Chair's solution to the conundrum of lawfulness and existence was as troubling as earlier decisions and again showed the Inquiry's entanglement in circular arguments around what constitutes the public interest to meet its Terms of Reference. Mitting reasoned that, as the public inquiry would discharge the function of getting to the truth and protecting citizens from bad policing, it was exempt from its GDPR obligation. Any other interpretation could not have been as parliament intended, he argued: 'A public inquiry set up under the Inquiries Act 2005 is the weapon of last resort available to the Government to get to the truth and inform remedial action' (UCPI, 2019b, p 5). If privacy protection legislation had the effect of slowing or hindering the discharge of the Inquiry's Terms, this would interfere in its ability to make recommendations that would, ultimately, ensure that abusive undercover policing could not occur in the future. Showing those targeted by undercover police their files would prevent the Inquiry from protecting those who could be targeted in the future. Once again, the circle squared itself.

## From human rights to political expression

Why did restrictions to disclosure and anonymity orders become the linchpin around which the public inquiry revolved for several years? How were they justified and to what extent did they undermine the public nature of the Inquiry itself? The answers I have given across this and previous chapters are reasonably obvious. While state and police core participants in the Inquiry shared an interest in maximum secrecy, those members of the public designated as non-state and non-police demanded maximum openness. Successive rulings by both Inquiry Chairs tended to find in favour of police arguments for confidentiality. Below this sits a more complex picture that tells us something about the ways that such arguments were based in law and enveloped in discourses of rights. The language of human rights and privacy, in particular, has become a powerful tool in the Inquiry. It is not a tool yielded, however, by those whose human rights and privacy were violated by undercover deployments.

I began this chapter by looking at Wendy Brown's well-known characterisation of rights-based claims in social movements as paradoxical – they can both be a route to emancipation *and* restrictions to emancipatory aims. Others, too, have considered the paradox of human rights as a tool for anti-oppressive practice 'from below' and at the same time as an instrument of law that can be used, or abused, by powerful interests. The point is an obvious one: despite the rootedness of human rights in the politics of social movements – they emerge, in the words of social movement theorist Neil Stammers, as 'struggle concepts' – their institutionalisation can mean that their original meaning gets lost or 'switched in ways that result in human rights becoming a tool of power, not a challenge to it' (Stammers, 2009, p 3). Recourse to human rights by social movements is therefore both complex and ambivalent. This ambiguity is not lost on social movements either. They may appeal to the language and law of human rights in challenging injustice and hegemonic expressions of power; yet they also push beyond them. It is what Stammers refers to as the 'paradox of institutionalisation'.

The public inquiry into undercover policing represents an institutionalisation of the human rights claims made by those targeted by undercover police operations. We can witness the paradox at play because the Inquiry was celebrated as a moment of official acknowledgement and at the same time it had become an institutional mechanism that was experienced as a form of state power over social movement activists.

The institutionalisation of human rights claims has had further, unintended consequences. The rights framework employed by activists was also available to their adversaries in state institutions. Those pursuing an investigation of the infringements of the rights to a private life under Article 8 now found this pursuit blocked by rival claims to privacy rights by the undercover officers and the police leadership. In particular, the determination of restriction order applications made on behalf of former police officers pushed the concerns of non-police, non-state core participants further into the background. Sir Christopher Pitchford had recognised that '[n]on-police, non-state witnesses participate as "victims" of invasion' of privacy. They are pursuing their Article 8 right to discover the truth' (UCPI, 2016j, p 9). Through the restriction orders process, it now fell to the former police officers, the 'wrongdoers', to pursue *their* Article 8 right to conceal elements of the truth.

Significant resources in the Undercover Policing Inquiry were invested into considering the human rights claims of undercover police officers. Media or activist interest in their post-undercover careers, their personal lives and that of their immediate family were all taken into consideration when determining the competing interests to openness and secrecy. As far as I know, there have been no cases in which former officers, or members of their families, have been physically harmed by those who they had infiltrated. Journalistic interest has been high in a small number of cases, such as those of Bob Lambert and Mark Kennedy, but has been defended by media companies as legitimate reporting on matters of public concern. In very few cases have there been vocal calls for accountability of former officers who had deceived women into long-term relationships, calls led or supported by those women themselves. Bob Lambert and Andy Coles have both faced protests at their places of work; Lambert eventually left his academic positions and Coles stood down as Cambridgeshire and Peterborough's Deputy Police and Crime Commissioner. Whether these protests constitute 'harassment' has not been tested in court and it is strongly rejected by the campaigners themselves.

Rights-based claims have of course been made by and on behalf of the 'victims' of undercover policing. In civil courts and in the Investigatory Powers Tribunal, for example, campaigners have achieved important victories, based on the acknowledged truth that they had indeed been victims of human rights abuses. In the Inquiry, on the other hand, non-police core participants have found other ways to raise their voices. Chapter 7 is therefore devoted to a discussion of acts of defiance and resistance by the targets of covert police surveillance, within the Inquiry and beyond it.

# 7

# In and against the Undercover Policing Inquiry

## Fighting for transparency

"The inquiry is a farce." These were the words of Alison, a pseudonym for a core participant in the Undercover Policing Inquiry who was deceived into a relationship with an undercover police officer. Alison was one of eight women who took legal action against the Metropolitan Police over the conduct of undercover officers. Writing in *The Guardian*, she named the hurdles that I detailed in the earlier chapters: 'hours of legalese and Kafkaeseque arguments based on redacted documents and closed sessions' (Alison, 2018). Like Alison, many of the core participants I spoke to for my research felt completely overwhelmed by the expectations put upon them. They reported that communication with and from the Inquiry was legalistic and lacked transparency. But more than anything else, they lacked the resources – the time and money – to engage with it fully. Some core participants told me that they felt unable to keep up with the details of the dispute that began to emerge around the entrenched position of the police lawyers and that they were overloaded with information.

For most of them, the formation of campaigns around the Inquiry was the best way to achieve some kind of impact on the process itself. By and large, they trusted those who emerged as unofficial spokespeople for the non-police, non-state core participants, as well as their legal representatives, to synthesise the most important information and to lead the challenge against the Neither Confirm Nor Deny (NCND) approach adopted by the police organisations. New transparency-focused campaign groups sprung up and they offered some of the most effective and critical challenges to the secrecy that prevailed in the official process. In this chapter, I specifically highlight the work of Police Spies Out of Lives, a group that offered support to the women who took legal action against the police. Others, too, such as the Campaign Opposing Police Surveillance and the Undercover Research Group (URG) have played a central role in scrutinising decisions taken in the Undercover Policing Inquiry. The Blacklist Support Group, the Monitoring Group and Netpol have also been vital in seeking justice for those affected by political undercover policing.

While the purpose of this chapter is to spotlight a few of the events in which spycops victims sought to challenge excessive secrecy, both inside and outside the public inquiry, it is also a reminder that many of the non-police, non-state core participants remain politically active. Though they were victims of spycops policing, I have been careful not to overuse the marker of victimhood in this book for this reason. The participants who are at the heart of the Inquiry, even while they find themselves marginalised from it, are also outspoken advocates for justice, transparency and accountability. They have refused to be silent and silenced. The public inquiry, seen through this lens, was therefore also a site of political agency and resistance to secrecy. Many of the arguments addressing secrecy and disclosure were fought over in this narrow confinement of a statutory inquiry, but they also extended beyond it, or in other words, 'in and against' the public inquiry.[1]

## Challenging the Terms of Reference

On 16 July 2015, Theresa May issued the Terms of Reference for the Undercover Policing Inquiry, which set out the purpose, scope and methods of the Inquiry (see Appendix A). There was no further public consultation on what they should entail.[2] There were some notable omissions. Foremost, the Terms of Reference ask the Inquiry Chair to stick only to narrow, national limits, namely to inquire into undercover policing 'by English and Welsh police forces in England and Wales'. The spycops operations extended to all nations of the United Kingdom and they were international. The Inquiry, by contrast, stops at the border. The activities of undercover officers when travelling outside England and Wales fall outside of its remit. But activists who were targeted in Scotland, Northern Ireland and other countries are ineligible for core participant status.

The Home Secretary's decision to not extend the Undercover Policing Inquiry's remit to cover Scotland was challenged early on. The protests in summer 2005 opposing the G8 summit held in the Scottish golf resort of Gleneagles were still fresh in people's minds. Several undercover officers were present here, getting centrally involved in the organisation of direct action to disrupt the meeting of world leaders. Activists who suspected that undercover officers had spied on them in Scotland found themselves excluded from the Inquiry. The Scottish government called on the Home Secretary to amend the Terms of Reference and allow the Inquiry to investigate the behaviour of police spies in Scotland. The Scottish Secretary for Justice wrote to Theresa May at the end of 2015 to ensure that Sir Christopher Pitchford would look at, for example, the role of English police officers in the Gleneagles protests (Hutcheon and Gordon, 2015). However, when their request was not accepted, the Scottish government denied campaigners an equivalent public inquiry there. Instead, it tasked the Inspectorate of Constabulary in Scotland to examine the matter. When the report came back it was decried as another whitewash: it had focused on a limited time period and failed to even mention the sexual relationships that officers had with their targets. Campaigners for transparency denounced it as another instance of the police marking their own homework (Campaign Opposing Police Surveillance, 2017).

The issue finally came to a head in a judicial review sought by the environmental campaigner Tilly Gifford. Gifford was an activist with the anti-aviation protest group Plane Stupid. In 2009, she was involved in an action to temporarily close down Aberdeen airport, protesting its plans for expansion (Lewis, 2009). The action drew the attention of the authorities. Two officers claiming to be from Strathclyde Police approached Gifford, then 24, and attempted to convince her to become an informant. In two meetings, one which Gifford covertly recorded, they offered her cash in exchange for information about the group and its tactics. The activist leaked the story to the national press, together with the recordings she had made of the police officers' approach. It demonstrated that the high-risk infiltration of protest groups remains just one line of intelligence work by the police; another is the recruitment of informants from within political movements themselves.[3]

The secret voice recording provided an insightful glimpse into the methods used to persuade campaigners to become police informants. Gifford had student loans to pay off and the officers seemingly offered her significant amounts of money in return for information about environmental activists in Plane Stupid. "UK plc can afford more than 20 quid", one is heard as saying. He is keen to point out that this would be "tax-free" money and that Gifford was free to give it to charity if she wanted to. But there would be more than financial incentives. The young activist could join a network of spies that, the officers said, stretched to hundreds of informants, including many in protest groups and organisations from across the political spectrum. One declared, without a hint of irony, that "people would sell their soul to the devil". There were warnings, too. Continued engagement with direct action and unlawful protest activity could have severe consequences for Gifford, the officers said. Without some kind of police protection, future arrests and convictions could mean that she may struggle to find employment or that she could be imprisoned together with "hard, evil" offenders (Lewis, 2009).

The experience made the Plane Stupid campaigner wonder about the extent of the police informants' network and the possibility of undercover officer infiltration in activist groups across Scotland. Gifford set up the Scottish chapter of the Campaign Opposing Police Surveillance, but her probing led to more questions than answers. Gifford wanted to know if police in Scotland had used undercover deployments into protest groups but was excluded from participating in the Undercover Policing Inquiry. Her judicial review was against the decision of the Home Secretary to not extend the Undercover Policing Inquiry to Scotland and simultaneously against the Scottish government's refusal to order its own public inquiry.

Ultimately, the legal challenge was unsuccessful. The apparent attempts by undercover police officers to recruit Tilly Gifford as an informant were not regarded as sufficiently grave infringements of the activist's rights to invoke their protection under the European Convention on Human Rights (see McKerrell, 2019).

This notwithstanding, the international dimension of the spycops scandal could not be denied. In October 2022, a German court found that Mark Kennedy's operation in the northern state of Mecklenburg-Vorpommern was unlawful as it lacked the necessary judicial authorisation (Oltermann and Evans, 2022). The case had been brought by Jason Kirkpatrick, a Berlin-based activist who had been befriended by Kennedy in Northern Ireland, in the run-up to the 2005 G8 summit in Scotland. Kennedy then visited Kirkpatrick in Germany several times in his undercover persona and was present at the protests against the G8 summit that took place in June 2007 in Heiligendamm. It remains a source of great frustration for many core participants that the Undercover Policing Inquiry does not investigate these spycops deployments abroad.

## Withdrawing from participation

Across this book I have described the public inquiry as a site of struggle, in which matters of scope, disclosure and participation were fought over by the assembled teams of legal representatives. Inside, the lawyers for the victims were outnumbered and largely failed to influence the Chair's stance towards secrecy and anonymity for former officers. Repeatedly, they had expressed their frustrations at the delay in the proceedings, which they attributed to deliberate police obfuscation. They continued to argue that the cover names of undercover officers should be published, alongside contemporaneous photographs, to allow more of those targeted by spycops to come forward. And they demanded access to their clients' intelligence files. Most of all, they highlighted that Sir John Mitting was an establishment figure who appeared to accept police testimony without critical interrogation.

Leading the way was Phillippa Kaufmann. She was one of the lawyers for the women who sued the police over the deceptive relationships initiated by undercover policemen. Since the start of the Undercover Policing Inquiry, she has been instructed to act on behalf of over two hundred non-police, non-state core participants. Kaufmann is an experienced human rights advocate who has acted in high-profile cases. In 2019, she successfully challenged the Parole Board's decision to release John Worboys from prison on behalf of two of his victims. In the Undercover Policing Inquiry, Kaufmann gave voice to the frustration of the victims of police spying and their worries about an investigation led by a man who appeared to possess little understanding of sexism and racism. Addressing a preliminary hearing on anonymity applications made by the Metropolitan Police, Kaufmann got straight to the point. 'I'm sorry to say this', she started her submission, and went on: 'we have the usual white, upper middle class, elderly gentleman whose life experiences are a million miles away from those who were spied upon' (UCPI, 2018h, p 9). It was a devastating characterisation of Mitting, but the Chair did not flinch. More was to come. Not only had Mitting demonstrated his unsuitability, he seemed to have accepted that his views on sexual relationships outside marriage might be 'a little naive and old-fashioned' (UCPI, 2018d, p 119). This unfortunate self-characterisation was seized upon by the lawyers for the women who had been tricked into intimate relationships with undercover officers. Yet, confronted with what Kaufmann called the 'astonished, disbelieving, uncomprehending and dismayed response of everybody here' (UCPI, 2018h, p 10), Mitting stuck to his views. He was incapable of learning and unwilling to comprehend the experiences of the spycops victims.

There was no coming back from this. Some of the non-police, non-state core participants clearly wanted Mitting 'sacked' from the Inquiry; in their eyes, he was entirely unsuited to the job. Others made concrete demands of a panel of experts, to include some with life experience of dealing with institutional racism and sexism, to sit alongside him. Kaufmann put this to him during the preliminary hearing:

> The core participants, the non-state, non-police core participants, do not want this important Inquiry, something that they so richly deserve to have conducted in an efficacious way, to be presided over by someone who is both naive and old-fashioned and does not understand the world that they or the police inhabit. (UCPI, 2018h, p 11)

It got to the point of the legitimacy that the Inquiry possessed in the eyes of two hundred of its participants:

> We are not prepared actively to participate in a process where the presence of our clients is pure window dressing, lacking all substance, lacking all meaning and which would achieve absolutely nothing other than lending this process the legitimacy that it doesn't have and doesn't deserve. (UCPI, 2018h, p 9)

Kaufmann knew that her submissions would not cut through. And she had been instructed to try something more forceful:

> Now, as matters stand, those clients who have given instructions ... are not prepared to continue to participate in today's hearing. I am instructed, therefore, together with the entire legal team, to withdraw

from this hearing while these issues are considered by you. That is all I have to say this morning. (UCPI, 2018h, p 12)

She gathered her files and left her seat. The non-state participants and their supporters, too, got up from their chairs at the back of court 73 in the Royal Courts of Justice and followed their legal representatives down the stairs and onto the pavement outside the front entrance. There, they unfurled a banner reading: *Tear down the #spycops inquiry's brick wall of silence*, a reference to Sir John Mitting's words when setting his expectations for total secrecy in some cases.

The walk out was a crucial moment in the Inquiry, even though it received little public acknowledgement from Mitting himself. It signalled the deep-seated frustrations of many who had chosen to participate in the proceedings and it showed their willingness to abandon the state-led investigation in favour of applying pressure from outside. Yet, it also betrayed a certain level of powerlessness. What could the threat to withhold participation in the Inquiry achieve, when the Chair had given little indication on when and how non-state witnesses would be invited to provide evidence? Mitting made it clear that he regarded the evidence from non-police sources as less than essential. In his 33-page strategic review of the Inquiry's progress, published in May 2018, he wrote that '[t]he absence of evidence from significant non-state witnesses would of course be regrettable and would mean that the foundation for the findings of fact which I could make would be less extensive than would be the case with it; but *it would not undermine the purpose of the Inquiry*' (UCPI, 2018i, p 4, emphasis added). The strategic review document further demonstrated the sanguine attitude of the Chair towards the issues raised by Kaufmann and others. He was determined to press on, regardless of their cooperation, and with only the police testimony to go by:

> It is not only the Inquiry which is at a crossroads. If, as has been reported, some non-state core participants are undecided whether or not to continue to participate in the Inquiry, the time for decision will soon arrive. The strategic review sets out how the Inquiry will attempt to find out what happened and why on the assumption that non-state core participants do participate. I do not intend to use coercive powers to make them do so. If they do not, the Inquiry will get as close to the truth as it can without them. (UCPI, 2018i, p 3)

The non-police, non-state core participants heeded that warning. They continued, to the best of their ability, to assist the Inquiry and their recognised legal representatives made opening statements on their behalf in November 2020. The question of whether their participation is meaningful, however, has not gone away. In a survey carried out in 2021 by Nathan

Stephens-Griffin (2022), activists affected by spycops deployments were almost unanimous in wanting the Inquiry to succeed, but they equally continued to express their lack of trust in the process. Three quarters of respondents, for example, agreed with the statement that the Undercover Policing Inquiry 'looks likely to be a whitewash'.

## 'Paid to lie'

The secrecy and opaqueness at the heart of the public inquiry was challenged from within, led by outspoken core participants and their legal representatives. They issued call after call for increased transparency, using the legal avenues available to them while simultaneously expanding the legal terrain on which they could act. In most part, they remained unsuccessful, coming up against the Chair's metaphorical brick wall of silence.

The lack of transparency in the public inquiry and the Chair's sole authority over the proceedings were also challenged from without, through campaigns that sought to garner wider public attention. One of the most intriguing, and controversial, attempts to open the public inquiry up to wider scrutiny was fronted by the cosmetics store Lush, a mainstay of British high streets and ethical shopping. Lush is no stranger to political and environmental campaigning. The company's founders and owners have been more than explicit in developing an ethical and animal cruelty free business model. Since 2007, the company has sold a popular hand and body lotion to raise money for small charities and grassroots activism on issues of animal protection, human rights and the environment. It has supported, for example, direct action groups like Sea Shepherd, UK Uncut and the Hunt Saboteurs Association.[4] Once this history is taken into account, it comes no longer as a surprise that Lush would take an interest in the spycops scandal. The very activists that received support from the company had been treated as 'domestic extremists' by police forces and subjected to covert surveillance.

In 2018, the company decorated its shop windows with fake police tape, spelling out the slogan 'police have crossed the line'. The displays also featured a poster depicting the portrait of a man whose appearance was split between that of a clean-shaven police constable and a bearded activist. In bold lettering, the image was subscripted with the words 'Paid to Lie'. It was intended to draw attention to the deceptive tactics used by the spycops units. Shoppers were invited to fill in postcards that would be sent to the Home Office. While the primary aim of this petition was for the Home Secretary to appoint a diverse panel of experts to sit with Sir John Mitting in the Undercover Policing Inquiry, it also included the wider aims of demanding the release of officers' cover names and of intelligence files.

Lush had worked closely with the support group Police Spies Out of Lives and the campaign was informed by several women's accounts of the spycops operations and the impact on their lives. The company's charitable giving coordinator, Rebecca Lush, stated the campaign's objectives:

> When Theresa May launched this public inquiry we all hoped that the truth about this scandal would finally be exposed and that the disgraceful police tactics would be examined. Instead, the public inquiry chair is making the inquiry more secretive and is granting the police anonymity in secret hearings. It is time the home secretary listened to the victims and appointed a diverse panel to hear the full evidence. (Cited in Belam, 2018)

Rebecca Lush was no stranger to activism herself. She had been a long-standing and well-known climate and sustainable transport campaigner and had been imprisoned for breaching a protest injunction at the Twyford Down direct action camp, which was set up to oppose the extension of the M3 motorway in 1992.

The company's efforts were quickly met with a wave of police and political backlash. The Home Secretary Sajid Javid replied to the demands by reiterating his belief that the Undercover Policing Inquiry would be conducted in a 'transparent, open manner', though he failed to address the wider public call for disclosure. Instead, he answered with a strongly worded condemnation that framed the transparency and anti-surveillance campaign as an anti-police crusade. Javid was quoted in a national newspaper: 'Never thought I would see a mainstream British retailer running a public advertising campaign against our hardworking police' (Javid, cited in Stephens-Griffin, 2020, p 186). In this way the Home Secretary repeated the logic of the undercover police units themselves, who placed police accountability groups under targeted surveillance with the justification that they represented the thin wedge of extremist hostility to legitimate policing.

Javid was not the only one. The vice-chair of the Police Federation wrote on Twitter: 'This is [a] very poorly thought out campaign and damaging to the overwhelmingly large majority of police who have nothing to do with this' (cited in Stephens-Griffin, 2020, p 186). Similar sentiments were expressed by the Director General of the National Crime Agency and other senior police leaders.

It was not so much that the campaign backfired, but Nathan Stephens-Griffin's study of how the media reported the fallout from the Lush intervention shows the extent to which narratives of 'rotten apples' re-emerged to counter the idea that the secretive culture of policing should receive public scrutiny. Transparency campaigners and victims of police spying had used the Twitter hashtag #spycops to build a community of activists and observers around the Undercover Policing Inquiry. Now, established online communities of police officers and their supporters employed the hashtag #notallcops to lead the backlash against the Lush campaign. Their concerted efforts had a huge impact on the media framing of the campaign. As Stephens-Griffin describes it, much of the media coverage that followed uncritically accepted the line that the Lush campaign was 'anti-police'. The *Daily Mail*, for example, used a quote by the former Metropolitan Police officer and prominent media commentator Peter Kirkham: 'Your anti police advertising campaign is an utter disgrace. It stereotypes ALL police officers as corrupt and includes some fundamental misrepresentations of the facts. I trust that you will never again seek police assistance if you are the victims of crime' (cited in Stephens-Griffin, 2020, p 186). In ways that echoed the legal strategy used by the Metropolitan Police in the public inquiry, influential figures in the press were allowed to turn attention away from the abuses against the women who had collaborated with Lush on their campaign and instead painted the calls for transparency and accountability as attacks on the police institution.

The company was forced to limit the damage. It issued a clarification of its support for mainstream policing and temporarily pulled the shop window displays. The controversial image of the police officer in disguise with the subtitle 'Paid to Lie' was permanently removed. Lush explained its decision to alter its campaign in the face of criticism, stating: 'we have taken away the distraction of, what turned out to be, a controversial visual to return the focus onto the shocking facts' (cited in Stephens-Griffin, 2020, p 181). The decision was made after several of its customer-facing staff reported being intimidated by people claiming to be former police officers (Evans, 2018). Among the media outrage and the hostility on social media, those affected by the undercover deployments struggled to be heard. Only sometimes their voices cut through, in unexpected ways. For instance, the son of an undercover police officer, who has been given the pseudonym initials 'TBS' as a core participant in the Undercover Policing Inquiry, supported the Lush campaign. In a letter published by *The Guardian*, he explained how the police were unwilling to provide him with any answers to his searching questions about who his biological father was and that he felt forced to seek disclosure through the courts (TBS, 2018).

The Lush incident reflects the tension between attempts to hold undercover policing to account and the idea that any criticism of the police would undermine its function. Lush's symbolic campaign and petition put pressure on the Home Secretary, and the company's action is a good example of how campaigns for greater transparency and public scrutiny can work as a catalyst for change. But while it certainly shone a spotlight on the undercover policing scandal, perhaps even reaching an audience that had remained unaware of the harms caused by the spycops operations, the immediate mainstream reaction continued to demonstrate its denial. The campaign apparently did not gain recognition from the official channels of the public inquiry itself. But in teaming up with the women of the Police Spies Out of Lives group, it succeeded in once again bringing to the foreground the voices of the victims of spycops policing. It is their stories, and their perseverance and resilience in re-telling these stories that has kept alive the hope for justice and accountability.

## Broadcasting the hearings

Established in 2015, the Undercover Policing Inquiry finally held its first evidence session at the end of 2020. For much of that year, public life had been placed under various restrictions due to the COVID-19 pandemic. Just days before the hearings were due to begin the UK government announced new measures. On the evening of Saturday, 31 October 2020, the then Prime Minister Boris Johnson gave a televised press conference to announce new, stricter public health regulations. From early November, he said, the public *must stay at home*. People residing in England could only leave their homes for specific reasons, for example education, essential work and limited outdoor recreation. Though the measures abandoned the regional and local 'tiered' approach that he had adopted only weeks earlier, Johnson was keen to stress that this was not a return to a full lockdown. Schools, colleges, universities and many workplaces, for example, would remain open.

What it meant for the Inquiry's face-to-face work was not entirely clear. The Chair had committed to hear oral evidence from non-state witnesses and former police officers during November 2020 but these proceedings were now overshadowed by the continuing public health crisis and the uncertainty surrounding the latest regulations. Unable to delay the evidence phase any further, the Inquiry's resolution to the problem could not have been satisfactory to anyone involved.

For the first seven days, the Inquiry heard opening statements made by David Barr, counsel to the Inquiry, and lawyers representing the state and non-state core participants. It also heard directly from Dave Smith of the Blacklist Support Group, Dónal O'Driscoll of the URG, Helen Steel, a category 'H' core participant, and Dave Morris of London Greenpeace. These statements were streamed in real time on the Inquiry's YouTube channel and recordings remain available on its website.

Following these, Sir John Mitting had invited oral evidence from nine state witnesses and two non-state witnesses, across a further six days of hearings. The procedure for obtaining the evidence from police witnesses whose identities were protected by restriction orders had been subject to considerable debate. Already before the first national lockdown, the Chair had ruled out a live video feed of the proceedings, as had become customary, for example, in the Grenfell Tower Inquiry, mostly to protect the identity of police witnesses. Instead of a publicly accessible video or audio feed, a single live stream of the oral evidence was to be transmitted to a venue in a central London hotel. Observers had to attend in person and register for one of the 60 available seats to view a video link to the virtual hearings.

With the new health protection regulations coming into effect, Sir John Mitting adopted new measures, which further restricted who could view or hear the evidence. They limited attendance at the hotel to view a live stream of the proceedings to core participants, their recognised lawyers and journalists only. The public was excluded. All that remained available was a transcript of what was said, which rolled across the Inquiry's YouTube channel in real time, but without video or audio. The situation was farcical, considering that the Inquiry had taken five years of dealing with preliminary matters to get to this point. There was no exemption to cover researchers or other observers and so I was reliant, in large part, on the volunteer work of transparency activists – foremost the core participant Tom Fowler – who tweeted from the hotel room.

The activists at the Campaign Opposing Police Surveillance rightly asked: 'Why can we watch Grenfell hearings on YouTube yet the [Undercover Policing Inquiry] only gives us what amounts to speeded-up Ceefax?' (Campaign Opposing Police Surveillance, 2020b). They were not alone. Dominic Casciani, then the home and legal correspondent for BBC News, complained in a thread he posted to Twitter:

> There is a livestream of the undercover policing inquiry here – but it is virtually unusable for reporters trying to follow it remotely. The words are appearing via a fast scrolling video feed that can't be paused or rewound.
>
> I can't type that fast to copy down everything. If I could hear the audio – which we are not allowed to do – I could take down quotes in shorthand. We cannot scroll back to check quotes. 20 years ago at the Bloody Sunday Inquiry, we could do that.
>
> This basically means, from a practical perspective as a working reporter, that a public inquiry becomes largely impossible to report. (Casciani, 2020)

Casciani pointed to other arrangements for remote access to legal proceedings, including also audio access to preliminary hearings of the Manchester Arena Inquiry during COVID-19 restrictions. The measures taken by Mitting went far beyond any of them.

Commenting underneath the Twitter thread, another user made a suggestion: could a BBC colleague work with Casciani and read out the rolling transcript, so that he was free to take notes? Casciani replied: 'The BBC does not have those kinds of resources – nor do other news organisations' (Casciani, 2020). It is testament to their resourcefulness, therefore, that the transparency campaigners at Police Spies Out of Lives found a way to overcome this obstacle. The group used its own YouTube channel to broadcast live readings of what they could see on the Inquiry's rolling transcript. In that way, followers could 'hear' what was being said in the Inquiry – though, of course, intonation, pauses or other features of the oral evidence remained lost and were transmitted with plenty of artistic licence. The idea caught on. For later hearings, the group enlisted support from high-profile actors, including Maxine Peake, to read out some of the evidence given at the hearings (Darling, 2020). It highlighted that an audio stream could have been provided by the Inquiry, even if it wanted to restrict the use of images to protect the identity of police witnesses. More fundamentally, it brought into sharp focus the importance of inquiry hearings that the public have access to. In this way, the transparency campaigners 'gave voice' – quite literally – to the police witnesses in these early evidence hearings.

## Human rights claims in the Investigatory Powers Tribunal

A year later, on 30 September 2021, a milestone was reached in terms of the human rights claims made by victims of undercover police abuses. Campaigners celebrated, yet this was unrelated to the public inquiry and also not a win achieved in the European Court of Human Rights. Instead, an obscure tribunal financed by the Home Office, yet independent from it, had issued a judgment in the case *Wilson v The Commissioner of Police of the Metropolis and the National Police Chiefs' Council*. The Investigatory Powers Tribunal (IPT) found, in a 158-page ruling, that the police had violated the human rights of an environmental and social justice activist, Kate Wilson. The Tribunal ruled that Wilson's European Convention rights were infringed on by the deployment of Mark Kennedy into her life and by the sexual relationship Kennedy had with her.

Kate Wilson had long been politically active in a range of social justice and environmental campaigns. After completing a university degree at Oxford, she moved to Nottingham where she met 'Mark Stone', the National Public Order Intelligence Unit (NPOIU) officer whose exposure by his partner Lisa brought the existence of spycops in social movements to public attention. 'Stone', the alias used by the undercover policeman Kennedy, had among others infiltrated Nottingham's Sumac Centre, a self-organised community space that was used by activists in the city and beyond. There are many remarkable facets to Wilson's experience. Not only was she deceived into a relationship with Kennedy, she has also been affected by the deployments of several other spycops. For example, 'Lynn Watson', who infiltrated the Sumac Centre's sister space in Leeds (the Common Place), appeared well aware that Wilson and Kennedy were in an intimate relationship. It seemed to prove that the use of relationships was at least acquiesced to, if not designed as a tactic within the undercover units.

Wilson's case was heard in the Investigatory Powers Tribunal, a fact that was at first seen as a defeat of the claimant's requests for disclosure and accountability. Like other women deceived by policemen into relationships after 1998, when the Human Rights Act took effect, Wilson had fought against the police's argument that her human rights claims should be heard in the secretive IPT. After a lengthy legal battle, the High Court ruled that it had no jurisdiction in the matter and the Court of Appeal later found that the IPT was the proper forum to consider the claims. Academic study of the IPT is rare and not without reason. Formed by the Regulation of Investigatory Powers Act (RIPA) 2000, the IPT adjudicates on matters related to, among others, the legality of state surveillance by security and intelligence agencies such as MI5 and GCHQ. Until the Investigatory Powers Act 2016, there was no effective right of appeal.

The IPT is, at least in part, a feature of the legal landscape in the UK following the implementation of the Human Rights Act 1998, and so fulfils the necessary function of securing compliance with the Convention's obligations. Yet, until recently, the Tribunal was hardly regarded as a safeguard against human rights abuses. Its reception in legal thinking has therefore often noted its skewed focus on national security considerations with little regard to open justice. One such recent commentary proposes that:

> [P]roceedings in the IPT are broadly regarded as outright 'secret justice', and critics have described its unique procedures as 'Kafkaesque'. Much of this reproach emanates from a friction between the need for intelligence activities to operate covertly, and the need for lawful and transparent governmental accountability. As a result of this struggle, reforms in this area have tended to be 'uniformly backward-looking and begrudging', with the intent being on protecting investigatory powers while barely meeting minimum human rights requirements. (Wilson, 2020, p 130)

There have been challenges to the IPT's status outside the normal principles of open justice. In 2019, the Supreme Court ruled in a case brought by the civil liberties organisation Privacy International that decisions made by the Tribunal's judges are liable to judicial reviews by the High Court. This was despite a clause in the relevant legislation, RIPA 2000, which apparently shielded IPT determinations from being questioned by other courts. In this case, the government argued that opening up the IPT to judicial reviews would undermine its role in considering secret evidence. A majority Supreme Court judgment found, however, that the RIPA wording was not explicit enough to place the Tribunal outside the jurisdiction of the High Court.

None of this fundamentally changed the way that cases heard in the IPT operate. At the discretion of the court, cases can be heard in private and complainants prevented from accessing the information relied on by the defence. Yet, it was here that Kate Wilson received more answers about the deployments targeting her than in the ostensibly *public* inquiry. Wilson's case against the police was wide ranging. More than questions of sexual relationships as a strategy for infiltration used by undercover officers, she sought admissions on her human rights protected by Articles 3, 8, 10, 11 and 14 of the European Convention. Her 'boyfriend', Mark Kennedy, had deceived her into a long-term relationship and played a major part in a period of her and her family's lives.

The judgment was made unanimously by the panel comprising of Lord Boyd of Duncansby, a former Lord Advocate for Scotland, Mrs Justice Lieven, a judge in the High Court's family division, and Graham Zellick, Emeritus Professor of Law, a former vice-chancellor of the University of London and former Chair of the Criminal Cases Review Commission. The three judges were clearly in recognition of the deep psychological impact that the police deployments had on Kate Wilson. And they acknowledged that any concessions on the part of the police were hard fought for: 'Were it not for [Wilson's] tenacity and perseverance, often in the face of formidable difficulties, much of what this case has revealed would not have come to light', they said (Investigatory Powers Tribunal, 2021, p 129). The judgment stated that the claimant had uncovered a 'formidable list of Convention violations' and that the handling of the police deployment revealed 'disturbing and lamentable failings at the most fundamental levels' (Investigatory Powers Tribunal, 2021, p 128). This was more than just a telling off and Wilson was awarded significant damages.

The ruling proved cathartic for Wilson and her supporters. This was even more so because the Metropolitan Police lawyers had taken every opportunity available to them to obfuscate and delay. As one legal scholar observed, the Tribunal's judgment showed that 'a still entrenched feature of policing in this country is the efforts that are made to evade scrutiny of procedures, protocols and chains of command when serious questions are raised about the conduct of particular officers' (Tuitt, nd). Faced with police resistance to accountability, the human rights claims had overcome a major obstacle.

Despite this victory, the ruling did not quite go as far as Wilson and others had hoped. The Tribunal found no evidence that the sexual relationships entertained by undercover officers were part of a 'deliberate tactic' and instead proposed that they resulted from a position of 'don't ask, don't tell'. It also allowed the Metropolitan Police to rely on its NCND position in regards to other men who Mark Kennedy introduced into Kate Wilson's life and who she suspected of being police officers.

Nonetheless, its findings were significant in recognising the human rights violations. The IPT found that the Metropolitan Police and the National Police Chiefs' Council had failed to protect Wilson's Article 3 Convention rights (no one shall be subjected to torture or to inhuman or degrading treatment or punishment). There were insufficient safeguards, inadequate training, failures of supervision and a lack of foresight in the police organisations that managed the Kennedy deployment. The Metropolitan Police and the National Police Chiefs' Council were also in breach of Wilson's Article 8 rights (the right to respect for her private and family life, her home and her correspondence). The deployment of an undercover officer into her private sphere, the length and the level of intrusion 'did not meet a pressing social need and was not necessary in a democratic society and not proportionate based on either the need for intelligence on the protest movement or on the claimant's own activities' (Investigatory Powers Tribunal, 2022, p 4). The Tribunal found the deployment to be unlawful and in breach of the provisions in the Regulation of Investigatory Powers Act. The ruling did, however, state that where undercover deployments were in accordance with RIPA, they would be justified.

The Tribunal also found that Wilson's rights under Article 14 of the Convention (prohibition of discrimination) had been violated. There had been no thought given by the police organisations to the differential impact of the sexual relationships on women, nor a justification for the disproportionate deployment of male officers into the lives of women. The judges said that the deployment of Mark Kennedy also infringed on Wilson's Article 10 and Article 11 rights – those to freedom of expression and freedom of peaceful assembly. It was unlawful, and 'not necessary in a democratic society' for the undercover officer to interfere with the applicant's personal and political beliefs or for him to directly influence the expression of these opinions.

The IPT ruling now takes a central place in the story of the women who seek answers and justice about the deceptions they experienced at the hands of the police. It may be that the public inquiry was a privileged arena in which they could participate – a form of 'official acknowledgement'. But it is the Tribunal's ruling on the violations of Wilson's human rights that provides that acknowledgement in terms of the harms the women have experienced. Perhaps most crucially, the Tribunal ruled that the police had infringed on Wilson's Article 10 and Article 11 rights. This was not just a matter of her bodily autonomy, as important as this is, but it offers the recognition that the policing operations had a political function. The Special Demonstration Squad (SDS) and NPOIU were secretive police units that undermined basic political rights to do with political expression and freedom of assembly and their operations could not be justified.

## Protest in a democratic society

The Undercover Policing Inquiry has faced a number of legal and political challenges along the way. It could not have been any other way. The subject matter it investigates is politically charged. Most of the non-police, non-state core participants have their backgrounds in political activism. They were 'victims' of targeted infiltration but also the driving force behind the search for answers. What they have unearthed only scratches the surface of secret political policing. They have done so in a political culture that continues to treat progressive activists with suspicion, regardless of their 'subversive' intent. It is a political climate that is anathema to democratic, political expression which is critical of the state and of large corporate interests.

The years since the Inquiry was set up with its Terms of Reference have seen successive conservative Home Secretaries come and go. Theresa May was replaced by Amber Rudd, then followed by Sajid Javid, Priti Patel, Grant Shapps (for about a week) and Suella Braverman. They have overseen government legislation that largely reinforces the hostility of the state and its enforcement agencies towards left-wing, anti-racist and environmental protest. There is little indication that they would have wanted to learn the lessons from the decades of political undercover policing, the blacklisting of workplace organisers or the surveillance of socialist politicians.

The Trade Union Act 2016 introduced minimum thresholds of participation in strike ballots and further restrictions to trade union activity. A report by the Trades Union Congress (TUC) called it 'the most serious attack on the rights of trade unions and their members in a generation' (TUC, 2017). Legislation passed in 2021 grants police forces, intelligence services and a wide range of public authorities the power to authorise the criminal conduct by its informants, with implications also for the regulation of undercover police deployments into protest groups. In England and Wales, the introduction of the Police, Crime, Sentencing and Courts Act 2022 sparked mass protests and some parliamentary opposition, yet has further eroded the space for civil society and social movements. The legislation increased police powers to impose conditions on protests assemblies, including limiting its noise levels. It also included new provisions for criminal damage to memorials, clearly intended to send a message to Black Lives Matter and others that they will face tougher penalties for the kind of actions that saw the statue of slave trader Edward Colston dumped in Bristol Harbour or the word 'racist' written on the statue of Winston Churchill in Parliament Square.

The government passed the Public Order Act through parliament in May 2023. It introduced new offences designed to deter and criminalise disruptive protest, including locking on, going equipped for locking on and disrupting key infrastructure. It also further extended police powers to stop and search protesters, including searches without suspicion. The Act also introduced Serious Disruption Prevention Orders, modelled on the policing responses to terrorism and serious organised crime. Where a person has previously been convicted of a 'protest-related' offence and commits a further offence that is deemed 'protest-related', a court can impose a restriction on further attendance at protests. Breaching an order is a serious matter, with a maximum sentence of 51 weeks in prison.

The Undercover Policing Inquiry may still offer accountability and lessons learnt for a truly democratic society that tolerates peaceful and disruptive protest activity as part of its civil society. But its final report can only be inadequate if it refuses to engage with the ever more authoritarian context in which governments seek to shrink the space for political activism and extra-parliamentary opposition.

# 8

# Public inquiries at a crossroads

## Limits to accountability

Throughout this book I have pointed to the significance of the spycops exposures in terms of the harms caused by the deployments, but also because they alert us to fundamental questions about the role of undercover policing in suppressing protest and dissent. Despite this, there has been a curious neglect in academic study of what I have called 'policing by deception'. Most discussion still assumes the overt and public function of policing in the British context, without as much as a cursory acknowledgement of the covert methods of police work. This should now change.

Police infiltration through the use of covert human intelligence sources is an area of statecraft that is necessarily secretive and has thus enjoyed the luxury of limited public scrutiny. But the tenacity of those who have been campaigning for 'truth' and accountability has lifted the lid on the function and tactics of political undercover units and their operations from 1968 onwards. There is no better site for this research to happen than the Undercover Policing Inquiry.

The existence of the public inquiry is already significant in itself. It is an official acknowledgement that the intrusive surveillance operations have really taken place and that the public concern around them is justified. Campaigners and targets of undercover policing, including those who were to become core participants in the Inquiry, knew that Theresa May's establishment of the investigation under the Inquiries Act 2005 was not about them. The architect of the hostile environment was not worried about the police infringement on civil liberties and political assembly rights. But as Home Secretary, May had picked fights with the police unions before, and she was determined to have a legacy that included police reform. The Stephen Lawrence case stood at the centre of this endeavour, as I have argued. Despite the question marks that hovered over the actual function of the Inquiry, it appeared certain that it would be able to shed light on undercover policing and infiltration. Most importantly, perhaps, it would reveal the extent of infiltration of political campaigns, parties, unions and movements, including contributing to the further exposure of spycops deployments.

I began scrutinising the work of the Inquiry in around 2015 as it began its task of scrutinising undercover policing. After almost nine years of delays, denial and legal dispute over the inquisitorial process, some things seem for certain. The Undercover Policing Inquiry has concealed the truth as much as it has revealed it, as the analysis in this book has shown. And yet it was much more than a cover-up. By its very function, public inquiries are public and allow for participation. This goes far beyond holding open hearings and designating core participants, but these are good indicators. The levels of public access and ability to participate in the proceedings were continually contested, attempts to limit them resisted by non-state core participants and strategies of denial reinvented by police lawyers.

Still, the public inquiry remains the go-to gold standard of investigation when things go wrong (for a recent discussion, see Cooper and Thomas, 2023). In this short, concluding chapter, therefore, I situate the conflicts and contestations in the Undercover Policing Inquiry in a broader debate about the role of public inquiries.

## Public inquiries in the conservative state

In my view, too much of the academic research on public inquiries has treated them as 'black box' investigations. Studies in disciplines such as political science, criminology or law have considered the accident, scandal or crisis that led to an inquiry and then offered reflection or analysis of the inquiry's report. Or, to use the black box metaphor, inquiries are studied through their observable inputs (the matters of concern that led to their establishment) and their observable outputs (their reports and recommendations), but what happens *inside* public inquiries remains unseen. In this book, I have argued that this approach is insufficient. The inner workings of the black box are crucial to our understanding of official discourse formation. Despite their inquisitorial role, public inquiries are inherently contested, and they are sites of struggle for a range of parties with divergent interests.

Grassroots voices frequently, and rightly, criticise public inquiries for their legalism, their positioning within establishment politics and their unwillingness to identify systemic failings of the prevailing political or economic system. But attacks on the idea of inquiries into past failures and abuses also come from the top and from the political Right. A reminder of that was a comment made by Boris Johnson in 2019, at the time a leadership-hopeful (he had resigned by then from Theresa May's cabinet over her Brexit plans), in an LBC Radio phone-in. Responding to a question about police budgets, Johnson declared that money spent on historical child abuse investigations, 'and all this malarkey', was money 'spaffed up a wall' (cited in Allegretti, 2019). The comment was immediately interpreted as an attack on the Independent Inquiry into Child Sexual Abuse, which had been set up by Theresa May in 2014. Fast forward a couple of years and following a scandal-hit premiership by Johnson himself, he appeared reluctant to set up a public inquiry into his government's preparedness and handling of the

COVID-19 pandemic. Theresa May's willingness to use the Inquiries Act 2005 to investigate crucial matters of public concern appeared to have gone with her disappearance from the front benches.

Why should anyone care? This was essentially my guiding research question for this study. Why did so many political activists spend so much time and energy pursuing what seemed to be a hopeless attempt to render the Undercover Policing Inquiry more transparent? Why, despite their continuous assertions that they were losing faith and that they regarded it as an expensive cover-up, did they persevere? In my answer I have gone somewhat against the grain of critical scholarship on public inquiries. Rather than treating their final reports and recommendations as state-imposed narratives to shut down debate and re-establish the legitimacy of its institutions (to be very clear, the final report of the Undercover Policing Inquiry may well turn out to be just that), I have suggested that opening the black box matters.

I have found a significant precursor for such an approach in Stuart Hall, the Jamaican-British academic and 'criminological activist-theorist' (Murji, 2020). Hall was among the founders of *New Left Review* in 1960 and acted as the first editor of the Marxist journal, which quickly established itself as an influential publication in the emerging British New Left. Later, it drew several of its editors from Trotskyist organisations such as the International Marxist Group and the International Socialists (the precursor organisation to the SWP) and actively supported the Vietnam Solidarity Campaign. Tariq Ali, a core participant and the first non-state witness to give evidence to the Undercover Policing Inquiry, is still on the editorial committee. Hall's collaborators and political affiliates had therefore been monitored by Special Branch and were infiltrated by officers from the Special Demonstration Squad (SDS). Apparently, officers from Special Branch also frequented the Partisan Coffee House in Soho that Hall had helped set up, alongside others such as the Marxist historians Raphael Samuel and Eric Hobsbawm (Thorpe, 2017), though it closed several years before the SDS was established. Hobsbawm and other historians with links to the Communist Party had been spied on by MI5, too, as files declassified in 2014 showed (Norton-Taylor, 2014).

In Chapter 4, I briefly cited Hall as one of the inspirations for attempting a reading of the specific political space occupied by public inquiries. More than just cover-ups, they can reveal 'cracks' in the positions of state institutions and provide openings for social struggle. In a short paper on the lessons that could be drawn from the Scarman report into the Brixton riots, Hall had suggested that Scarman's findings needed to be understood as politically relevant, a 'moment of rupture' even, not simply as an establishment cover-up (Hall, 1982, p 67). Hall explicitly directed his short essay 'against the grain' of Scarman's reception in left-wing circles. This reception had identified the report's liberal reformism as little more than a screen for the continuation of authoritarian policing. Hall pointed also to the reception of the report among the police establishment, one of 'full-throated vengeance and outrage' as he put it. This establishment response was so hostile that Hall almost showed sympathy for the judge. He wrote: 'Lord Scarman may not have known what some of us meant by a "politicised police" which has become an organised and open faction of the populist right. He does now' (Hall, 1982, p 67).

I think that we should remember Hall's intervention into the politics of inquiries, especially if we want to exploit such openings to interrogate the fault lines and contradictions in official discourse or narratives pushed by state and corporate actors. It is equally important for academic analysis. As Karim Murji (2020, p 452) expresses it, political activities that are concretely engaged in state-run inquests and inquiries 'showcase a critical criminological perspective that seeks to bring the state and history back into an analysis of what might otherwise be treated as just particular cases'. Through his research, Murji reminds us that Hall was named as an advisor to the Independent Committee of Inquiry, established in 1985 by the Roach Family Support Campaign, and that he provided a foreword to its published report. The campaign was set up following the death in Stoke Newington police station of Colin Roach, a 21-year-old black man, in 1983. An inquest jury decided by a majority verdict that the cause of death was suicide. The family called for a full public inquiry and made formal complaints over the police's handling of the case. No disciplinary action was brought.

The Roach family's campaign and its supporters set up an independent inquiry with the help of the Labour-run Hackney council. Murji writes of the constitution of the inquiry's panel: 'Why Hall was an adviser to the inquiry, rather than a panellist, is not known, though it is possible his then recent or ongoing work with another inquiry into the 1985 riots in Handsworth, Birmingham could have limited his time' (Murji, 2020, p 453).

In his foreword, Hall wrote that the commissioned report was willing to ask questions that had all been pushed to the background by the police investigation, the press reporting and the inquest. In fact, Hall appeared to advance an argument for independent public inquiries that could contextualise single cases and address them as social phenomena. He suggested that 'Coroner's inquests were never designed or intended to be, and cannot function as, a substitute for an independent public inquiry into matters of this kind which affect public confidence in the expectation of justice under the rule of law from the courts and the police' (Hall, 1988). Perhaps Hall would now agree that independent public inquiries, as they are currently constituted, cannot function as a substitute for genuine, community-driven accountability campaigns either.

Hall also took an interest in another inquiry: that into the death of Stephen Lawrence and the police response to the murder. Together with colleagues, he produced a short report for the legal team of Duwayne

Brooks, the friend of Stephen Lawrence who was with him on the night he was killed in South London in 1993. Brooks is now a core participant in the Undercover Policing Inquiry. As a traumatised young man following the murder of his friend and the racist attack on himself, anti-racist groups that he campaigned alongside were monitored by SDS officer HN81, assuming the cover name 'David Hagan'. Murji did some digging: 'Hall came into this work through a commission by the lawyers for Duwayne Brooks … and they told me they invited Hall because, "[h]e may just be the best known person [on race]"' (Murji, 2020, p 453). Hall's involvement here seemed to have not had any lasting impact, but to a large extent these engagements speak to the ambivalent responses to calls for public inquiries. A study by the historian Simon Peplow revealed how some felt that the call for a public inquiry following the 1980 Bristol 'riot' was a 'tactical manoeuvre to apply pressure'. Peplow argues that 'appeals for a public inquiry from sections of the local community demonstrates the value awarded to them by this politically marginalized group' (Peplow, 2018, p 129). But he also found opposition to inquiries, mainly from younger community activists. This ambivalence over the effectiveness of public inquiries carries through to current inquiries held under the Inquiries Act 2005. In their own particular ways, they can represent both political closure and political openings.

## Can a public inquiry bring accountability?

In the Undercover Policing Inquiry, this ambivalence expressed itself in the struggle over secrecy and disclosure and resulted from the paradoxical task to inquire *publicly* into state *secrets*. There is a different paradox that I have concerned myself with in this book: those who proclaim a well-founded critique of state policy must rely on a state accountability mechanism to get to the truth. It is extraordinary how people who have been victimised by state agencies over and over again, many of whom in fact held views critical of the state long before they exposed police infiltration into their lives, put so much effort and trust into an official public inquiry established by the Home Office. These people were not naive, but the public inquiry provided them with one form of official acknowledgement of what happened. Of course, the Undercover Policing Inquiry has heard dissenting voices. Many of them were well articulated, personal testimonies that not only indicated the personal and structural harm done by undercover police deployments. They also strongly exposed the Inquiry's failings and the personal and political toll experienced by its core participants of being victims 'a second time'. But was this not to be expected? Many of the core participants are activists, perhaps not resourced in terms of money and influence but certainly aware of their moral standing.

As Sir John Mitting was preparing a first interim report after hearing about the methods and justifications for the undercover work of SDS from 1968 to 1982, few could be satisfied with the time it had taken to get there. Asked about this at a session of the Home Affairs Committee on 22 June 2022, the permanent secretary to the Home Office, Matthew Rycroft, reminded parliament of the formal independence from government that the Undercover Policing Inquiry enjoyed. But he also conceded that, as the Inquiry's sponsor, the Home Office remained acutely aware of the delay and its associated costs – ultimately, the Inquiries Act 2005 gave the sponsoring minister the power to terminate the Inquiry.

When in February 2023, the Inquiry Chair invited written and oral closing statements from core participants about the Tranche 1 era (1968–82), few could have had any hopes. The Inquiry's most senior lawyer, David Barr, summed up the evidence the Inquiry had received in the preceding years and made his own submission to Sir John Mitting. He submitted that, all being said, whatever the rationale for sending police spies into political groups planning follow-up demonstrations to the Grosvenor Square anti-Vietnam war rally, the SDS should have been wound up almost as soon as it started. Barr said that the Home Office's annual renewal of funding for the spycops unit should have presented it with the opportunity to ask searching questions over its justification. He also found that the Metropolitan Police's senior leadership was aware of its operations but failed to consider its wider function. Barr said that:

> [N]o one appears to have considered whether the level of intrusion occasioned by SDS long-term undercover police deployments was justified. No one appears to have addressed their mind specifically to the legality of the SDS' operations ... Had they done so, there is a strong case for concluding that they should have decided to disband the SDS. (UCPI, 2023b, p 36)

The fact that the Inquiry's own legal team had concluded that the Metropolitan Police and the Home Office should have closed down the secretive SDS unit almost as soon as it started was a vindication of sorts for the activists who were spied on. Rajiv Menon, the barrister representing some of those spied on, went further in his devastating conclusion that the 'intrusive espionage' against political dissidents should never have been permitted in the first place. As he put it:

> The primary objective of the SDS was never to prevent crime or engage in genuine law enforcement. It was always to spy on those perceived to be political opponents of the state or the status quo. It was always to prevent positive social change and allow the established order to thrive. (UCPI, 2023c, p 2)

The non-police, non-state core participants knew all this already. But hearing the senior lawyer for a government-sponsored inquiry sum it up in these terms reaffirmed them in their search for an official acknowledgement of the political policing operations. They remain acutely aware, also, that any such admissions are hard fought for. As they stated themselves at the conclusion of the Inquiry's Tranche 1 evidence phase: 'The Metropolitan Police can be sure that we, and the thousands of others affected by this unjustifiable and invasive political policing, are not going away' (Campaign Opposing Police Surveillance, 2023).

It has been a long and arduous journey to get to this point. Any spycops policing that occurred after 1982 is yet to be examined by the Undercover Policing Inquiry. By the time it has done so, and it has produced its final report and recommendations to the Home Office, it may well have surpassed the Bloody Sunday Inquiry as the longest running public inquiry in recent history.

# APPENDIX A

# Terms of Reference

## Purpose

To inquire into and report on undercover police operations conducted by English and Welsh police forces in England and Wales since 1968 and, in particular, to:

- investigate the role and the contribution made by undercover policing towards the prevention and detection of crime;
- examine the motivation for, and the scope of, undercover police operations in practice and their effect upon individuals in particular and the public in general;
- ascertain the state of awareness of undercover police operations of Her Majesty's Government;
- identify and assess the adequacy of the:
  1. justification, authorisation, operational governance and oversight of undercover policing; and
  2. selection, training, management and care of undercover police officers;
- identify and assess the adequacy of the statutory, policy and judicial regulation of undercover policing.

## Miscarriages of justice

The inquiry's investigations will include a review of the extent of the duty to make, during a criminal prosecution, disclosure of an undercover police operation and the scope for miscarriage of justice in the absence of proper disclosure.

The inquiry will refer to a panel, consisting of senior members of the Crown Prosecution Service and the police, the facts of any case in respect of which it concludes that a miscarriage of justice may have occurred as a result of an undercover police operation or its non disclosure. The panel will consider whether further action is required, including but not limited to, referral of the case to the Criminal Cases Review Commission.

### Scope

The inquiry's investigation will include, but not be limited to, whether and to what purpose, extent and effect undercover police operations have targeted political and social justice campaigners.

The inquiry's investigation will include, but not be limited to, the undercover operations of the Special Demonstration Squad and the National Public Order Intelligence Unit.

For the purpose of the inquiry, the term 'undercover police operations' means the use by a police force of a police officer as a covert human intelligence source within the meaning of section 26(8) of the Regulation of Investigatory Powers Act 2000, whether before or after the commencement of that Act. The terms 'undercover police officer', 'undercover policing', 'undercover police activity' should be understood accordingly. It includes operations conducted through online media. The inquiry will not examine undercover or covert operations conducted by any body other than an English or Welsh police force.

### *Method*

The inquiry will examine and review all documents as the inquiry chairman shall judge appropriate.

The inquiry will receive such oral and written evidence as the inquiry chairman shall judge appropriate.

### *Report*

The inquiry will report to the Home Secretary as soon as practicable. The report will make recommendations as to the future deployment of undercover police officers. It is anticipated that the inquiry report will be delivered up to three years after the publication of these terms of reference.

# APPENDIX B

# Timeline

### 14 March 2010

Peter Francis, a former Special Demonstration Squad officer, gives a 'whistleblowing' interview about the undercover unit to *The Observer*. On film, he appears disguised with his face in silhouette and his voice distorted. He later 'unmasks' himself for the Channel 4 *Dispatches* documentary 'The Police's Dirty Secret', broadcast in 2013.

### 21 October 2010

A post on the website Indymedia UK makes public the exposure of 'Mark Stone', real name Mark Kennedy, as an undercover police officer in the National Public Order Intelligence Unit.

### 10 January 2011

The criminal proceedings of protesters on charges of conspiracy to sabotage a power station collapse after it emerges that the infiltration of the group by Mark Kennedy was not disclosed. The Court of Appeal quashes the sentences of another group of protesters later that year.

### 15 October 2011

London Greenpeace campaigners confront Bob Lambert MBE at an event held by the Trades Union Congress. They demand an apology for his infiltration of their group in the 1980s when he posed as the activist 'Bob Robinson'.

### October 2011

The Metropolitan Police sets up a criminal investigation into allegations of misconduct by undercover police officers in its former Special Demonstration Squad. The investigation is known as Operation Herne and led by Derbyshire Chief Constable Mick Creedon.

## December 2011

Eight women deceived into intimate relationships with undercover officers inform the Metropolitan Police of their intention to take legal action, including for breaches of their human rights.

## July 2012

The Home Secretary asks Mark Ellison to lead a review into, among others, 'inappropriate undercover activity directed at the Lawrence family'. The findings are published in the Stephen Lawrence Independent Review.

## 13 July 2013

The Commissioner of the Metropolitan Police, Sir Bernard Hogan-Howe, issues a public apology for the 'morally repugnant' use of deceased children's identities by the SDS. He refuses to inform the affected parents and families.

## 6 March 2014

The Home Secretary Theresa May makes a statement to the House of Commons on the findings of the Stephen Lawrence Independent Review. She commits to a judge-led statutory inquiry into undercover policing and the role of the SDS. She also commissions a further report into possible miscarriages of justice resulting from undercover police work.

## 12 March 2015

The Home Secretary establishes the public inquiry under the 2005 Inquiries Act and appoints Sir Christopher Pitchford as the Chair, pre-empting the conclusion of the criminal investigation. Stephen Taylor, former Director at the Audit Commission, publishes the findings from his investigation into the links between the SDS and the Home Office.

## 16 July 2015

The Home Secretary announces the Terms of Reference. They anticipate a three-year Inquiry with a report to be published in 2018. Mark Ellison and Alison Morgan deliver their report on the impact of undisclosed undercover police activity on the safety of convictions.

## 28 July 2015

The Undercover Policing Inquiry formally opens with a call for applications to be designated core participant status under Rule 5 of the 2006 Inquiry Rules.

## 7 October 2015

Sir Christopher Pitchford holds a first preliminary hearing on the designation of core participant status at the Royal Courts of Justice. Submissions are made by legal representatives and by some applicants personally. Some 380 applications are received by the following month.

## 4 November 2015

The Chair convenes a preliminary hearing on recognised legal representation for designated core participants.

## 20 November 2015

The Metropolitan Police Service issues a public apology to seven of the women who brought a legal claim against them. Assistant Commissioner Martin Hewitt reads out the apology, which acknowledges that the 'relationships were a violation of the women's human rights'. The wording is a result of a legal settlement. Only the eighth claimant, Kate Wilson, continues her case in the Investigatory Powers Tribunal (IPT).

## 22–23 March 2016

The Inquiry holds a much-anticipated preliminary hearing on the legal approach it should apply to restriction order applications.

## 27 April 2016

The Chair convenes a preliminary hearing on the nature of the undertaking that he should seek from the Attorney General to ensure that nothing said by witnesses to the Inquiry can be used in criminal proceedings against them.

## 3 May 2016

Sir Christopher Pitchford issues his ruling on the legal principles applied to decisions on restriction orders and on their determination on a case-by-case basis.

## 22 June 2016

The Chair holds a preliminary hearing to determine whether the state has a duty to disclose to the parents of a deceased child that the identity of that child was used for police purposes.

## 14 July 2016

The Chair rules on the Inquiry's obligations towards the families and close relatives of deceased children whose identities were used by undercover officers. Following the ruling, the Inquiry issues a public notice inviting any parent or close relative of a child who was born between 1938 and 1975 to make contact with the Inquiry should they wish to know if the child's identity was used by police for covert purposes, even though the Inquiry may not be able to give them an answer either way.

## 28 August 2016

The Attorney General grants an undertaking that no evidence or information given by a witness to the Inquiry will be used against them in any future criminal proceedings.

## 5–6 April 2017

The Inquiry holds a preliminary meeting on anonymity for SDS officers. Its specific purpose is to consider the Metropolitan Police's request for an extension for making anonymity applications and for a change to the Inquiry's approach to restriction orders.

## July 2017

Sir Christopher Pitchford steps down as Chair for reasons of ill health. Sir John Mitting succeeds him.

## 20 November 2017

The new Chair convenes a preliminary hearing on the impact of the Rehabilitation of Offenders Act 1974 on the Inquiry's work

## 20–21 November 2017

Sir John Mitting holds a second preliminary hearing on anonymity for SDS officers.

## 29 November 2017

The Chair issues a ruling on the effect of the Rehabilitation of Offenders Act 1974 on the Inquiry's work. He sets out that he will admit evidence related to a person's spent convictions when considering applications for restriction orders. He invites the Justice Secretary to amend the Act accordingly to put the decision on a statutory footing.

## 5 February 2018

The Inquiry convenes a third preliminary hearing on anonymity for SDS officers.

## 21 March 2018

The Inquiry holds a fourth preliminary hearing on anonymity for SDS officers. Following a short submission to the Chair, some 60 core participants and their supporters led by their legal representative Phillippa Kaufman, 'walk out' of the hearing and hold a protest outside the Royal Courts of Justice.

## 9 May 2018

The Chair holds a fifth preliminary hearing on anonymity for SDS officers.

## 10 May 2018

The Chair publishes a strategic review of the Undercover Policing Inquiry, setting out an anticipated timeline for its completion. He announces his intention to deliver his final report and recommendations to the Home Secretary before the end of 2023.

## 18 May 2018

The Chair convenes an oral hearing to discuss with core participants the matters that need to be resolved and the police resources that need to be committed in order to meet his 'ambitious timeline' set out in the Inquiry's strategic review.

## 25 May 2018

The General Data Protection Regulation (GDPR) and the Data Protection Act 2018 come into effect.

## 31 January 2019

The Inquiry holds its first preliminary hearing on privacy. The Chair hears submissions on how his approach to disclosure can guarantee individuals' rights to privacy without undermining the Inquiry's obligation to conduct its proceedings as publicly as possible.

## 25 March 2019

The Inquiry holds a second preliminary hearing on privacy to determine to what extent the introduction of GDPR and the Data Protection Act 2018 imposes new obligations on it. The Chair rejects calls from non-police, non-state core participants that the exercise of their privacy rights should grant them access to 'their' intelligence files.

## June 2019

The Rehabilitation of Offenders Act 1974 is amended at the request of the Chair to make exceptions for inquiries under the Inquiries Act 2005 and allow questions to be asked about spent convictions.

## 24 September 2020

The government introduces new legislation to parliament, which it says will protect national security. The Covert Human Intelligence Sources (CHIS) Bill provides a legal basis for the police and other public authorities to allow involvement in criminality by undercover operatives. The legislation is nicknamed the spycops bill.

## 15 October 2020

The Labour Party leadership orders MPs to abstain in the third reading of the spycops bill in the House of Commons. Several Labour MPs defy the whip and resign from the frontbench to oppose the legislation. The Covert Human Intelligence Sources (Criminal Conduct) Act becomes law in 2021.

## 2–19 November 2020

Long awaited, the Inquiry begins its public evidential phase with opening statements and oral hearings They are conducted remotely due to the COVID-19 pandemic. In these 'Tranche 1/Phase 1' hearings, the Inquiry heard evidence from former undercover officers and non-state witnesses about the establishment and work of the SDS in the period from 1968 to 1972.

## 26 January 2021

The Chair convenes a Directions hearing to determine the practicalities of the proceedings to be used in 'Tranche 1/Phase 2' evidence hearings later that year.

## 21 April–13 May 2021

Opening statements and 'Tranche 1/Phase 2' evidence hearings are held by the Inquiry, conducted remotely due to the COVID-19 pandemic.

## 30 September 2021

Kate Wilson wins her case against the Metropolitan Police and the National Police Chiefs' Council (NPCC) in the IPT. The IPT rules that the undercover policing operations against her were unlawful and infringed on her rights enshrined in Articles 3, 8, 10, 11 and 14 of the European Convention on Human Rights.

## 9–20 May 2022

Opening statements and 'Tranche 1/Phase 3' evidence hearings are held in person at the Thistle Marble Arch Hotel in London. Invited witnesses are primarily former managers of the SDS covering a period up to 1982.

## 29 June 2023

The Inquiry publishes its 'Tranche 1' interim report on 'Special Demonstration Squad officers and managers and those affected by deployments (1968–82)'. A separate closed interim report, based on evidence heard in secret, is presented to the Home Office at the same time.

# Notes

## Chapter 1

Some sections of this chapter were published in a previous research paper (Schlembach, 2016), which has also informed the discussions in Chapters 2 and 4. Permission to reproduce materials here has been granted by the publisher.

1. Throughout the book I have preferred the use of its proper title – the Undercover Policing Inquiry – instead of the colloquial Pitchford Inquiry or Mitting Inquiry. I have preferred the lower-case spelling of 'public inquiry' in general, but the upper-case 'Inquiry' is used as shorthand for the Undercover Policing Inquiry in particular. The exception is for the purpose of in-text references, where I have used the common abbreviation UCPI to aid readability. An important disclaimer: UCPI in a reference does *not* in general mean that the Undercover Policing Inquiry is the author of the text cited or referred to. It merely means that the document is in its possession and publicly available on its website. Authorship should be clear from the way my sources are introduced or contextualised. This referencing system is preferable, in my view, to avoid confusion in instances where the source author(s) were unable to be determined or documents contained contributions from more than one source (such as hearing transcripts).

2. Interested readers would find no reference at all to the scandal or the public inquiry in most criminology or policing textbooks of the past decade. There are exceptions. For example, in the fifth edition of *The Politics of the Police,* Bowling, Reiner and Sheptycki declare that the spycops scandal uncovered a 'thirty-seven-year campaign by undercover police to infiltrate the Socialist Workers party' (2019, p 250). Although they question the ability of the public inquiry to provide accountability, they credit it mistakenly for uncovering the history of spycops in 'extreme left- and right-wing groups' and for shedding light on 'the deception of women into intimate relationships as a tactic'. Rowe's aptly titled *Policing the Police: Challenges of Democracy and Accountability* (2020) identifies the increased role of the Office of Surveillance Commissioners in regulating covert surveillance but does not further comment on the 'Pritchard Inquiry [sic]' (2020, p 35).

3. The role of MI5 did, however, become a major theme once the Inquiry began to consider evidence.

4. For example, three anti-apartheid campaigners – Jonathan Rosenhead, Christabel Gurney and Ernest Rodker – had their criminal convictions going back to 1972 quashed in January 2023 after it was revealed that one of their co-defendants was an undercover Special Demonstration Squad (SDS) officer.

5. The paradox has been the defining feature of the preliminary matters considered by the Inquiry. Its first Chair, Sir Christopher Pitchford, named it in the following terms: 'there is no escape from and no short cut to avoid the complexities of the issues raised by the nature of a public inquiry into state activity that is carried out secretly' (UCPI, 2017a, p 42).

## Chapter 3

1. This chapter is an updated and extended version of a text published as 'Resisting the surveillance state: Deviant knowledge and undercover policing' (Schlembach, 2020). Permission was granted by the publisher to reproduce these materials here.

## Notes

2   This was denied by Barry Moss, the former SDS manager (1980–82) and overall head of Special Branch (1996–99), when questioned by Counsel to the Inquiry. Moss was the first Special Demonstration Squad (SDS) manager to give evidence to the Inquiry and insisted that its priority had been the prevention of public order. As he put it, anything useful to MI5 in monitoring subversive activity 'was a by-product of the public order work we were doing' (UCPI, 2022d, p 71).

3   Harvie and Milburn experienced the university sector's readiness to make academics redundant on commercial and ideological grounds, rather than ethical ones, when they lost their posts at the University of Leicester apparently due to their involvement in 'critical' and 'political economy' research at the start of 2021. Redundancy was threatened against 16 staff in the School of Business, half of whom were trade union officials, in the university's efforts to disinvest from critical management studies. In response, the national trade union, the University and College Union (UCU), called for a global academic boycott of the institution. Incidentally, my own university employer faced the same UCU sanction in response to plans for mass redundancies in 2023.

## Chapter 4

1   In a ruling published on 11 April 2018, the Chair finally explained that he had refused the anonymity application made by Mark Jenner in respect of his real and assumed names. This followed a closed hearing and the full reasoning was supplied to Jenner in a closed note. In summary, the open ruling stated that issuing a restriction order would serve 'no purpose' as the applicant had been named in the media. Further, he had admitted to the relationship with Alison. 'To the extent that there are differences in the account of the relationship between HN15 [Jenner] and Alison, they can and should be publicly explored', the ruling stated (UCPI, 2018c).

## Chapter 5

1   In a statement following his appointment, Sir John Mitting wrote: 'Questions of national security do arise in a small minority of the deployments to be investigated by the Inquiry. Where they do, I will do nothing to harm the interests of national security. But in the great majority of cases in which anonymity is sought, the reason has nothing to do with national security and everything to do with the human rights of the individuals concerned' (UCPI, 2017j, p 4).

## Chapter 6

1   The question of anonymity for police witnesses was so central to the procedure of the Inquiry that it continued to dominate the preliminary matters long after Pitchford's ruling. In fact, the Inquiry was forced to hold further hearings on anonymity, as the Metropolitan Police sought to change the approach. In essence, the Metropolitan Police argued that it lacked the resources to provide the materials it needed to justify anonymity applications for all Special Demonstration Squad (SDS) officers and that the Inquiry, in effect, should resort back to offering blanket protection from disclosure for most of them.

2   It is frequently used in the UCPI to refer to the practice of redacting (sections of) documents and replacing the redactions with short summaries of the redacted content (without disclosing any details).

3   Police lawyers also argued that other Convention rights could be engaged in the determination of restriction orders, particularly Article 2 which protects the right to life and is an absolute right. Risk assessments could potentially show that the publication of an officer's name may result in threats to his or her life. The examples of restriction orders

I mention here are merely a snapshot of some decisions taken by the Chair. A fuller, more systematic analysis was carried out by Chris Brian (2019).

## Chapter 7

1. 'In and against the state' was the phrase used in the title of an influential pamphlet issued by the London Edinburgh Weekend Return Group, members of the Conference of Socialist Economists, in 1979. It has recently been re-published by Pluto Press with a new foreword by John Holloway and an interview with John McDonnell (London Edinburgh Weekend Return Group, 2021).
2. The Terms propose that undercover operations by police units other than the Special Demonstration Squad (SDS) and the National Public Order Intelligence Unit (NPOIU) shall be examined. In practice, the Inquiry has not signalled an intention to actively do so, as of yet. This may be a blessing in disguise. The vagueness of the purpose as outlined in the Terms of Reference could have allowed the Inquiry's team to hide beyond a generic assessment of undercover policing. The focused work on these two units does at least allow it to assess the politically-targeted deployments. How the Inquiry is supposed to go about its business is a question left open; the Terms simply suggest an analysis of documentation and the soliciting of oral and written evidence 'as the inquiry chairman shall judge appropriate'. Reference is also made to undercover operations 'conducted through online media', an aspect which has been absent from the Inquiry's public-facing work so far.
3. Activists with Plane Stupid had previously exposed a corporate spy. A young Oxford graduate had seemingly found employment in a private security company and infiltrated Plane Stupid's London group before he was outed in 2008 (Lubbers, 2012, p xii).
4. Lush has funded hundreds of grassroots campaign organisations. For transparency's sake I should mention that an anti-austerity print and online publication, *Shift Magazine*, that I co-edited between 2007 and 2012, was the recipient of a small Lush start-up grant.

# References

Ali, T. (2018) *Street Fighting Years: An Autobiography of the Sixties*. London: Verso.

Alison (2018) Undercover police abused female activists. But the inquiry is a farce. *The Guardian*, 9 February 2018. Available at: https://www.theguardian.com/commentisfree/2018/feb/09/undercover-police-female-activists-inquiry-farce. Last accessed 8 November 2022.

Alison, Belinda, Helen Steel, Lisa and Naomi (2022) *Deep Deception: The Story of the Spycops Network by the Women Who Uncovered the Shocking Truth*. London: Ebury Spotlight.

Allegretti, A. (2019) Boris Johnson faces calls to apologise for claiming child sex abuse inquiry money "spaffed up the wall". *Sky News*, 13 March 2019. Available at: https://news.sky.com/story/boris-johnson-faces-calls-to-apologise-for-claiming-child-sex-abuse-inquiry-money-spaffed-up-the-wall-11664043. Last accessed 22 December 2022.

Badger, M. (2017) The law unto themselves: Spycops and miscarriages of justice. *Real Media*, 13 February 2017. Available at: https://realmedia.press/law-unto-spycops-miscarriages-justice/. Last accessed 22 June 2022.

Barkan, S. (2006) Criminal prosecution and the legal control of protest. *Mobilization*, 11(2): 181–95.

Barrett, D. (2011) Scotland Yard fights to keep Jack the Ripper files secret. *The Telegraph*, 15 May 2011. Available at: https://www.telegraph.co.uk/news/uknews/crime/8514000/Scotland-Yard-fights-to-keep-Jack-the-Ripper-files-secret.html. Last accessed 20 January 2023.

BBC (2019) Ex-undercover officer wins case against Police Scotland. *BBC News*, 31 January 2019. Available at: https://www.bbc.co.uk/news/uk-scotland-47076733. Last accessed 26 October 2022.

Belam, M. (2018) Cosmetics retailer Lush criticised by police over 'spycops' ad campaign. *The Guardian*, 1 June 2018. Available at: https://www.theguardian.com/media/2018/jun/01/cosmetics-retailer-lush-criticised-by-police-over-spycops-ad-campaign. Last accessed 18 January 2023.

Belknapp, J. (2015) Activist criminology. *Criminology*, 53(1): 1–22.

Bell, E. (2013) Normalising the exceptional: British colonial policing cultures come home, *Mémoire(s), identité(s), marginalité(s) dans le monde occidental contemporain*, 10. Available at: http://journals.openedition.org/mimmoc/1286. Last accessed 8 November 2022.

Birchall, C. (2021) *Radical Secrecy: The Ends of Transparency in Datafied America*. Minneapolis: University of Minnesota Press.

Boffey, D. (2014) Scotland Yard in new undercover policing row. *The Observer*, 8 March 2014. Available at: https://www.theguardian.com/uk-news/2014/mar/08/scotland-yard-undercover-police-row. Last accessed 27 January 2023.

Bonino, S. (2015) Why a controversial undercover cop should keep his academic post. *Times Higher Education*, 22 January 2015, Available at: https://www.timeshighereducation.com/comment/opinion/why-a-controversial-undercover-cop-should-keep-his-academic-post/2018046.article. Last accessed 8 May 2022.

Bonino, S. and Kaoullas, L.G. (2015) Preventing political violence in Britain: An evaluation of over forty years of undercover policing of political groups involved in protest. *Studies in Conflict & Terrorism*, 38(10): 814–40.

Bowling, B., Reiner, R. and Sheptycki, J. (2019) *The Politics of the Police* (5th edn). Oxford: Oxford University Press.

Bowling, B. Iyer, S., Reiner, R. and Sheptycki, J. (2016) Policing: Past, present and future. In R. Matthews (ed.) *What Is to Be Done about Crime and Punishment?* London: Palgrave Macmillan, pp 123–58.

Brian, C. (2020) Spy, shred – and repeat. *Undercover Research Group*, 21 April 2020. Available at: https://undercoverresearch.net/2020/04/11/spy-shred-and-repeat/. Last accessed 22 March 2023.

Brian, C. (2019) Secrecy, power and the Undercover Policing Inquiry. Unpublished MSc Dissertation. Cardiff University.

Brown, W. (2000) Suffering rights as paradoxes. *Constellations*, 7(2): 230–41.

Burgess, A. (2011) The changing character of public inquiries in the (risk) regulatory state. *British Politics*, 6(1): 3–29.

Burton, F. and Carlen, P. (1979) *Official Discourse: On Discourse Analysis, Government Publications, Ideology and the State*. London: Routledge and Kegan Paul.

Campaign Opposing Police Surveillance (2017) Scottish inquiry – reputation before justice, 15 January 2017. Available at: http://campaignopposingpolicesurveillance.com/2017/01/15/scottish-inquiry-reputation-before-justice/. Last accessed 22 December 2022.

Campaign Opposing Police Surveillance (2018) Spycops inquiry: Banging your head against a brick wall, 26 February 2018. Available at: http://campaignopposingpolicesurveillance.com/2018/02/26/spycops-inquiry-banging-your-head-against-a-brick-wall/. Last accessed 19 October 2022.

Campaign Opposing Police Surveillance (2020a) UCPI Daily Report, 5 November 2020. Available at: http://campaignopposingpolicesurveillance.com/2020/11/06/ucpi-daily-report-5-nov-2020/. Last accessed 20 April 2022.

Campaign Opposing Police Surveillance (2020b) UCPI Daily Report, 11 November 2020. Available at: http://campaignopposingpolicesurveillance.com/2020/11/11/ucpi-daily-report-11-nov-2020/. Last accessed 22 February 2023.

Campaign Opposing Police Surveillance (2023) Unlawful, unjustifiable and useless: Inquiry condemns spycops, 16 March 2023. Available at: http://campaignopposingpolicesurveillance.com/2023/03/16/unlawful-unjustifiable-useless-inquiry-condemns-spycops/. Last accessed 22 March 2023.

Canning, V, Martin, G. and Tombs, S. (2023) (eds) *The Emerald International Handbook of Activist Criminology*. Bingley: Emerald Publishing.

Carlen, P. and Ayres França, L. (2017) (eds) *Alternative Criminologies*. London: Routledge.

Carrabine, E. et al (2014) *Criminology: A Sociological Introduction* (3rd edn). Abingdon: Routledge.

Casciani, D. (2020) Twitter @BBCDomC, 11 November 2020. Available at: https://twitter.com/BBCDomC/status/1326478268682235905. Last accessed 19 February 2023.

Channel 4 News (2014) I'll tell all to Lawrence inquiry – Peter Francis. *Channel 4 News*, 11 March 2014. Available at: https://www.channel4.com/news/peter-francis-stephen-lawrence-public-inquiry-prosecution. Last accessed 5 April 22.

Channel 4 News (2017) *Channel 4 News*, 12 May 2017. Available at: https://www.youtube.com/watch?v=obyJPByHgNE. Last accessed 7 April 2022.

Cohen, N. (2014) Why must we tolerate police spies in our midst? *The Observer*, 21 December 2014. Available at: https://www.theguardian.com/commentisfree/2014/dec/21/why-tolerate-police-spies-in-our-midst. Last accessed 8 May 2022.

Cohen, S. (1993) Human rights and crimes of the state: The culture of denial. *Australian and New Zealand Journal of Criminology*, 26(2): 97–115.

Cohen, S. (1996) Government responses to human rights reports: Claims, denials, and counterclaims. *Human Rights Quarterly*, 18(3): 517–43.

Cohen, S. (2001) *States of Denial: Knowing about Atrocities and Suffering*. Cambridge: Polity.

Cooper, S. and Thomas, O. (2023) Judge-led public inquiries in the UK: The gold standard? In S. Prasser (ed.) *New Directions in Royal Commissions and Public Inquiries: Do We Need Them?* Cleveland, QLD: Conor Court.

Darling, Z. (2020) Spycops inquiry: 'An establishment cover up taking place before our eyes'. *The Justice Gap*, 20 November 2020. Available at: https://www.thejusticegap.com/spycops-inquiry-an-establishment-cover-up-taking-place-before-our-eyes/. Last accessed 19 February 2023.

Davies, A. (2013) I was weak and cruel, admits ex-undercover police boss. *Channel 4 News*, 5 July 2013. Available at: https://www.channel4.com/news/undercover-police-bob-lambert-exclusive. Last accessed 20 June 2022.

Della Porta, D. and Reiter, H. (1998) Introduction. In D. Della Porta and H. Reiter (eds) *Policing Protest: The Control of Mass Demonstrations in Western Democracies*. Minneapolis: University of Minnesota Press.

Dembour, M.B. (2010) What are human rights? Four schools of thought. *Human Rights Quarterly*, 32(1): 1–20.

Dick, C. (2019) Evidence to the Home Affairs Committee. The Macpherson report: Twenty years on, 10 July 2019. Video available at: https://www.parliamentlive.tv/Event/Index/cd010bb3-558c-4575-9a23-ec4a5070a3cb. Last accessed 24 February 2022.

Dixon, H. and McCann, K. (2017) Exclusive: Special Branch monitored Jeremy Corbyn for 20 years amid fears that he was 'undermining democracy'. *The Daily Telegraph*, 7 June 2017. Available at: https://www.telegraph.co.uk/news/2017/06/06/exclusive-special-branch-monitored-jeremy-corbyn-20-years-amid/. Last accessed 14 May 2022.

Elliott-Cooper, A. (2020) 'Britain is not innocent': A Netpol report on the policing of Black Lives Matter protests in Britain's towns and cities in 2020. *The Network for Police Monitoring*. Available at: https://netpol.org/wp-content/uploads/2020/11/Britain-is-not-innocent-web-version.pdf. Last accessed 24 February 2022.

Ellison, M. (2014) *The Stephen Lawrence Independent Review: Possible corruption and the role of undercover policing in the Stephen Lawrence case*. London: HM Government. Available at: https://assets.publishing.service.gov.uk/government/uploads/system/uploads/attachment_data/file/287030/stephen_lawrence_review_summary.pdf. Last accessed 7 September 2022.

Evans, R. (2011) Top prosecutor rejects calls for deeper inquiry into police spies. *The Guardian*, 7 December 2011. Available at: https://www.theguardian.com/uk/undercover-with-paul-lewis-and-rob-evans/2011/dec/07/police-spies-row-continues?CMP=gu_com. Last accessed 22 June 2022.

Evans, R. (2014) Police forced to name undercover officers who duped women. *The Guardian*, 15 August 2014. Available at: https://www.theguardian.com/uk-news/2014/aug/15/metropolitan-police-forced-to-name-undercover-officers. Last accessed 22 January 2023.

Evans, R. (2015a) Police apologise to women who had relationships with undercover officers. *The Guardian*, 20 November 2015. Available at: https://www.theguardian.com/uk-news/2015/nov/20/met-police-apologise-women-had-relationships-with-undercover-officers. Last accessed 18 March 2022.

Evans, R. (2015b) Ex-undercover officer who infiltrated political groups resigns from academic posts. *The Guardian*, 23 December 2015. Available at: https://www.theguardian.com/uk-news/2015/dec/23/bob-lambert-ex-undercover-officer-quits-st-andrews-london-metropolitan. Last accessed 8 May 2022.

Evans, R. (2015c) University under pressure to sack controversial former undercover spy Bob Lambert. *The Guardian*, 6 January 2015. Available at: https://www.theguardian.com/uk-news/undercover-with-paul-lewis-and-rob-evans/2015/jan/06/university-under-pressure-to-sack-controversial-former-undercover-spy-bob-lambert. Last accessed 8 May 2022.

# References

Evans, R. (2016) Officer claims Met police improperly destroyed files on Green party peer. *The Guardian*, 8 January 2016. Available at: https://www.theguardian.com/uk-news/2016/jan/08/officer-claims-met-police-improperly-destroyed-files-on-green-party-peer. Last accessed 29 September 2022.

Evans, R. (2018) Lush removes police spies posters after 'intimidation of staff'. *The Guardian*, 7 June 2018. Available at: https://www.theguardian.com/uk-news/2018/jun/07/lush-removes-posters-undercover-police-spies-campaign?CMP=share_btn_tw. Last accessed 19 February 2023.

Evans, R. (2021) Police spies inquiry: Five officers allowed to give evidence in secret. *The Guardian*, 18 October 2021. Available at: https://www.theguardian.com/uk-news/2021/oct/18/police-spies-inquiry-five-officers-allowed-to-give-evidence-in-secret. Last accessed 21 January 2023.

Evans, R. and Lewis, P. (2011a) Police accused of allowing undercover officers to lie in court. *The Guardian*, 19 October 2011. Available at: https://www.theguardian.com/uk/2011/oct/19/police-undercover-officers-court-perjury-claim. Last accessed 20 June 2022.

Evans, R. and Lewis, P. (2011b) Activists walk free as undercover officer prompts collapse of case. *The Guardian*, 10 January 2011. Available at: https://www.theguardian.com/environment/2011/jan/10/activists-undercover-officer-mark-kennedy. Last accessed 11 January 2023.

Evans, R. and Lewis, P. (2013) *Undercover: The True Story of Britain's Secret Police*. London: Faber and Faber.

Fatsis, L. and Lamb, M. (2022) *Policing the Pandemic: How Public Health Becomes Public Order*. Bristol: Policy Press.

Foucault, M. (1991 [1977]) *Discipline and Punish: The Birth of the Prison*. London: Penguin Books.

Francis, P. (2014) Former officer: Findings of inquiry 'will be shocking'. *ITV News*, 6 March 2014. Available at: https://www.itv.com/news/update/2014-03-06/former-officer-findings-of-inquiry-will-be-shocking/. Last accessed 28 February 2022.

Gilligan, G. (2013) Official inquiry, truth and criminal justice. In G. Gilligan and J. Pratt (eds) *Crime, Truth and Justice: Official Inquiry, Discourse, Knowledge*. Abingdon: Routledge, pp 11–25.

Gilmore, J. and Tufail, W. (2015) Justice denied: Police accountability and the killing of Mark Duggan. In D. Whyte (ed.) *How Corrupt Is Britain?* London: Pluto Press, pp 94–101.

Grenfell Tower Inquiry (2020a) Transcript – Day 5, 3 February 2020. Available at: https://assets.grenfelltowerinquiry.org.uk/inline-files/Appendix%20C.2%20Transcript%203%20February%202020.pdf. Last accessed 29 September 2022.

Grenfell Tower Inquiry (2020b) Ruling on an application to seek an undertaking from the Attorney General, 6 February 2020. Available at: https://assets.grenfelltowerinquiry.org.uk/inline-files/Ruling%20on%20the%20Application%20for%20an%20Undertaking%2006.02.2020.pdf. Last accessed 27 September 2022.

Greer, C. and McLaughlin, E. (2011) 'This is not justice': Ian Tomlinson, institutional failure and the press politics of outrage. *British Journal of Criminology*, 52(2): 272–93.

Greer, C. and McLaughlin, E. (2016) Theorizing institutional scandal and the regulatory state. *Theoretical Criminology*, 21(2): 112–32.

Gutmann, A. and Thompson, D. (2004) *Why Deliberative Democracy?* Princeton, NJ: Princeton University Press.

Hadjimatheou, K. (2017) Neither Confirm nor Deny: Secrecy and disclosure in undercover policing. *Criminal Justice Ethics*, 36(3): 279–96.

Hameed, Y. and Monaghan, J. (2012) Accessing dirty data: Methodological strategies for social problems researchers. In M. Larsen and K. Walby (eds) *Brokering Access: Politics, Power and Freedom of Information in Canada*. Vancouver: UBC Press, pp 142–68.

Hall, S. (1982) The lessons of Lord Scarman. *Critical Social Policy*, 2(5): 66–72.

Hall, S. (1988) Foreword. In Independent Committee of Inquiry, *Policing in Hackney 1945–1984*. London: Karia Press/RFSC. Available at: https://hackneyhistory.wordpress.com/2011/03/12/policing-in-hackney-1945-1984/. Last accessed 10 March 2023.

Harkin, J. (2020) Unmasking Stakeknife: The most notorious double agent in British history. *GQ Magazine*, 1 November 2020. Available at: https://www.gq-magazine.co.uk/politics/article/stakeknife-ira-mole. Last accessed 10 July 2022.

Higgerson, D. (2011) How Jack the Ripper is helping to shape FOI rules, 14 July 2011. Available at: https://davidhiggerson.wordpress.com/2011/07/14/how-jack-the-ripper-is-helping-to-shape-foi-rules/. Last accessed 13 July 2022.

Home Affairs Committee (2013a) Undercover Policing: Interim Report, 26 February 2013. Available at: https://publications.parliament.uk/pa/cm201213/cmselect/cmhaff/837/837.pdf. Last accessed 4 April 2022.

Home Affairs Committee (2013b) Minutes of Evidence HC837, 5 February 2013. Available at: https://publications.parliament.uk/pa/cm201213/cmselect/cmhaff/837/130205i.htm. Last accessed 17 May 2022.

Home Office (2012) Definition of policing by consent: FOI release. Available at: https://www.gov.uk/government/publications/policing-by-consent/definition-of-policing-by-consent. Last accessed 3 May 2022.

House of Commons (2015) Daily Hansard – Debate, 26 March 2015. Available at: https://publications.parliament.uk/pa/cm201415/cmhansrd/cm150326/debtext/150326-0001.htm#15032622000001. Last accessed 6 April 2022.

Hutcheon, P. and Gordon, T. (2015) Justice Secretary Michael Matheson backs investigation into police spying in Scotland. *The Herald*, 20 December 2015. Available at: https://www.heraldscotland.com/news/14157243.justice-secretary-michael-matheson-backs-investigation-police-spying-scotland/. Last accessed 22 December 2022.

Information Commissioner's Office (nd) When to refuse to confirm or deny information is held: The Freedom of Information Act. Available at: https://ico.org.uk/media/for-organisations/documents/1166/when_to_refuse_to_confirm_or_deny_section_1_foia.pdf. Last accessed 28 February 2022.

Institute for Government (2018) Explainer: public inquiries, 21 May 2018. Available at: https://www.instituteforgovernment.org.uk/explainers/public-inquiries. Last accessed 9 November 2022.

Investigatory Powers Tribunal (2021) *Wilson v (1) Commissioner of Police of the Metropolis (2) National Police Chiefs' Council*, 30 September 2021. Available at: https://www.ipt-uk.com/judgments.asp?id=61. Last accessed 28 November 2022.

Investigatory Powers Tribunal (2022) *Remedy Order: Wilson v. Commissioner of Police of the Metropolis and National Police Chiefs' Council*, 24 January 2022. Available at: https://www.ipt-uk.com/docs/Remedy%20Order%2024%20Jan%202022.pdf. Last accessed 28 November 2022.

IOPC (2019a) Baroness Jenny Jones – Final Report. *Independent Office for Police Conduct*, 14 February 2019. Available at: https://s3.documentcloud.org/documents/6812417/Baroness-Jenny-Jones-Final-Report-for-Publication.pdf. Last accessed 24 September 2022.

IOPC (2019b) Operation Hibiscus – Final Report. *Independent Office for Police Conduct*, 17 November 2019. Available at: https://policeconduct.gov.uk/sites/default/files/Op_Hibiscus_Final_report_for_publication.pdf. Last accessed 24 September 2022.

IOPC (2020) Op Hibiscus/Baroness Jenny Jones/Op Gilbert – Summary of IOPC conclusions. Available at: https://policeconduct.gov.uk/sites/default/files/Op%20Hibiscus_Baroness%20Jenny%20Jones_Op%20Gilbert_Summary_of_IOPC_conclusions.pdf. Last accessed 28 September 2020.

Ireton, E. (2018) How public is a public inquiry? *Public Law* (April 2018): 277–98.

Jackson, R. (2007) The core commitments of critical terrorism studies. *European Political Science*, 6(3): 244–51.

Jackson, R., Gunning, J. and Breen Smyth, M. (2009) Critical terrorism studies: Framing a new research agenda. In R. Jackson, M. Breen Smyth and J. Gunning (eds) *Critical Terrorism Studies: A New Research Agenda*. Abingdon: Routledge, pp 216–36.

JUSTICE (2017) To 'Neither Confirm Nor Deny': Assessing the response and its impact on access to justice. Available at: https://files.justice.org.uk/wp-content/uploads/2018/02/06170605/NCND-Brochure_FINAL_WEB_Spreads2.pdf. Last accessed 17 May 2022.

Lambert, R. (2014) Researching counter-terrorism: A personal perspective from a former undercover police officer. *Critical Studies on Terrorism*, 7(1): 165–81.

Leahy, T. (2020) *The Intelligence War against the IRA*. Cambridge: Cambridge University Press.

Lentz, S.A. and Chaires, R.H. (2007) The invention of Peel's principles: A study of policing 'textbook' history. *Journal of Criminal Justice*, 35(1): 69–79.

Lewis, P. (2009) Police caught on tape trying to recruit Plane Stupid protester as spy. *The Guardian*, 24 April 2009. Available at: https://www.theguardian.com/uk/2009/apr/24/strathclyde-police-plane-stupid-recruit-spy. Last accessed 22 December 2022.

Lewis, P. and Evans, R. (2013) Police spies: In bed with a fictional character. *The Guardian*, 1 March 2013. Available at: https://www.theguardian.com/uk/2013/mar/01/police-spy-fictional-character. Last accessed 20 April 2022.

Lewis, P., Evans, R. and Pollak, S. (2013) Trauma of spy's girlfriend: 'Like being raped by the state'. *The Guardian*, 24 June 2013. Available at: https://www.theguardian.com/uk/2013/jun/24/undercover-police-spy-girlfriend-child. Last accessed 17 April 22

Loadenthal, M. (2014) When cops 'go native': Policing revolution through sexual infiltration and panopticonism. *Critical Studies on Terrorism*, 7(1): 24–42.

Loftus, B. (2019) Normalizing covert surveillance: The subterranean world of policing. *The British Journal of Sociology*, 70 (5): 2070–91.

Loftus, B. and Goold, B. (2012) Covert surveillance and the invisibilities of policing. *Criminology & Criminal Justice*, 12(3): 275–88.

Loftus, B., Goold, B. and MacGiollabhui, S. (2015) From a visible spectacle to an invisible presence: The working culture of covert policing. *British Journal of Criminology*, 56(4): 629–45.

London Edinburgh Weekend Return Group (2021) *In and against the State: Discussion Notes for Socialists* (2nd edn). London: Pluto Press.

Lubbers, E. (2012) *Secret Manoeuvres in the Dark: Corporate and Police Spying on Activists*. London: Pluto Press.

Lubbers, E. (2015) Undercover research: Corporate and police spying on activists. An introduction to activist intelligence as a new field of study. *Surveillance & Society*, 13(3/4): 338–53.

Lubbers, E. (2018) 'Mary' received the real name of #spycop 'Rick Gibson'. *Undercover Research Group*, 7 May 2018. Available at: https://undercoverresearch.net/2018/05/07/mary-received-the-real-name-of-spycop-rick-gibson/. Last accessed 20 September 2022.

Lubbers, E. (2019) Undercover research: Academics, activists and others investigate political policing. In A. Choudry (ed.) *Activists and the Surveillance State*. London: Pluto Press.

Mac Giollabhuí, S., Goold, B. and Loftus, B. (2016) Watching the watchers: Conducting ethnographic research on covert police investigation in the United Kingdom. *Qualitative Research*, 16(6): 630–45.

Macpherson, W. (1999) The Stephen Lawrence Inquiry. Available at: https://assets.publishing.service.gov.uk/government/uploads/system/uploads/attachment_data/file/277111/4262.pdf. Last accessed 7 February 2022.

Marx, G. (1984) Notes on the discovery, collection, and assessment of hidden and dirty data. In J. Schneider and J. Kitsuse (eds) *Studies in the Sociology of Social Problems*. Norwood, NJ: Ablex, pp 78–113.

Marx, G. (1988) *Undercover: Police Surveillance in America*. Berkeley, CA: University of California Press.

May, T. (2014) Oral Statement to Parliament: The Ellison Review, 6 March 2014. Available at: https://www.gov.uk/government/speeches/the-ellison-review. Last accessed 7 February 2022.

McDonald, C. (2019) External review questions Police Scotland's insistence that officers being told to burn secret files in a carpark was routine housekeeping. *Sunday Post*, 24 November 2019. Available at: https://www.sundaypost.com/fp/if-it-looks-like-a-cover-up-smells-like-a-cover-up-if-even-the-met-cant-deny-its-a-cover-up-then-trust-me-its-a-cover-upmarch-3-2019/. Last accessed 28 September 2022.

McDonnell, J. (2022) Introduction. In S. Reel, *Silence Is Not an Option*. London: Bookmarks, pp 3–6.

McGovern, M. (2013) Inquiring into collusion? Collusion, the state and the management of truth recovery in Northern Ireland. *State Crime Journal*, 2(2): 4–29.

McGovern, M. (2016) The contradictions of harm: Police spies, 'domestic radicals' and denying accountability. Presentation at the University of Brighton CAPPE annual conference, 7–9 September 2016. Unpublished.

McGovern, M. (2022) Legacy, truth and collusion in the North of Ireland. *Race & Class* 64 (3): 59–89.

McKerrell, N. (2019) 'Spycops' in Scotland: Matilda Gifford's judicial review – no right to the truth? *Edinburgh Law Review*, 23(2): 253–8.

McKerrell, N. (2022) Sheku Bayoh – immunity of evidence in public inquiries: Truth versus the administration of justice? *Edinburgh Law Review* 26(3): 453–8.

McLaughlin, E. (2007) *The New Policing*. London: Sage.

McLean, D. (2022) *Small Town Girl: Love, Lies and the Undercover Police*. London: Hodder and Stoughton.

Metropolitan Police (2023) Met Police response to the Undercover Policing Inquiry Tranche 1 Interim Report. Available at: https://news.met.police.uk/news/met-police-response-to-the-undercover-policing-inquiry-tranche-1-interim-report-469230. Last accessed 6 September 2023.

Mills, H. (2017) The undercover policing of political protest. Briefing 21. *Centre for Crime and Justice Studies*. Available at: https://www.crimeandjustice.org.uk/sites/crimeandjustice.org.uk/files/Undercover%20policing%20October.pdf. Last accessed 14 June 2022.

Muir, H. (2014) Lawrence family lawyer Imran Khan: 'We see what the state is capable of'. *The Guardian*, 25 March 2014. Available at: https://www.theguardian.com/law/2014/mar/25/stephen-lawrence-family-lawyer-imran-khan-state-capable-police. Last accessed 4 November 2022.

Murji, K. (2020) Stuart Hall as a criminological theorist-activist. *Theoretical Criminology*, 24(3): 447–60.

NIQB (2003) Judgement: In the matter of an application by Freddie Scappaticci for Judicial Review, 18 August 2003. Available at: https://www.judiciaryni.uk/sites/judiciary/files/decisions/In%20the%20matter%20of%20an%20application%20by%20Freddie%20Scappaticci%20for%20Judicial%20Review.pdf. Last accessed 3 January 2023.

Norton-Taylor, R. (2014) MI5 spied on leading British historians for decades, secret files reveal. *The Guardian*, 24 October 2014. Available at: https://www.theguardian.com/world/2014/oct/24/mi5-spied-historians-eric-hobsbawm-christopher-hill-secret-files. Last accessed 16 March 2023.

O'Driscoll, D. (2017) What is the spycops inquiry hearing about? *Campaign Opposing Police Surveillance*, 20 November 2017. Available at: http://campaignopposingpolicesurveillance.com/2017/11/20/what-is-the-spycops-inquiry-hearing-about/. Last accessed 10 November 2022.

O'Driscoll, D. and Lubbers, E. (2016) Another #spycop exposed: Carlo Neri confirmed as an undercover. *Undercover Research Group*, 18 January 2016. Available at: https://undercoverresearch.net/2016/01/18/how-we-proved-carlo-neri-was-an-undercover-police-officer/. Last accessed 12 September 2022.

Oltermann, P. and Evans, R. (2022) British police spy unlawfully operated in Germany, court finds. *The Guardian*, 11 October 2022. Available at: https://www.theguardian.com/uk-news/2022/oct/11/british-police-spy-unlawfully-operated-in-germany-court-finds. Last accessed 22 December 2022.

Operation Herne (2013) *Report 1: Use of cover identities*. Available at: https://www.met.police.uk/SysSiteAssets/foi-media/metropolitan-police/priorities_and_how_we_are_doing/corporate/operation-herne---report-1---use-of-covert-identities. Last accessed 14 June 2022.

Operation Herne (2014a) *Report 3*, July 2014. Available at: https://www.met.police.uk/SysSiteAssets/foi-media/metropolitan-police/priorities_and_how_we_are_doing/corporate/operation-herne---report-3---special-demonstration-squad-reporting-mentions-of-sensitive-campaigns. Last accessed 22 November 2022.

Operation Herne (2014b) *Report 2: Allegations of Peter Francis (Operation Trinity)*. Available at: https://www.met.police.uk/SysSiteAssets/foi-media/metropolitan-police/priorities_and_how_we_are_doing/corporate/operation-herne---report-2-allegations-of-peter-francis-operation-trinity. Last accessed 20 June 2022.

Peplow, S. (2018) 'A tactical manoeuvre to apply pressure': Race and the role of public inquiries in the 1980 Bristol 'riot'. *Twentieth Century British History*, 29(1): 129–55.

Peterborough Telegraph (2018) Woman at centre of allegations against former spy cop and current Peterborough City Councillor hits out at police. 21 March 2018. Available at: https://www.peterboroughtoday.co.uk/news/politics/woman-centre-allegations-against-former-spy-cop-and-current-peterborough-city-councillor-hits-out-police-investigations-315896. Last accessed 4 April 2022.

Police Spies Out of Lives (2011) Legal action against Metropolitan Police, 16 December 2011. Available at: https://policespiesoutoflives.org.uk/legal-action-against-metropolitan-police/. Last accessed 20 January 2023.

Police Spies Out of Lives (2019) Statement on Carlo Soracchi (Neri) HN104. Available at: https://policespiesoutoflives.org.uk/statement-on-carlo-soracchi-neri-hn104. Last accessed 18 September 2022.

Police Spies Out of Lives (nd) Donna's story. Available at: https://policespiesoutoflives.org.uk/our-stories/donnas-story-new/. Last accessed 4 April 2022.

Police Spies Out of Lives (nd) Helen's story. Available at: https://policespiesoutoflives.org.uk/our-stories/helens-story-2/. Last accessed 4 April 2022.

Police Spies Out of Lives (nd) Jessica's story. Available at: https://policespiesoutoflives.org.uk/our-stories/jessicas-story-2/. Last accessed 4 April 2022.

Reel, S. (2022) *Silence Is Not an Option*. London: Bookmarks.

Reiner, R. (2016) Foreword. In M. Brunger, S. Tong and D. Martin (eds) *Introduction to Policing Research: Taking Lessons from Practice*. London: Routledge, p xiii.

Rolston, B. and Scraton, P. (2005) In the full glare of English politics: Ireland, inquiries and the British state. *British Journal of Criminology*, 45(4): 547–64.

Rose, N. (2011) *Ratcliffe-on-Soar power station protest: Inquiry into disclosure*. London: Office of Surveillance Commissioners.

Rotberg, R.I. and Thompson, D. (2000) (eds) *Truth v. Justice: The Morality of Truth Commissions*. Princeton, NJ: Princeton University Press.

Rowe, M. (2020) *Policing the Police: Challenges of Democracy and Accountability*. Bristol: Policy Press.

Schlembach, R. (2016) The Pitchford inquiry into undercover policing: Some lessons from the preliminary hearings. *Papers from the British Criminology Conference* 16: 57–74. Available at: http://www.britsoccrim.org/wp-content/uploads/2016/12/pbcc_2016_Schlembach.pdf. Last accessed 20 April 2022.

Schlembach, R. (2018) Undercover policing and the spectre of 'domestic extremism': The covert surveillance of environmental activism in Britain. *Social Movement Studies*, 17(5): 491–506.

Schlembach, R. (2020) Resisting the surveillance state: Deviant knowledge and undercover policing. In E.L. Hart, J. Greener and R. Moth (eds) *Resisting the Punitive State*. London: Pluto Press, pp 171–86.

Schlembach, R. and Hart, E.L. (2022) Towards a criminology of public inquiries: From cautious optimism to contestation in the Brook House Inquiry. *Criminology & Criminal Justice*, Online First at https://doi.org/10.1177/17488958221115797.

Scott, S. (nd) Stafford Scott talks about undercover policing. *The Monitoring Group*. Available at: https://tmg-uk.org/news/stafford-scott-talks-about-undercover-policing. Last accessed 27 November 2022.

Scraton, P. (1999) Policing with contempt: The degrading of truth and denial of justice in the aftermath of the Hillsborough disaster. *Journal of Law and Society*, 26(3): 273–97.

Scraton, P. (2002) Lost lives, hidden voices: 'Truth' and controversial deaths. *Race & Class*, 44(1): 107–18.

Scraton, P. (2013a) From deceit to disclosure: The politics of official inquiries in the United Kingdom. In G. Gilligan and J. Pratt (eds) *Crime, Truth and Justice: Official Inquiry, Discourse, Knowledge*. Abingdon: Routledge, pp 46–68.

Scraton, P. (2013b) The legacy of Hillsborough: Liberating truth, challenging power. *Race & Class*, 55(2): 1–27.

Smith, D. and Chamberlain, P. (2015a) On the blacklist: How did the UK's top building firms get secret information on their workers? *The Guardian*, 27 February 2015. Available at: https://www.theguardian.com/uk-news/2015/feb/27/on-the-blacklist-building-firms-secret-information-on-workers. Last accessed 8 November 2022.

Smith, D. and Chamberlain, P. (2015b) *Blacklisted: The Secret War between Big Business and Union Activists*. Oxford: New Internationalist Publications.

Spalek, B. and Lambert, R. (2008) Muslim communities, counter-terrorism and de-radicalisation: A reflective approach to engagement. *International Journal of Law, Crime and Justice*, 36(4): 257–70.

Spalek, B. and O'Rawe, M. (2014) Researching counter-terrorism: A critical perspective from the field in light of allegations and findings of covert activities by undercover police officers. *Critical Studies on Terrorism*, 7(1): 150–64.

# References

Stammers, N. (2009) *Human Rights and Social Movements*. London: Pluto Press.

Stephens-Griffin, N. (2020) #Notallcops: Exploring 'rotten apple' narratives in media reporting of Lush's 2018 'Spycops' undercover policing campaign. *International Journal for Crime, Justice and Social Democracy*, 9(4): 177–94.

Stephens-Griffin, N. (2021) 'Everyone was questioning everything': Understanding the derailing impact of undercover policing on the lives of UK environmentalists. *Social Movement Studies*, 20(4): 459–77.

Stephens-Griffin, N. (2022) 'Nothing has changed …': A report from a survey of political activists targeted by undercover police in the UK. Northumbria University. Available at: https://researchportal.northumbria.ac.uk/ws/portalfiles/portal/70346815/Spycops_Survey_Report_FINAL_April_2022.pdf. Last accessed 1 August 2023.

Stone, R. (2015) *Hidden Stories of the Stephen Lawrence Inquiry: Personal Reflections*. Bristol: Policy Press.

Sulitzeanu-Kenan, R. (2010) Reflection in the shadow of blame: When do politicians appoint Commissions of Inquiry? *British Journal of Political Science*, 40(3): 613–34.

Syal, R. and Wainwright, M. (2011) Undercover police: Officer A named as Lynn Watson. *The Guardian*, 19 January 2011. Available at: https://www.theguardian.com/uk/2011/jan/19/undercover-police-officer-lynn-watson. Last accessed 6 April 2022.

Taylor, S. (2015) Investigation into links between Special Demonstration Squad and Home Office, 6 January 2015. Available at: https://assets.publishing.service.gov.uk/government/uploads/system/uploads/attachment_data/file/411785/2015-01-06_FINAL_Report_on_HO_links_to_SDS_v2.4_REDACTED_FINAL.pdf. Last accessed 7 June 2022.

TBS (2018) Letters: As the son of an undercover cop, I support what Lush did. *The Guardian*, 10 June 2018. Available at: https://www.theguardian.com/uk-news/2018/jun/10/as-the-son-of-an-undercover-cop-i-wholeheartedly-support-lush. Last accessed 21 February 2023.

Thomas, O. (2020) Security in the balance: How Britain tried to keep its Iraq War secrets. *Security Dialogue*, 51(1): 77–95.

Thomas, O. and Cooper, S. (2020) Understanding issue salience, social inequality and the (non)appointment of UK public inquiries: A new research agenda. *Public Money & Management*, 40(6): 457–67.

Thompson, T. (2010) Inside the lonely and violent world of the Yard's elite undercover unit. *The Observer*, 14 March 2010. Available at: https://www.theguardian.com/uk/2010/mar/14/undercover-police-far-left-secret. Last accessed 7 February 2022.

Thorpe, V. (2017) How a Soho coffee house gave birth to the New Left. *The Observer*, 23 April 2017. Available at: https://www.theguardian.com/politics/2017/apr/22/cafe-cnd-new-left. Last accessed 19 March 2023.

Trautwein, A. (2017) 'Seit 28 Jahren ist die Rote Flora infiltriert': Interview with Andreas Blechschmidt. *Zeit Online*, 22 June 2017. Available at: https://www.zeit.de/hamburg/2017-06/rote-flora-verdeckte-ermittler-prozess-interview. Last accessed 17 March 2022.

TUC (2017) Trade Union Act 2016 – A TUC guide for union reps, 17 April 2017. Available at: https://www.tuc.org.uk/research-analysis/reports/trade-union-act-2016-tuc-guide-union-reps. Last accessed 6 March 2023.

Tuitt, P. (nd) Don't Ask, Don't Tell: Police responses to police misconduct. Available at: https://www.patriciatuitt.com/single-post/don-t-ask-don-t-tell-police-responses-to-police-misconduct. Last accessed 26 February 2023.

Ture, K. and Hamilton C.V. (1992) *Black Power: The Politics of Liberation in America*. New York: Vintage Books.

UCPI (2015) Chairman's opening remarks, 28 July 2015. Available at: https://www.ucpi.org.uk/wp-content/uploads/2015/07/Opening-Remarks.pdf. Last accessed 15 June 2022.

UCPI (2016a) Submissions on behalf of the NPCC on the issue of restriction orders. 12 February 2016. Available at: https://www.ucpi.org.uk/wp-content/uploads/2016/02/160212-submissions-on-the-legal-approach-to-restriction-orders-NPCC.pdf. Last accessed 16 June 2022.

UCPI (2016b) Restriction orders: Legal Principles and Approach Ruling, 3 May 2016. Available at: https://www.ucpi.org.uk/wp-content/uploads/2016/05/160503-ruling-legal-approach-to-restriction-orders.pdf. Last accessed 28 November 2022.

UCPI (2016c) Submissions on restriction orders – Metropolitan Police Service, 12 February 2016. Available at: https://www.ucpi.org.uk/wp-content/uploads/2016/02/160212-submissions-on-the-legal-approach-to-restriction-orders-Met-Police.pdf. Last accessed 14 June 2022.

UCPI (2016d) Transcript – Preliminary Hearing: Restriction order approach, Day 2, 23 March 2016. Available at: https://www.ucpi.org.uk/wp-content/uploads/2016/03/160323-transcript-of-hearing-on-23-March-2016-1.pdf. Last accessed 14 June 2022.

UCPI (2016e) Press notice: The ruling in respect of the test for restriction orders, 3 May 2022. Available at: https://www.ucpi.org.uk/wp-content/uploads/2016/05/160503-press-note-restriction-orders.pdf. Last accessed 20 June 2022.

UCPI (2016f) Submission on behalf of the NPCC on the principle of Neither Confirm Nor Deny, 21 January 2016. Available at: https://www.ucpi.org.uk/wp-content/uploads/2016/03/160121-submissions-on-the-NCND-principle-NPCC.pdf. Last accessed 2 August 2022.

UCPI (2016g) Skeleton argument on behalf of various non-police, non-state core participants, 26 April 2016. Available at: https://www.ucpi.org.uk/wp-content/uploads/2016/04/160426-skeleton-argument-undertakings-DPG-and-PIL.pdf. Last accessed 29 September 2022.

# References

UCPI (2016h) Counsel to the Inquiry's supplementary note to undertakings, 25 April 2016. Available at: https://www.ucpi.org.uk/wp-content/uploads/2016/05/160425-supplementary-note-by-Counsel-to-the-Inquiry-re-undertakings-v2.pdf. Last accessed 29 September 2022.

UCPI (2016i) Transcript – Preliminary Hearing: Undertakings, 27 April 2016. Available at: https://www.ucpi.org.uk/wp-content/uploads/2016/04/160427-transcript-of-undertakings-hearing.pdf. Last accessed 29 September 2022.

UCPI (2016j) Undertakings – Ruling, 26 May 2016. Available at: https://www.ucpi.org.uk/wp-content/uploads/2016/05/160526-ruling-undertakings.pdf. Last accessed 6 February 2023.

UCPI (2016k) Applications for restriction orders on behalf of police officers – risk assessments: Note to core participants, 20 October 2016. Available at: https://www.ucpi.org.uk/wp-content/uploads/2016/10/161020-note-to-CPs-risk-assessments.pdf. Last accessed 28 October 2022.

UCPI (2017a) Applications by the Metropolitan Police Service for an extension of time for the making of restriction order applications and for a change by the Inquiry to its approach to investigation – Ruling, 2 May 2017. Available at: https://www.ucpi.org.uk/wp-content/uploads/2017/05/20170502-ruling-MPS-applications-re-SDS.pdf. Last accessed 14 December 2022.

UCPI (2017b) Index to media coverage, November 2017. Available at: https://www.ucpi.org.uk/wp-content/uploads/2017/11/Media-coverage-bundle.pdf. Last accessed 22 December 2022.

UCPI (2017c) The 'Mosaic Effect' and the potential risk to officers. Metropolitan Police Service report, 1 December 2015. Available at: https://www.ucpi.org.uk/wp-content/uploads/2017/08/Mosaic-report-open-version.pdf. Last accessed 5 July 2022.

UCPI (2017d) Transcript – Preliminary Hearing, 20 November 2017. Available at: https://www.ucpi.org.uk/wp-content/uploads/2018/01/20171120-transcript-SDS-anonymity.pdf. Last accessed 5 July 2022.

UCPI (2017e) Chairman's statement, 20 November 2017. Available at: https://www.ucpi.org.uk/wp-content/uploads/2017/11/20171120-Chairman-statement.pdf. Last accessed 13 September 2022.

UCPI (2017f) Application for restriction order (anonymity) re: N297, MPS, Department of Legal Services, 3 July 2017. Available at: https://www.ucpi.org.uk/wp-content/uploads/2017/08/HN297-Open-application-from-the-MPS.pdf. Last accessed 11 September 2022.

UCPI (2017g) N297 – Risk Assessment, 3 July 2017. Available at: https://www.ucpi.org.uk/wp-content/uploads/2017/08/HN297-Open-risk-assessment-from-the-MPS.pdf. Last accessed 11 September 2022.

UCPI (2017h) 'Minded-to' note: Applications for restriction orders in respect of the real and cover names of officers of the Special Operations Squad and the Special Demonstrations Squad, 3 August 2017. Available at: https://www.ucpi.org.uk/wp-content/uploads/2017/08/20170803-Minded-to.pdf. Last accessed 11 September 2022.

UCPI (2017i) Written submissions of Guardian News and Media Limited, 4 October 2017. Available at: https://www.ucpi.org.uk/wp-content/uploads/2017/10/20171004-Media-submissions-re-SDS-Minded-to.pdf. Last accessed 11 September 2022.

UCPI (2017j) Submissions on behalf of the NPNS core participants re: the Chairman's 'Minded-to' note dated 3 August, 5 October 2017. Available at: https://www.ucpi.org.uk/wp-content/uploads/2017/10/20171004-NPNSCPs-submissions-re-SDS-Minded-to.pdf. Last accessed 11 September 2022.

UCPI (2017k) Transcript – Preliminary Hearing: SDS anonymity, Hearing 2, 21 November 2017. Available at: https://www.ucpi.org.uk/wp-content/uploads/2018/01/20171121-transcript-final.pdf. Last accessed 20 September 2022.

UCPI (2017l) Witness statement – Neil Hutchison, 17 June 2017. Available at: https://www.ucpi.org.uk/wp-content/uploads/2017/08/Hutchison-WS-R9-8-and-R9-12.pdf. Last accessed 29 September 2022.

UCPI (2017m) Sixth Update Note, October 2017. Available at: https://www.ucpi.org.uk/wp-content/uploads/2017/11/20171103-sixth-update-note.pdf. Last accessed 6 October 2022.

UCPI (2017n) Transcript – Preliminary Hearing: SDS anonymity, Hearing 1 / Day 1, 5 April 2017. Available at: https://www.ucpi.org.uk/wp-content/uploads/2017/04/20170405-transcript-MPS-applications-re-SDS-1-of-2.pdf. Last accessed 8 November 2022.

UCPI (2017o) Rehabilitation of Offenders Act 1974: Position statement on behalf of the MPS, 28 April 2017. Available at: https://www.ucpi.org.uk/wp-content/uploads/2017/05/20170428-submissions-re-ROA-1974-MPS.pdf. Last accessed 3 December 2022.

UCPI (2017p) MPS submissions on the Rehabilitation of Offenders Act 1974, 8 November 2017. Available at: https://www.ucpi.org.uk/wp-content/uploads/2017/11/20171108-ROA-1974-submissions-MPS.pdf. Last accessed 3 December 2022.

UCPI (2017q) Non-police, non-state core participants' submissions on the Rehabilitation of Offenders Act 1974, 2 May 2017. Available at: https://www.ucpi.org.uk/wp-content/uploads/2017/05/20170502-submissions-re-ROA-1974-NPNSCPs.pdf. Last accessed 3 December 2022.

UCPI (2018a) Anonymity: Special Demonstration Squad – Ruling 3, 20 February 2018. Available at: https://www.ucpi.org.uk/wp-content/uploads/2018/02/20180220-ruling-SDS-anonymity.pdf. Last accessed 6 April 2022.

UCPI (2018b) Special Demonstration Squad Tradecraft Manual. Available at: https://www.ucpi.org.uk/wp-content/uploads/2018/03/20180319-TC-Documents_Final_Version.pdf. Last accessed 8 March 2022.

UCPI (2018c) Application for restriction order in respect of the real and cover names of HN15 – Ruling. Available at: https://www.ucpi.org.uk/wp-content/uploads/2018/04/20180410_ruling_HN15.pdf. Last accessed 19 June 2022.

UCPI (2018d) Transcript – Preliminary Hearing: SDS anonymity, 5 February 2018. Available at: https://www.ucpi.org.uk/wp-content/uploads/2018/02/20180502-transcript.pdf. Last accessed 20 September 2022.

UCPI (2018e) Ruling 12 – HN104. Available at: https://www.ucpi.org.uk/wp-content/uploads/2018/08/20180807-SDS_anonymity_Ruling_12_HN104_real_name-1.pdf. Last accessed 28 September 2022.

UCPI (2018f) Applications for restriction orders in respect of the real and cover names of officers of the Special Operations Squad and the Special Demonstrations Squad – 'Minded to' note 9 and Ruling 8, 23 May 2018. Available at: https://www.ucpi.org.uk/wp-content/uploads/2018/05/20180523-Minded_to_note_9_and_ruling_8.pdf. Last accessed 5 December 2022.

UCPI (2018g) Transcript – Strategic Review Hearing, 18 May 2018. Available at: https://www.ucpi.org.uk/wp-content/uploads/2018/05/20180518-Hearing-Transcript-Strategic-Review-full-day.pdf. Last accessed 19 November 2022.

UCPI (2018h) Transcript – Preliminary Hearing, 21 March 2018. Available at: https://www.ucpi.org.uk/wp-content/uploads/2018/03/20180321-draft-transcript-.pdf. Last accessed 8 November 2022.

UCPI (2018i) The Inquiry into Undercover Policing – Strategic Review, May 2018. Available at: https://www.ucpi.org.uk/wp-content/uploads/2018/06/20180510-strategic_review.pdf. Last accessed 23 March 2023.

UCPI (2019a) Eighth Update Note, July 2019. Available at: https://www.ucpi.org.uk/wp-content/uploads/2019/07/20190715-eighth-update-note.pdf. Last accessed 15 April 2022.

UCPI (2019b) Preliminary Issue: Privacy and Data Protection Note regarding the Inquiry's evidence gathering process, 26 February 2019. Available at: https://www.ucpi.org.uk/wp-content/uploads/2019/02/20190226_Privacy_hearing_supplemental_note_FINAL.pdf. Last accessed 21 September 2022.

UCPI (2019c) Chairman's statement on Data Protection and Privacy, 11 April 2019. Available at: https://www.ucpi.org.uk/wp-content/uploads/2019/04/20190411-Chairmans_Statement_on_Data_Protection_and_Privacy.pdf. Last accessed 8 October 2022.

UCPI (2019d) Letter to the Inquiry Chair by academic researchers, 12 April 2019. Available at: https://www.ucpi.org.uk/wp-content/uploads/2019/04/20190412_chairmans_letter_to_dr_schlembach_inquiry.pdf. Last accessed 8 October 2022.

UCPI (2019e) Chairman's letter to Dr Schlembach, 25 March 2019. Available at: https://www.ucpi.org.uk/wp-content/uploads/2019/04/20190325-letter_by_academics_to_ucpi_evidence_gathering_process.pdf. Last accessed 8 October 2022.

UCPI (2019f) Transcript – Preliminary Issue: Privacy (First Hearing), 31 January 2019. Available at: https://www.ucpi.org.uk/wp-content/uploads/2019/01/20190131-transcript-Privacy_hearing.pdf. Last accessed 19 November 2022.

UCPI (2019g) Transcript – Preliminary Issue: Privacy (Second Hearing), 25 March 2019. Available at: https://www.ucpi.org.uk/wp-content/uploads/2019/04/20190325-transcript-Privacy_hearing.pdf. Last accessed 26 October 2022.

UCPI (2020a) Transcript – Opening statements, 17 November 2020. Available at: https://www.ucpi.org.uk/wp-content/uploads/2020/11/20201117-ucpi_opening_statements_transcript.pdf. Last accessed 20 January 2023.

UCPI (2020b) Transcript – Opening statements, 10 November 2020. Available at: https://www.ucpi.org.uk/wp-content/uploads/2020/11/20201110-ucpi_opening_statements_transcript.pdf. Last accessed 20 January 2023.

UCPI (2020c) Peter Francis: Opening statement of Undercover Policing Inquiry, 29 October 2020. Available at: https://www.ucpi.org.uk/wp-content/uploads/2020/11/20201029-Opening_Statement-Peter_Francis.pdf. Last accessed 7 February 2022.

UCPI (2020d) Written opening statement on behalf of 'Alison', 'Bea', 'C', 'Ellie', Denise Fuller, Donna, Belinda Harvey, 'Jane', 'Jenny', 'Jessica', 'Lisa', 'Lizzie', 'Maya', 'Monica', 'Naomi', 'Rosa', 'Ruth', 'Sara', Helen Steel, 'Wendy', Kate Wilson, 26 October 2020. Available at: https://www.ucpi.org.uk/wp-content/uploads/2020/11/20201026-Opening_Statement-CAT_H_Birnbergs-PKQC-AMENDED_09.11.20.pdf. Last accessed 13 April 2022.

UCPI (2020e) Opening statement on behalf of the Category M core participants, 23 October 2020. Available at: https://www.ucpi.org.uk/wp-content/uploads/2020/11/20201023-Opening_Statement-Cat_M_CPs-Hickman_Rose.pdf. Last accessed 13 April 2022.

UCPI (2020f) UCPI Evidence Hearings, Tranche 1 (Phase 1), Day 8. Transcript. Available at: https://www.ucpi.org.uk/wp-content/uploads/2020/11/20201111-ucpi_evidence_hearings_transcript.pdf. Last accessed 21 April 2022.

UCPI (2020g) Opening statement of the Metropolitan Police Service, 22 October 2020. Available at: https://www.ucpi.org.uk/wp-content/uploads/2020/11/20201022-Opening_Statement-MPS_CL.pdf. Last accessed 7 June 2022.

UCPI (2020h) Transcript – Opening statements, 3 November 2020. Available at: https://www.ucpi.org.uk/wp-content/uploads/2020/11/20201103-ucpi_opening_statements_transcript.pdf. Last accessed 7 August 2022.

UCPI (2020i) Transcript – Opening statements, 6 November 2020. Available at: https://www.ucpi.org.uk/wp-content/uploads/2020/11/20201106-ucpi_opening_statements_transcript.pdf. Last accessed 29 September 2022.

UCPI (2021a) Council for the Inquiry opening statement for Tranche 1/Phase 2, 21 April 2021. Available at: https://www.ucpi.org.uk/wp-content/uploads/2021/04/20210421-CTIs_T1P2_Opening_Statement.pdf?v1. Last accessed 12 April 2022.

UCPI (2021b) Written opening statement of Madeleine, 20 April 2021. Available at: https://www.ucpi.org.uk/wp-content/uploads/2021/04/20210420-_Opening-Statement-Madeleine-Amended.pdf. Last accessed 12 September 2022.

UCPI (2021c) Letter from Steven Bramley CBE (on behalf of the Commissioner of the Metropolitan Police Service), 8 January 2021. Available at: https://www.ucpi.org.uk/wp-content/uploads/2021/01/20210119-letter_from_mps_to_dr_paul_bishop.pdf. Last accessed 29 April 2022.

UCPI (2021d) Transcript – Directions Hearing, 26 January 2021. Available at: https://www.ucpi.org.uk/wp-content/uploads/2021/01/20210126-directions_hearing_transcript.pdf. Last accessed 21 August 2022.

UCPI (2022a) Opening statement in Tranche 1/Phase 3 to the Undercover Policing Inquiry on behalf of Lindsey German, Richard Chessum, 'Mary', 24 April 2022. Available at: https://www.ucpi.org.uk/wp-content/uploads/2022/05/20220425-T1P3-LG_RC_M-Opening-Statement.pdf. Last accessed 12 May 2022.

UCPI (2022b) Opening statement on behalf of Tariq Ali, Ernie Tate and Piers Corbyn for Tranche 1/Phase 3, 27 April 2022. Available at: https://www.ucpi.org.uk/wp-content/uploads/2022/05/20220427-T1P3-TA_ET_PC-Opening_Statement.pdf. Last accessed 13 May 2022.

UCPI (2022c) First witness statement of David Smith, 2 December 2020. Available at: https://www.ucpi.org.uk/wp-content/uploads/2022/05/MPS_0747443.pdf. Last accessed 22 December 2022.

UCPI (2022d) Evidence hearing, Tranche 1/(Phase 3), Day 5. Transcript, 13 May 2022. Available at: https://www.ucpi.org.uk/wp-content/uploads/2022/05/20220513-ucpi-t1_p3-evidence_hearings-transcript.pdf. Last accessed 12 January 2022.

UCPI (2022e) Transcript – Opening statements, Tranche 1/Phase 3, Day 2, 10 May 2022. Available at: https://www.ucpi.org.uk/wp-content/uploads/2022/05/20220510-ucpi-t1_p3-opening_statements-transcript.pdf?v1. Last accessed 28 November 2022.

UCPI (2022f) Eleventh Update Note, July 2022. Available at: https://www.ucpi.org.uk/wp-content/uploads/2022/07/20220729-eleventh_update_note.pdf. Last accessed 19 October 2022.

UCPI (2022g) Applications for restriction orders in respect of the real and cover names of officers of the Special Operations Squad and the Special Demonstrations Squad, and those connected with these squads – 'Minded to' note 15, 22 July 2022. Available at: https://www.ucpi.org.uk/wp-content/uploads/2022/07/20220722-SDS_anonymity_Minded_to_15.pdf. Last accessed 6 October 2022.

UCPI (2022h) Applications for restriction orders in respect of the real and cover names of officers of the National Public Order Intelligence Unit and its predecessor/successor units – 'Minded to' Note 4, 18 January 2022. Available at: https://www.ucpi.org.uk/wp-content/uploads/2022/01/20220118-Minded_to_4-NPOIU_anonymity-batch_3.pdf?v2. Last accessed 23 October 2022.

UCPI (2022i) Ruling 22. Available at: https://www.ucpi.org.uk/wp-content/uploads/2022/10/20221026-sds_anonymity-ruling_22.pdf. Last accessed 26 November 2022.

UCPI (2023a) Undercover Policing Inquiry Tranche 1 Interim Report, June 2023. Available at: https://www.ucpi.org.uk/wp-content/uploads/2023/06/Undercover-Policing-Inquiry-Tranche-1-Interim-Report.pdf. Last accessed 6 September 2023.

UCPI (2023b) Counsel to the Inquiry's opening statement for Tranche 1 Modules 2b and 2c, 27 January 2023. Available at: https://www.ucpi.org.uk/wp-content/uploads/2023/01/20230127-CTIs_M2B-C_Opening_Statement.pdf. Last accessed 20 March 2023.

UCPI (2023c) Tranche 1 closing submissions on behalf of Tariq Ali, Ernie Tate and Piers Corbyn, 22 February 2023. Available at: https://www.ucpi.org.uk/wp-content/uploads/2023/02/20230222-T1-Closing_Statement-Ali-Corbyn-Tate.pdf. Last accessed 22 March 2023.

Ullrich, P. (2019) Data and obstacle: Police (non)visibility in research on protest policing. *Surveillance & Society*, 17(2): 405–21.

Undercover Research Group (2015) Bob Lambert controversy intensifies. Available at: https://undercoverresearch.net/2015/02/09/399/. Last accessed 14 May 2022.

Undercover Research Group (2020) Spycops Inquiry: Opening statement from Dónal O'Driscoll, 5 November 2020. Available at: https://undercoverresearch.net/2020/11/05/spycops-inquiry-opening-statement-from-donal-odriscoll/. Last accessed 21 September 2022.

Undercover Research Group (nd) Bob Lambert. Available at: https://powerbase.info/index.php/Bob_Lambert. Last accessed 14 December 2022.

Waddington, P.A.J. (1994) *Liberty and Order: Public Order Policing in a Capital City*. London: UCL Press.

Waddington, P.A.J. (2016) Is undercover policing worth the risk? Oxford University Press Blog. Available at: https://blog.oup.com/2016/08/undercover-policing-risk-law/. Last accessed 20 April 2022.

Walby, K. and Monaghan, J. (2011) Private eyes and public order: Policing and surveillance in the suppression of animal rights activists in Canada. *Social Movement Studies*, 10(1): 21–37.

Walters, R. (2003) *Deviant Knowledge: Criminology, Politics and Policy*. Cullompton: Willan.

Walters, W. (2021) *State Secrecy and Security: Refiguring the Covert Imaginary*. Abingdon: Routledge.

White, L. (2010) Discourse, denial and dehumanisation: Former detainees' experiences of narrating state violence in Northern Ireland. *Papers from the British Criminology Conference*, 10: 3–18.

Wilson, K. (2020) The European Convention on Human Rights and the Investigatory Powers Tribunal: Rationalising a law unto itself? *Trinity College Law Review*, 23: 129–54.

Wilson, T. and Walton, R. (2019) Extremism Rebellion: A review of ideology and tactics. *Policy Exchange*. Available at: https://policyexchange.org.uk/publication/extremism-rebellion. Last accessed 28 February 2022.

Woodman, C. (2018) Comment: A brick wall of silence at Undercover Policing Inquiry. *Centre for Crime and Justice Studies*, 7 February 2018. Available at: https://www.crimeandjustice.org.uk/resources/brick-wall-silence-latest-undercover-policing-inquiry-0. Last accessed 29 September 2022.

Wright, S. (2016) Police chief accused of covering up secret ploy to spy on the family of murdered Stephen Lawrence dodges disciplinary action by retiring. *Mail Online*, 16 January 2016. Available at: https://www.dailymail.co.uk/news/article-3401884/Police-chief-accused-covering-secret-ploy-spy-family-murdered-Stephen-Lawrence-dodges-disciplinary-action-retiring-early.html. Last accessed 7 March 2022.

# Index

#notallcops 155
#spycops 154
9/11 Commission 98

## A

abuse 3, 9, 23, 89, 165
  police (state) 2, 39, 20, 60, 70, 90–1
  sexual 42, 44
  *see also* women
academics 49
acceptance 70
access 50, 157
accessibility 71, 157
  academic 111–13
accountability 24–5, 168–70
  deviant knowledge 48, 65–6
  dirty data 96, 102, 114
  in and against the inquiry 154–5, 163
  limits 164–5
  site of struggle 69–73, 83
  *see also* human rights and data protection
accounts, official 49
acknowledgement, official 2, 27, 47, 161
  crossroads 164, 168, 170
  dirty data 94, 114, 145
  site of struggle 68, 90
acknowledgement, police 22, 39
activation 25
activism 35, 36, 37, 59, 153
  workplace 51
activist communities 22, 60, 99
activists 24–6, 34, 103, 145, 168
  political 91
  site of struggle 76, 78, 83
  *see also* deviant knowledge
activities, political
  anti-fascist 67
  deviant knowledge 50, 52
  dirty data 105, 107, 111
  *see also* scandals, undercover policing
actors, high-profile 157
Adams, Rolan 31
agency 26
Aldermaston 35
Ali, Tariq 52–3, 54, 166
Alison 67–8, 75, 94, 147
ambiguity 144
amplification 24, 25
anarchists 40
Andrea 102
animal rights 54–5, 59, 89
anonymity 150
  deviant knowledge 42, 65–6

dirty data 96, 99, 101
site of struggle 79–81, 92–3
*see also* human rights and data protection
Anwar, Aamer 115
archives 113
Armstrong, Franny 89
arrests 53
assemblies, political 56
Association of Chief Police Officers (ACPO) 54
atrocities 70
audiences 155
audio streams 157
audits 25
authorities 24
authority 72, 96
autonomy 71

## B

banners 94
Barker, John 43, 89–90
Barr, David 53–4, 156, 169
Bercow, John 34
bias 23
Big Flame 99
black boxes 165, 166
black communities 27
Black Lives Matter 28, 162
*Black Power* 27
Blacklist Support Group 147
blacklisting 52
blackmail, emotional 103
blame 69, 71
bombings 96
Bonino, Stefano 50, 51, 63, 64
Bonser, Kathryn Lesley 35
borders 148
Boyling, Jim 38, 76, 91
Bramley, Steven 117
Brander, Ruth 121
breakdowns 72
Brian, Chris 40
British National Party 30–1
broadcasting hearings 156–8
Brook House Inquiry 115
Brooks, Duwayne 167–8
Brown, Wendy 123, 144
Burton, F. 72
business interests 23

## C

Cairo 125
Camp for Climate Action 64, 77
campaign groups 53

# Index

Campaign Opposing Police Surveillance  53, 62, 127, 147, 149, 157
campaigners  26, 40, 103, 154, 157
  political  91
campaigns  24, 35–6, 89, 167
  animal rights  83
  deviant knowledge  51, 65
  environmental  16–18, 158
  in and against the inquiry  147, 153, 155
  justice  59
  political  10, 37–8, 69, 164
  *see also* deviant knowledge
Carlen, P.  72
Carmichael, Stokely  27
Carswell, Robert, Baron  86–7
Casciani, Dominic  157
Cassidy, Mark  67–8
  *see also* Jenner, Mark
Centre for Crime and Justice Studies  109
Channel 4  40
Clark, Richard  100
  *see also* Gibson, Rick (Richard)
Clifford, Max  69
climate change protestors  55
closure  73
codenames  82
  *see also* cyphers
Cohen, Nick  63
Cohen, Stanley  69, 70, 71
Coles, Andy  40–1, 145
Colin Roach Centre  67
collaborations  62
Collins, Peter  136
colonialism  47
common law  38–9
communication  49, 147
communities  6, 71
concealment  73, 94, 95
conferences  64
conferences, press  156
confidentiality  79–80, 81, 98, 127, 144
conspiracy theories  57, 87, 113
construction companies  34
contestations  165
contradictions, internal  73
convictions
  previous (spent)  129–31
  wrongful  34
cooperation  48
Corbyn, Jeremy  64
Corbyn, Piers  52
corruption  28, 29, 104
  institutional  33
counselling  67–8
counter-terrorism  33, 60–5
Counter Terrorism Command (SO15)  32
*Countering Al-Qaeda in London: Police and Muslims in Partnership*  64
court trials  75

cover names  150, 153
COVID-19 pandemic  52, 118, 156, 166
credibility  61
Creedon, Mick  75
crime  50
  state  70
criminological knowledge from below  65–6
criminology  48
crises  71
*Critical Studies on Terrorism*  60
Critical Terrorist Studies  60–1
Cunningham, Ian  78
cyphers
  EN35  132
  EN37  132
  EN59  138
  EN107  137–8
  EN108  133–4
  EN508  132
  HN10  58
  HN15  67
  HN80  135–6
  HN104  101, 103, 135
  HN106  136
  HN297  99–101
  HN303  136–7
  HN332  138
  HN348  35
  N81  32

## D

data  66
data, dirty
  academic access to the evidence  111–13
  file giving  119–21
  and hidden data  108–11
  morality  100–4
  obstruction and obfuscation  117–19
  political mediation  98–100
  secrecy, security, disclosure  95–6
  from secrecy to dis/closure  96–8
  self-incrimination  113–17
  technical data management  104–8
Data Protection Act, UK  124, 139
Davey, Andy  40–1
Dearlove, Sir Richard  88
death certificates  30
deception  48, 53, 119
*Deep Deception*  67, 89
delays  70
Della Porta, Donatella  56
Dembour, Marie-Bénédicte  122–3
democracies  161–3
demonstrations  28, 50, 53, 54
denial  95, 155, 164
  deviant knowledge  57, 61
  site of struggle  69–71, 73
deployments  51

*Deviant Knowledge* 48
devices
  of dis/closure 96–7
  morality 100–4
  political mediation 98–100
  technical data management 104–8
Diana, Princess 87–8
Dick, Cressida 27–8
Dines, John 91, 128, 129
  *see also* Barker, John
disclosure 96–8, 126, 148, 168
  failures 77–9
  *see also* data, dirty; struggle, public enquiry as site of
discourse, official 167
discrimination 27, 161
disorder 47, 50, 51, 54
*Dispatches* 25, 29–30
disputes, legal 164
dissent 23
Dobson, Gary 29
documentation (documents) 40, 68
  restriction of 92
  *see also* data
double lives 50

# E

elites 72, 73
Ellison, Mark 23, 28–9, 31–3, 104, 112
Emmerson, Ben 82, 84–5
empowerment 61
environmental destruction 89
equality 28
ethics, academic 64
ethnic minority communities 27
European Convention on Human Rights (ECHR) 38, 114, 122, 150
Evans, Rob 22, 25, 29–30, 63, 76, 106
evidence hearings 53
expertise 63, 64, 65
experts 151, 153
exploitation 44
Extinction Rebellion 33
extremism, domestic 23, 54, 61, 62

# F

Facenna, Gerry 141–3
failings 24
  institutional 26, 165
fairness 130–1
Fayed, Dodi 87
al-Fayed, Mohamed 88
feminism 35, 51, 123
field agents 53
file giving 119–21
files 98, 105
  intelligence 150, 153
  *see also* documentation (documents)
fly-posters 65–6

Foucault, Michel 36, 48–9, 95
Fowler, Tom 157
Francis, Peter 25, 29–31, 33–4, 59, 69, 82
Francis, Sir Robert 140
freedom of expression 161
freedom of information laws 54
Freedom of Information Tribunal 81
funding 106, 169

# G

G8 summit 148, 150
gatekeepers 60
General Data Protection Regulation (GDPR) 139–44
German, Lindsay 110
Germany 150
Gibson, Rick (Richard) 99–100
  *see also* Clark, Richard
Gifford, Tilly 149, 150
Gillard, Michael 103
Gilmore, Joanna 65
Goold, Benjamin 50
governance, market 48
Greenham Common Peace Camp 35
Greer, Chris 24, 25, 26
Grenfell Tower Inquiry 115, 156
grooming 40
groups, political 52
Guardian News and Media 100
*Guardian, The* 22, 25, 106, 147, 155
  site of struggle 67, 76, 78

# H

Hadjimatheou, Katerina 80
Hagan, David 32, 168
  *see also* Hall, Stuart
Hall, Jonathan 71, 140
Hall, Stuart 73, 166–7
  *see also* Hagan, David
Hamburg 46
Hamilton, Charles 27
harm 133–5, 168
Harvie, David 64
Hewitt, Martin 39
hidden data 108–11
*Hidden Voices* 112
Home Office 105, 106, 112
honesty 90
horse charges 53
human rights 39, 60, 91, 114, 121, 158–61
human rights and data protection
  anonymity in numbers 132–3
  anonymity, risk and harm 133–5
  contesting risk assessments 129–31
  different kind of paradox 124–6
  human rights to political expression 144–6
  police officer anonymity 126–9

# Index

posthumous rights 135–8
privacy and data protection 139–43
statutory reach abroad 135
spy's right to privacy 122–4
weapon of last resort 143–4

## I

identities 24, 30, 34, 37, 41, 103
  covert 76
  dead children 59
  deviant knowledge 50, 61
  site of struggle 68, 70, 83–4
immigration detainees 115
immunity (from prosecution) 72, 116
impact, psychological 57
impartiality 47
impunity 73
incentives, financial 149
independence 47
Independent Office for Police Conduct (IOPC) 107
Independent Police Complaints Commission (IPCC) 32–3
*Indymedia UK* 22, 25
infiltration 23, 34, 44, 57
  sexual 100
  *see also* sexual infiltration
informants 50
information 33, 74
  from activists 61
information gathering 30
information management systems 104
information reliability 62
informers 49
Inquiries Act (2005) 71–2, 79, 112, 131
insecurity 36
insiders, outside 58, 62
Institute for Government 23
institutionalisation, paradox of 145
institutions 25–6, 69, 72
intelligence gathering 51, 52
intelligence sources, covert human 50
internet 83
*Introduction to Policing Research: Taking Lessons from Practice* 57
investigations 33, 59
Investigatory Powers Act 2016 159
Investigatory Powers Tribunal (IPT) 158–61
invisibility 57, 61
Islington Against Police Spies 63

## J

Jack the Ripper 81
Jacobs, Marco 132
Jacqui 38, 59
Jaipur 82–3, 125
Javid, Sajid 154, 162
Jenner, Mark 67–8
  *see also* Cassidy, Mark
Jessica 40–1
Johnson, Boris 156, 165
Jones, Edward David 132
Jones, Jenny, Baroness 106–7
Jordan, John 76
justice 26, 65, 66
JUSTICE 74

## K

Kaoullas, Lambros 50, 51
Karachi 82–3
Kaufmann, Philippa 93, 94, 150, 151, 152
Kennedy, Mark 22–3, 25, 28, 55
  dirty data 107, 120
  human rights and data protection 132, 134, 145
  in and against the inquiry 150, 158, 160–1
  site of struggle 69, 77, 83
Khan, Imran 68
Khan, Sadiq 28
killings, racially motivated 31
Kilroy, Charlotte 76
Kirkham, Peter 155
Kirkpatrick, Jason 150
Kissinger, Henry 98
knowledge 94
knowledge, deviant 48–9
  covert policing and activist knowledge 46–8
  criminological knowledge from below 65–6
  critical studies in counter-terrorism 60–5
  NPOIU 54–5
  police targeting 49–52
  public order policing and political protest 55–9
  special demonstration squad 52–4
knowledges of resistance 49

## L

Lambert, Bob (Robert) 38, 129, 145
  deviant knowledge 58–60, 62–5
  site of struggle 75–6, 89–90
latency 24
law enforcement 51
lawfulness 143
Lawrence, Baroness 33
Lawrence family 25, 30
Lawrence, Stephen 28, 164, 167
  *see also* Stephen Lawrence Inquiry
leaflets 89
legacy bill 72
legal disputes 164
legal rules 26
legitimacy 25, 45, 61–2, 72, 123, 151
  police 23
letters 64
Lewis, Paul 22, 25, 29, 30, 76

Lewis, Simon 64
liability 70
libel suits 59
liberty 57
*Liberty and Order* 56, 57
literature 56, 69, 72
live streams 157
lives, double 50
Loadenthal, Michael 36–7
lockdowns 156
Loftus, Bethan 49–50
London Greenpeace 43
love 67
Lubbers, Eveline 59, 83, 100, 101, 102
Lush 153, 155
Lush, Rebecca 154
lying 76, 153–6

## M

Macpherson Inquiry 26, 28, 30, 32
Macpherson, Sir William, of Cluny 26–7, 28
malpractice 72, 105
management, data 104–8
manipulation 119
Mansfield, Michael 115–16
Marriot, Trevor 81
Marx, Gary 56, 108, 113
Mary 100
May, Theresa 25, 28–30, 33, 68, 164–6
  in and against the inquiry 148, 162
McDonalds 59, 89
McGovern, Mark 72–3
McLaughlin, Eugene 24, 25, 26
McLean, Donna 41–2
*McLibel* 89
media 23–4, 145, 154–5
  dirty data 99, 109
  site of struggle 70, 86, 91
  *see also* social media
mediation, political 98–100
medical histories 134
memorials, criminal damage to 162
Menon, Rajiv 169
MI5 52
Milburn, Keir 64
Mills, Helen 75, 109
Mitting, Sir John 35, 92–3, 169
  human rights and data protection 127–8, 130–1, 133–8, 140–4
  in and against the inquiry 150–2, 156–7
  *see also* data, dirty
monitoring 51
Monitoring Group 147
Moore-Bick, Sir Martin 115–16
moral ambiguity 56, 60
morality 64, 100–4
Morris, Dave 156
mosaic effect 81–6, 93

movements, social 31, 35, 44
Murji, Karim 167

## N

names, cover 40
narratives, official 167
national security *see* security, national (state)
National Domestic Extremism and Disorder Intelligence Unit (NDEDIU) 106, 107–8
National Public Order Intelligence Unit (NPOIU) 28, 50, 51, 54–5, 126
nationalism 31
Neither Confirm Nor Deny (NCND) strategy 65, 67–70, 128, 147, 160
  contesting 88–92
  limits 73–9
Neri, Carlo 41, 101–3
  *see also* Soracchi, Carlo
Netpol 147
*New Left Review* 166
news, internet 24
*Newsnight* 78
newspapers 90
Norris, David 29
Northern Ireland 86–7
Northern Ireland Troubles 72
numbers, anonymity in 132–3
  *see also* codenames; cyphers

## O

obfuscation 117–19, 150, 160
*Observer, The* 29, 90
obstruction and obfuscation 117–19
O'Discroll, Dónal 83, 101–2, 120–1, 131, 156
Officer A 29–35
opaqueness 153
openness 22
  dirty data 95, 117, 119
  human rights and data protection 125, 127, 144
  site of struggle 71, 73, 79–80, 84
Operation FileSafe 104
Operation Herne 23, 75–6, 105, 107
Operation Hibiscus 107–8
Oppenheim, Jonathan 64
opposition, anti-capitalist 55
oppression 123
O'Rawe, Mary 60–1, 62
organisations 52
  police 73–4
othering 40
oversight 65–6

## P

paradox of institutionalisation 145
participants, core 5, 11–17, 20, 26, 31
  deviant knowledge 51, 53

# Index

human rights and data protection 125–31, 139, 141, 143–6
  in and against the inquiry 147–8, 150–3, 156–7, 162
  inquiry crossroads 164–5, 168–70
  site of struggle *see* struggle, public enquiry as site of
participants, corporate 115
parties 42
partnerships 65
Paxman, Jeremy 78
Peel, Robert 47
Peplow, Simon 168
performance management 25
personal data (details) 51, 109
personas, cover (fictional) 30, 37
  *see also* identities
perspectives, critical 48
Peterloo Massacre 47
Pickford, Jim 38
Pitchford, Sir Christopher 28, 148
  dirty data 99, 114
  human rights and data protection 124, 126–7, 130, 145
  *see also* struggle, public enquiry as site of
Plane Stupid 149
Police, Crime, Sentencing and Courts Act 2022 162
police powers, abuse of 60
police secrets 6–7
Police Spies Out of Lives 44, 62, 102–3, 147, 153, 156–7
police targeting 49–52
policing 57, 73–4
policing by consent 19, 45, 47, 48, 55
policing by deception 19, 44–5, 47, 55, 164
policing, covert 21, 22, 46–8
policing hierarchies 34, 52
policing (police), secret 19, 35, 47, 53, 64, 117
policing units, undercover 23
political activity 2, 13, 18, 20, 31, 35
  deviant knowledge 50, 52
  dirty data 105, 107, 111
political expression 144–6, 161–2
political policing 10, 19, 45, 162, 170
  deviant knowledge 48, 49–52, 65–6
politicians 11, 13, 23, 34, 44, 106
politics, establishment 165
posthumous rights 135–8
power 36, 70, 108, 116, 123, 128
powerlessness 152
powers, enhanced 96
preliminary matters 11–12
press 24, 25, 80, 149, 155
privacy 109, 161
privacy and data protection 139–43
  spy's rights 122–4
Privacy International 159

prosecution, immunity from 72
protection 31
protest policing 45, 50, 55–6, 61–2
protesters 8–9, 23, 76–7, 162
  deviant knowledge 53, 55–6, 62
  environmental 19, 40
protests 51, 53, 62, 69, 161–3
  political 55–9, 61, 81
pseudonyms 41
  *see also* codenames
public access 15, 21, 165
  dirty data 80, 113
  human rights and data protection 124, 136
public acknowledgement 6, 23, 152
public concern 53, 88, 114, 164, 166
  human rights and data protection 136–7, 145
  policing scandal 24–5, 37
public disorder 30
public health crises 156
public inquiries
  bringing accountability 168–70
  in conservative state 165–8
  limits to accountability 164–5
  politics of 1–6
public interest 44
  dirty data 95, 99–100, 118
  *see also* human rights and data protection; struggle, public enquiry as site of
public order 32, 45, 51, 53, 55–9
Public Order Act
  1986 56
  2023 162
public scrutiny 19, 46, 138, 154–5, 164
public trust 28, 74, 105
publication, restriction 92

# R

racism 51, 150
  institutional 9, 16–18, 23, 26–8, 44, 151
radicalism, student 35
Ratcliffe-on-Soar 77–8
reaction 25
Reclaim the Streets 76
recognition 27
record keeping 104, 105
recordings, voice 149
redactions 41, 96–7, 119, 128–9
reference terms 10–11
regulation 48
Regulation of Investigatory Powers Act (RIPA) 2000 65, 159, 161
regulations 157
Rehabilitation of Offenders Act (ROA) 1974 129–31
Reiner, Rob 57–8
Reiter, Herbert 56
Reith, Charles 47

relationships 23, 30, 32, 35–41, 44
  deviant knowledge 48, 62, 65
  site of struggle 67–8, 89
repression 36, 47, 95
research background 7–10
research methods 14–18
researchers 7–8, 19, 83–4, 122, 157
  dirty data 98, 100, 102, 111–13
  *see also* knowledge, deviant
resources 147
restriction orders 79–81, 121, 124, 130, 132, 145
Richardson, Louise 63
Richardson, Rod 132
rights, posthumous 135–8
risk and harm 133–5
risk assessment 129–31
risks 61, 96
Roach Family Support Campaign 167
Robinson, Bob 58
Rose, Christopher, Sir 78
Rycroft, Matthew 169

## S

safeguards 161
Sanders, Oliver 126–7, 140–1
Sandra 35
scandals, undercover policing 22–3
  greatest possible scrutiny 26–8
  Home Secretary's announcement 28–9
  institutional sexism 41–4
  making of 23–6
  Officer A 29–35
  personal is political 35–9
  policing by deception 44–5
  tradecraft manual 39–41
Scappaticci, Freddie 86–7
scepticism 62
scholarship 96, 166
Schwarz, Mark 77
Scobie, Jame 52
Scotland 148, 149
Scottish Police 105
Scraton, Phil 65, 70
scrutiny 26–8
secrecy 22, 168
  deviant knowledge 48, 57, 65–6
  dirty data 95–8, 118, 120
  human rights and data protection 126, 144
  in and against the inquiry 147–8, 150, 152–3
  *see also* struggle, public enquiry as site of
secret policing 64
security 84
security, national (state) 50–1, 87, 95–6, 109, 133
self-incrimination 113–17
sensitivity 61

Serious Disruption Prevention Orders 162
sexism, institutional 23, 36, 41–4, 151
sexual infiltration 29, 36, 39, 100
Sheku Bayoh Inquiry 115
silence, wall of 92–4
Skelton, Peter 117
slogans 31
*Small Town Girl* 41
smearing 30
Smith, Dave 156
social media 154–5
social movements 48, 51, 144
Socialist Workers Party 110
Soracchi, Carlo 104
  *see also* Neri, Carlo
Spalek, Basia 60–1, 62
Special Branch 53, 65
Special Demonstration Squad (SDS) 29–31, 50–4, 105–6, 126, 166, 169
Stakeknife *see* Scappaticci, Freddie
Stammers, Neil 144–5
Starmer, Keir 78, 89
state, conservative 165–8
*State Secrecy and Security* 96
*States of Denial: Knowing about Atrocities and Suffering* 69
statutory reach 135
Steel, Helen 42–3, 88–92, 94, 128–9, 156
Stephen Lawrence case 44
Stephen Lawrence Independent Review 29, 104
Stephen Lawrence Inquiry 26–7, 112
Stephens-Griffin, Nathan 36–7, 152–3, 154, 155
stereotypes 61
Stone, Mark 158
  *see also* Kennedy, Mark
Stone, Roger 112–13
Stop the War 110
*Street Fighting Years: An Autobiography of the Sixties* 54
struggle, public enquiry as site of
  confirm nor deny 67–70
  contesting NCND 88–92
  Diana, Princess 87–8
  legal approach to restriction orders 79–81
  mosaic effect 81–6
  NCND limits 73–9
  political accountability 70–3
  Scappaticci 86–7
  wall of silence 92–4
subversion 23, 45, 51, 54, 55
suffering 44
Sumac Centre 158
surveillance 23, 36, 68, 108–10, 164
  *see also* knowledge, deviant
suspicion 36
Sutton, Jim *see* Boyling, Jim
systemic failings 165

## T

Tate, Ernie 52–3
Taylor, Stephen 105–6
*Telegraph, The* 106
Terms of Reference 148–50
terrorism (terror attacks) 60–4, 82, 162
Thomas, O. 84–5
*Times Higher Education* 64
Tomkins, Barry 136
Trade Union Act 2016 162
trade unions 67, 162
tradecraft manual 39–41
Trades Union Congress (TUC) 162
transparency 32
   deviant knowledge 48, 62
   in and against the inquiry 147–8, 153, 155
   site of struggle 71, 79–80, 90
   *see also* data, dirty
trauma 44, 90
trial by media 24
Troops Out Movement 99
trust 61–2, 67, 74, 100, 113, 153
truth 25, 65, 68–71, 73, 94, 165
truth, official 24
Tufail, Waqas 65
Twyford Down 154
Tyndall, John 31

## U

undercover 49
*Undercover* 30
Undercover Policing Inquiry, in and against
   broadcasting hearings 156–8
   challenging Terms of Reference 148–50
   fighting for transparency 147–8
   human rights claims in Investigatory Powers Tribunal 158–61
   paid to lie 153–6
   protest in a democratic society 161–3
   withdrawing from participation 150–3

Undercover Research Group (URG) 58, 62, 83, 147
*Undercover: The True Story of Britain's Secret Police* 22
universities 48

## V

vetting 52
victims 24, 101, 121
video feeds 156
Vietnam Solidarity Campaign (VSC) 53
violations 60
violence 55
   political 45, 50, 63–4
victims, relatable 24

## W

Waddington, P.A.J. 56, 57, 60
Walters, Reece 48, 49, 65
Walters, William 69, 95–8, 100, 104, 108
Walton, Richard 32–3
Watson, Lynn 35, 132, 158
wellbeing 134
whistleblowing 106
   Officer A 29–35
Wilson, Kate 125, 158–9, 160, 161
witnesses 68, 114, 115, 116
women 23, 29, 34–5, 39, 44, 161
   deviant knowledge 63, 65
   dirty data 101, 103
   human rights and data protection 128, 145
   site of struggle 67, 76, 90
Women's Liberation Front (WLF) 35
Woodman, Connor 110
Worboys, John 150
wrongdoing 69, 72, 114, 127, 137

## Y

Youth against Racism in Europe (YRE) 29, 31
YouTube 156

www.ingramcontent.com/pod-product-compliance
Lightning Source LLC
Chambersburg PA
CBHW051542020426
42333CB00016B/2052